ABOUT THE EDITOR

Teotonio R. de Souza (18 February 1947 – 20 February 2019). He was the Founder-Director of the Xavier Centre of Historical Research, Goa since 1979. He is the author of Medieval Goa and edited Indo-Portuguese History: Old Issues, New Questions(1985), Essays in Goan History (1987), Goa through the Ages: An Economic History (1990), Jesuits in India: In Historical Perspective (1992). He has also written extensively on Indo-Portuguese History and Church History in various academic and cultural journals in India and abroad. He is post-graduate teacher and Ph.D. research guide of the Goa University, and is Life-Member and Fellow of various associations of Historians, including Indian History Congress and the Portuguese Academy of History. He has convened national and international seminars since 1981, including the Third International Seminar on Indo-Portuguese History (ISIPH-3). He has convened the 7th Seminar of the same series for January 1994.

He retired as Cathedratic professor of the Universidade Lusófona, after representing, since 1996, the interests of History teaching and research on the Scientific and Pedagogic Councils, of the Faculty of Social and Human Sciences, Education and Administration of the Universidade Lusófona, as an ex-officio member. While acting as coordinator / Director of the MA and M.Phil courses in History, he guided M.Phil and Ph.D researchers in Political Science and Diplomatic Relations, and directed a line of research related to "Colonial and Post-Colonial Societies", and Memories of CPES (Centro de Pesquisa e Estudos Sociais) of the Faculty of Social and Human Sciences, Universidade Lusófona, Lisboa.

Indo-Portuguese History
Old Issues, New Questions

Edited by
TEOTONIO R. de SOUZA

CONCEPT PUBLISHING COMPANY PVT. LTD.
NEW DELHI-110059

witnessed in works published anywhere from Iberia to Japan. No note on his contribution can hope to be more than tentative, for even as this is being written he has doubtless much more on the way to instruct, entertain and enlighten us as only he can.

Pembroke College,
Cambridge, U.K.

G.V. SCAMMELL.

Editor's Preface

I WISH to take the lead from our octogenarian historian-guide, Prof. C.R. Boxer, to whom this book is being dedicated as a token of gratitude of the Editor, of the XCHR, and of the ISIPH group of historians, all of whom owe Prof. Boxer a kind of debt that can be repaid only by burning ever more brightly the flame of Indo-Portuguese studies. Somewhere in his classic survey of the Portuguese seaborne empire Prof. Boxer has quoted Valignano, the great organizer of the Jesuit eastern missions, remarking despondently "that Portuguese India was a frontier land of war and trade, rather than one of learning and study". Fortunately for us, the times have changed: War and trade may not have declined, but the erstwhile Portuguese India has begun tasting the fruits of the tree of knowledge.

Till a decade ago whatever critical study we have on the basis of Portuguese archival documentation has come to us from across the Portuguese national borders. Such work was done by non-Portuguese nationals, like Prof. Boxer, or by the Portuguese nationals in exile, like Prof. Magalhäes-Godinho. Within the reach of the Portuguese government control some historical objectivity was safeguarded, by men like Prof. Pissurlencar, by limiting most of their energies to publication of documents. We owe much to the intellectual honesty and courage displayed by these stalwarts of Indo-Portuguese scholarship. In the improved political climate, the new generation of Indo-Portuguese historians will have no lack of scope to display their honesty and courage as well.

Following the liberation of Goa, the historic nerve-centre of the Portuguese *Estado da India*, it was only to be expected that there would be a re-assessment of history and historiography in a post-colonial spirit. Fortunately for the Indian historians, a radical change in the political climate of Portugal in 1974, made it possible to join hands with their Portuguese counterparts in this task of historical reassessment. While the diplomatic wheels moved slowly, as they are still doing, a concrete step was taken by Dr. John Correia-Afonso by convoking ISIPH (international seminar on Indo-Portuguese history) in Goa in 1978. It was a great success and it was considered worthwhile to convoke it again with conveniently regular frequency. An important institutional off-shoot of this renaissance of Indo-Portuguese studies in India was the establishment of the Xavier Centre of Historical Research (XCHR) in Goa at the same time as ISIPH-1, and I feel myself justly proud of having been instrumental for its creation, and for building it up and shaping its various projects from nothingness into what can be seen after its six years of existence.

The first ISIPH delved on *sources* and paid some attention to *problems* of Indo-Portuguese history. ISIPH-2 in Lisbon in October 1980 continued the story of success, and we can recall it mixed with sadness caused by the premature death of its dynamic organizer, Admiral Avelino Teixeira da Mota. As it was only to be expected, ISIPH-2 faced the problems of the deep sea with greater vigour. Encouraged by the results of the first two seminars of the ISIPH series, I took it upon myself to organize ISIPH-3 in Goa in January (28-30) 1983. Indo-Portuguese historians and other social scientists from 12 different countries presented 35 papers. The focus of ISIPH-3 captured navigation, trade and cultural exchanges, all of them *old issues*, but subjecting them to *new questions*. Vice-Admiral M.P. Awati (Flag Officer Commanding-in-Chief Western Naval Command, and Chairman of Maritime History Society, Bombay) summed up the scope of the seminar in characteristic terms of the *Carreira da India* in his inaugural key-note address :

> In spite of all these baffling factors, mis-management and callous disregard for the mariners the carreira went on, though at a much reduced pace. The only answer perhaps to this puzzle is the Portuguese resilience which has enabled them to weather many storms and upheavals. The 'Carreira da India' went on because of the indomitable spirit of the few honest individuals and a few skilled and seasoned pilots who were the very backbone of the sea passage to the Indies. A study of their backgrounds at home, of what

> motivated them, their aspirations and frustrations, the ships they manned, their life style in the conquered territories and their interaction with the people of the west coast, their treaties and parleys with the local powers and the then paramount Emperor in Delhi and his Viceroys in the Deccan, the cultural synthesis that resulted between Portugal and her small enclaves in Goa, Daman and Diu, is indeed a vast field for research and writing for students of Indo-Portuguese history and historiography.

The transactions of the seminar went definitely beyond the expectations of Vice-Admiral Awati as the present selection from a wide range of papers can testify. Unfortunately due to several good reasons, it has not been possible for us to publish the proceedings of ISIPH-3 in their entirety. However, we do have a good representative and scholarly sampling. K.S. Mathew, Niels Steensgaard, Mme Bouchon, and Lea Williams have raised questions relating to the *Carreira da India* : Who were the cargo feeders of the *Carreira* in India ? Why did the Portuguese fail to break the stranglehold of the Muslim middle-men ? What was the impact of the *Carreira* upon the society and economy of Malabar ? Is it justifiable to study *Carreira* and Portuguese expansion in the early 16th century independently from the Spanish efforts ? What archival information do we have for the early history of the *Carreira* ? Why do we not find appreciable increase in cargo with the increase of tonnage in the Carreira's *monsters* ? How did the *Carreira* fare in Chinese waters ? Luis Filipe Thomaz, Leonard Blusse, George Winius, and Artur Teodoro de Matos discuss the success and failure of the Portuguese presence in the *Estado da India*, raising such questions as : How did the native communities in Malacca face the challenge of Portuguese presence ? Why did the Dutch adopt an aggressive stance, while they had been friendly earlier ? Did the *Estado da India* really face financial bankruptcy during the Phillipine regime ? John Correia-Afonso leads us on the land (*caminho da India*) by routes that were much older than the *Carreira.* A.R. Kulkarni has filled in a gap in Maratha historiography with the help of new documents from Portuguese archives, and raises a very important question : Can we regard the Portuguese as a spent force in Indian politics in the 17th century ? His answer is clearly in the negative. Teotonio R. de Souza and Caroline Ifeka have raised questions regarding approach to Goan history and they have their own specific contributions to offer from economic and anthropological angles respectively. The second death centenary of Marquis de Pombal evoked papers from J.P. Bacelar e Oliveira and Henry Scholberg. While Bacelar e Oliveira handles the case of Jesuits victimized by the Marquis, Scholberg analyses the work of an eminent Goan biographer of the Marquis. As it could be expected, much attention was paid in ISIPH-3 to the more lasting effects of the Portuguese presence in the *Estado da India*, that is, to cultural exchanges and influences. While Lotika Varadarajan examined the artistic influences and exchanges, M.H. Goonatilleka, Rocky Miranda, and Fernando Castelo-Branco discussed the linguistic and literary crossings. Niels Steensgaard had the final word in his concluding address. He raised the question whether the Indo-Portuguese historians would not do better by talking in terms of just one continent, instead of Asia and Europe. He also drew attention to one recurring issue throughout the seminar discussions, and invited Indo-Portuguese historian to focus more attention in future on the concept of *coastal society* in order to find more satisfactory answers to many of the questions raised and answered so far.

It is our hope that the ISIPH forum will continue to promote greater international understanding and relations and will use historical research for this noble purpose. Old issues and new questions should not divide, but unite. The Governments of India and Portugal, Calouste Gulbenkian Foundation, Heras Institute, Xavier Centre of Historical Research, Maritime History Society, Indian Council of Historical Research, Indian Council of Cultural Relations, our benefactors from Süssen Church and Fr. Joe übelmesser S.J. in West Germany deserve a mention of gratitude for their moral and financial backing in making ISIPH-3 a successful event. May their generosity continue to sustain the good work they have begun.

Porvorim, Goa
15th June, 1984

TEOTONIO R. DE SOUZA

List of Contributors

John Correia-Afonso
Director, Heras Institute of Indian History and Culture, Bombay. Author of *Jesuit Letters and Indian History.* Has edited *Letters from the Mughal Court* (1980) and *Indo-Portuguese History : Sources and Problems* (1981).

Leonard Blussé
Professor at the Centre for the History of European Expansion and the Reactions to it, Leiden University. Editors of *Itinerario.*

G. Bouchon
She is specialized in history of India (15th-17th centuries) and is presently professor in charge of research at the Centre National de la Recherche Scientifique, Paris. Has published *Mamale de Cananor* (1975), *A Propos de L'Inscription de Colombo* (1501), *Joao de Nova Dans L'Ocean Indian* (1980).

Fernando Castelo-Branco
Lectures at the Universidade Livre, Lisboa. Has published *Actividade dos Missionarios Portugueses em Ceilão* (1957), *Modelos da Fortaleza de Diu* (1962), and *Comemorações do Centenario da India em Lisboa* (1977).

Maria dos Remedios Castelo-Branco
Has specialized in literary history, and is a member of the Teachers' Training Advisory Board (Ministry of Education), Lisbon. Has published *Filosofia do cómico em Ludwig Tieck* (1955) and *A Missão do Coronel Wylde atravéssde Algumas Cartas Inéditas de D. Fernando* (1957).

M.H. Goonatilleka
Head, Department of Fine Arts, University of Kelanyia, Sri

Lanka. Specialized in Portuguese theatre and language in Sri Lanka.

Caroline Ifeka
Lecturer, Department of Pre-History and Anthropology, Australian National University. Has published *Peoples and Empires of West Africa* (1969).

A.R. Kulkarni
Professor of History, University of Poona. Author of *Maharashtra in the Age of Shivaji* (1969), and *James Cunningham Grant Duff* (1971). Was Chairman of the Indian Council of Historical Research (1978-81).

K.S. Mathew
Reader in the Department of History, University of Baroda. Has specialized in 16th century economic history, and has published *Society in Medieval Malabar* (1979), and *Portuguese Trade in 16th Century India* (1983).

Artur Teodoro de Matos
Professor of History, Universidade dos Acores. Has published *Timor Portuguese* (1974). *O Estado da India nos anos de 1581-1588 : Estrutura Administrativa e Econômica* (1982).

Rocky Miranda
Associate Professor, Department of Linguistics, University of Minnesota, USA. Has specialized in historical and Indo-European linguistics.

J.P. Bacelar e Oliveira
Rector, Universidade Catolica Portuguesa, Lisboa. Specialized in Philosophy, directed the publication of the encyclopaedia VERBO of Luso-Brazilian culture.

G.V. Scammell
Director of studies in History, Pembroke College, Cambridge. Author of *The World Encompassed* (1981).

Henry Scholberg
Librarian, Ames Library of South Asia, University of

Minnesota, USA. Author of *Bibliography of Goa and the Portuguese in India* (1982).

Teotonio R. de Souza
Director, Xavier Centre of Historical Research, Goa. Editor, XCHR Studies Series. Author of *Medieval Goa*, has specialized in socio-economic history (16th-17th centuries).

Niels Steensgaard
Professor at the Institute of History, University of Copenhagen. Has specialized in the international trade, and published *The Asian Trade Revolution of the Seventeenth Century* (1975).

Luis Filipe Thomaz
Has specialized in the history of Portuguese expansion in Asia. Is presently Professor of History at the University of Lisbon.

Lotika Varadarajan
Lecturer in History, Jawaharlal Nehru University, New Delhi. Has published *India in the Seventeenth Century* (1981) and *South Indian Traditions of Kalamkari* (1982).

Lea E. Williams
Professor of History, Brown University, Rhode Island. Is also Director of East Asia Language and Area Centre. Has published *South-east Asia : A History* (1976) and *The Future of the Overseas Chinese in Southeast Asia* (1966).

George Winius
Professor at the Centre for the History of European Expansion on the Reactions to it, Leiden University. Editor of *Itinerario.*

Contents

Prof. C.R. Boxer v

Editor's Preface vii

List of Contributors xi

1. Indian Merchants and the Portuguese Trade on the Malabar Coast during the Sixteenth Century .... *K.S. Mathew* 1

2. The Return Cargoes of the *Carreira* in the 16th and Early 17th Century .... *Niels Steensgaard* 13

3. Inauspicious Ambience : The Historical Setting of Early Luso-Chinese Contacts .... *Lea E. Williams* 32

4. Glimpses of the Beginnings of the *Carreira da India* (1500-1518) .... *Geneviève Bouchon* 40

5. The Indian Merchant Communities in Malacca under the Portuguese Rule .... *Luis Filipe Thomaz* 56

6. The Origin and Rhythm of Dutch Aggression against the *Estado da India*, 1601-1661 .... *Leonard Blussé & George Winius* 73

7. Manuel Godinho's Alternatives to the *Carreira da India* .... *John Correia-Afonso* 84

8. The Financial Situation of the State of India during the Philippine Period, 1581-1635 .... *Artur Teodoro de Matos* 90

9. Capital Input in Goa's Freedom Struggle : The Bombay Connection .... *Teotonio R. de Souza* 102

10. Portuguese in the Deccan Politics: A Study of New Marathi Documents from Lisbon .... *A.R. Kulkarni* 114

11. Arrest, Spoliation and Exile of the Goa Jesuits according to Father Caeiro's *De Exilio* .... *J.P. Bacelar é Oliveira* 123

12. Indian Textiles in Portuguese Collections: A Problem of Provenance .... *Lotika Varadarajan* 133

13. A Portuguese Creole in Sri Lanka: A Brief Socio-Linguistic Survey .... *M.H. Goonatilleka* 147

14. The Image of Goa .... *Caroline Ifeka* 181

15. Diogo Ribeiro's *Vocabulario da Lingoa Canarim* and its Historical Significance .... *Rocky V. Miranda* 196

16. The Writings of Francisco Luis Gomes .... *Henry Scholberg* 203

17. The Presence of Indian Culture in the Work of some Portuguese Writers .... *Maria dos Remedios Castelo-Branco &* .... *Fernando Castelo-Branco* 216

18. Asian Trade and World Economy from the 15th to 18th Centuries .... *Niels Steensgaard* 225

Index 237

1

Indian Merchants and the Portuguese Trade on the Malabar Coast during the Sixteenth Century

K.S. MATHEW

IT IS generally accepted that one of the aims of the Portuguese adventurers and the Crown of Portugal in discovering the perilous sea-route to India was to establish direct commercial contacts with the spice-producing areas of the Orient and derive the maximum profit by doing away with the middle-men and probably also the Indian merchants. The King of Portugal issued specific instructions to this effect and the local authorities in Portuguese India tried their best to materialise this goal. The Portuguese expansion in the East was considered to be the continuation of the attempts of the *reconquista* of the Iberian Peninsula and so wresting the trade in Oriental commodities out of the hands of the Muslim merchants was one of the ramifications of the same "crusading" enterprise. Perhaps, realising it unfeasible to do away with the local merchants altogether, the Portuguese government gave specific instructions to the governors and viceroys to encourage Hindu and Christian merchants on the subcontinent of India to the disadvantage of the Muslim merchants. In the light of these facts it is judged worthwhile to inquire if the Portuguese succeeded or not in avoiding the local merchants in their commercial transactions with India, and if not, what the main reasons were. One could also ask if the Portuguese met with success in avoiding the Muslim merchants or not. Further, some light could be thrown on the nature of services rendered to the Portuguese by the Indian merchants. Moreover, if the Hindus and the Christians who were professionally not merchants were brought into the field of trade and commerce, there could be some changes in the social life of the people and this also may be discussed at least in passing. An attempt is made here in this paper to highlight these problems drawing on the Portuguese sources of the sixteenth century.

The Portuguese, from the very beginning, took necessary measures to avoid the local traders and enter on direct relations with the Kings on the western coast, who, according to their conception, were the owners of the commodities, and the cultivators themselves. Vasco da Gama, intent on concluding direct contracts of trade with the Kings on the Malabar coast, arrived at Cannanore on October 18, 1502. In his interview with the King of Cannanore on the following day, he pressed the matter of fixing the prices of spices and other commodities. The King told him that he had nothing to do with this and that it was a matter which should be settled with the merchants who were the proprietors of the commodities. So, the King sent for the Muslim merchants to deal the subject directly with the Portuguese. Offended as he was with such a reaction on the part of the King, Vasco da Gama left for Cochin,[1] where he met the King with a letter of introduction from the King of Portugal.[2] When he insisted on the fixation of the price of spices, the King confessed the fact that it was the merchants who were the proprietors of spices and that the matter should be finalised with them. At last on January 3, 1503, Vasco da Gama reached an agreement with the local merchants regarding the price and other details of trade.[3] Thus the Portuguese were frustrated in their attempts to establish direct relations with the Kings or the cultivators with regard to the purchase of commodities.

However, they did not cease trying to avoid the local merchants and contact the cultivators directly. Dom Francisco da Almeida, the first viceroy, instructed the officials in India in 1508 to announce to the cultivators at the sound of trumpet that they would be immediately paid in cash and copper for the pepper they brought directly to the Portuguese factory. The response, however, was not encouraging: only an *Ilava* gentleman was reported to have brought some pepper to the factory at Cochin and received payment in cash and copper[4] Generally those who produced pepper were not the Muslims but the Christians and the Hindus who delivered it to the Muslim merchants for the goods they needed. Later in 1518, Pero Nunes. the Comptroller of Finance, contacted the Christians of Cranganore, who were the producers of pepper in that area, and concluded an agreement to the effect that they should not sell their pepper to the Muslim merchants, but should sell it directly to the Portuguese officials in future. He sought the help of the Armenian priest, Jacome Abuna, in charge of the Christians, and the latter along with the factor, Manuel Botelho, visited the Christians and instructed them to do the same.[5] However, the attempts did not meet with success and the Portuguese had to get the help of local merchants in various ways.

One of the most important services rendered to the Portuguese by the local merchants consisted in supplying commodities on credit. The Muslim merchants of Cannanore, namely, Mamale, Mohammed Ali and Pokkarachan used to deliver merchandise on credit at the Portuguese factory.[6] Sometimes these merchants supplied commodities on the guarantee of the Kings on the Malabar coast. This practice continued also in the late sixteenth century when the Portuguese capital meant for trade began to dwindle.[7] The local merchants after receiving an advance from the Portuguese captain or the factor of the respective ports, collected commodities from the cultivators and stored them in their own godowns and delivered them to the Portuguese at the time of the arrival of the ships from Portugal.[8]

Apart from supplying commodities on credit, the local merchants advanced loans to the Portuguese officials in charge of the Indian affairs.[9] According to the report given by Lourenço Moreno in 1513, the Portuguese had taken a loan of 10,000 *pardaos* from the Malabar coast.[10] Khoja Shams-ud-din of the province of Gilan,[11] who had his base in Cannanore after 1543, is reported to have given a loan of 750,000 *pardaos* of gold to the Portuguese governor.[12] He had a great treasure in Cannanore and was taken in confidence by the Portuguese governor,[13] and the latter personally went to meet the former at his place in Cannanore[14] and to collect a huge amount of loan from him. In fact, there were several people who had their doubts about this loan and so during the tenure of the office João de Castro made inquiry into the matter.[15]

Some resourceful local merchants supplied their own vessels to the Portuguese for the transportation as well as defence. Thus Nino Marakkar of Cochin sent his ship to Malacca for the sake of the Portuguese activities there. Since the Portuguese did not have any ships ready or any pilot, the merchant came forward with his ship and helped them.[16] A few of the Gujarati merchants gave their vessels to the Portuguese for transporting the textile goods from Cambay to the Portuguese factories on the Malabar coast from where these items were again carried to Malacca to purchase spices from there.[17] The vessels of Chilay Marakkar were used in transporting elephants from the Malabar coast to Goa and from there to Portugal.[18]

Some of the local merchants went so far as to defend the Portuguese against their enemies. Thus Nino Marakkar with the co-operation of his brother who had trading establishments in the Coramandel coast arranged 1,500 fighters to overpower the enemies of the Portuguese in that region.[19]

Most of the local merchants acted as contractors to the Portuguese and contacted the cultivators directly by going from one place to another; giving rice, cloth and cash with a view to getting pepper, ginger and so on at the time of harvest. They took cotton textiles from Cambay to the Malabar coast to exchange for the commodities available there.[20] In certain cases they themselves stored the merchandise after receiving the advance from the Portuguese officials and delivered them at the time of loading the ships bound for Portugal.[21] These merchants presumably collected the commodities from the cultivators at whatever price they succeeded in finalising and then delivered them to the Portuguese factories at the price fixed in advance. Thus Cherina Marakkar of Cochin supplied 3,000 *bhars*[22] of pepper to the Portuguese in 1504[23] according to the terms of the contract. Therefore, the local merchants tried to derive the maximum profit by purchasing the commodities at the cheapest price possible from the cultivators and selling them to the Portuguese at the stipulated rate. Since, in many a case these merchants exchanged goods such as textiles, rice and so on for the spices, they had the opportunity of increasing the rate of their profit.

Some of the merchants who supplied pepper and other goods to the Portuguese were given some remuneration for their services. Thus Ali Apula, a Muslim merchant of Edappally, was given twenty *crusados* a year as the remuneration for the services he rendered to the Portuguese. Similarly, Mathias and Bragaida Taquatome of Kayamkulam who, from the beginning of the Portuguese contacts with the southern part of Malabar coast helped in finding the necessary cargo, were given special allowance by the Portuguese. Presumably such merchants acted as paid agents of the Portuguese rather than independent merchants who supplied commodities according to the terms of a contract.

The local merchants, especially the resourceful ones, did not confine themselves to supplying commodities only to the Portuguese. They also conducted trade with other parts of the world with the knowledge of the Portuguese. Thus Cherina Marakkar of Cochin used to take *cartazes* from the Portuguese officials and sent commodities to Eden.[24] A great merchant, Khoja Shams-ud-din, had his commercial establishments in Arabia and Persia. He received the *cartazes* from the Portuguese to send his cargo ships to Mecca and Ormuz.[25] In 1543 he sent three ships with commodities to Mecca and the Persian Gulf area.[26] He had his brother Abdul Jabbar in Arabia and there were great trading houses in the Red Sea area. It was through this way that the spices reached Cairo and the marts of the Mediterranean, and finally to the various parts of the Continent. Thus Khoja Shams-ud-din had a large network of international trade besides being one of the most important merchants of India collaborating with the Portuguese. It is held by a number of historians that Indian spices were available in Cairo, Alexandria, Antioch and Beirut in the forty's of the sixteenth century.[27] Probably, the revival of the Levantine trade in the period after 1540 may be explained in the light of the activities of the local merchants like Khoja Shams-ud-din and the difficulty of the Portuguese to withhold the permits to these merchants to whom they were greatly indebted.

In fact, the freedom granted to the influential local merchants to conduct trade with the Persian Gulf and the Red Sea areas helped the Portuguese to a great extent. These merchants acted also as spies collecting information for the Portuguese. The details regarding the movements of the Turks passed on to the Portuguese through Khoja Shams-ud-din were of paramount importance and enabled the Portuguese to be ready to face the threat.[28] He had a great number of spies all over[29] and collected information from the various parts in India and passed it on to the Portuguese in right time.

These merchants who rendered services of various types to the Portuguese belonged to different groups such as the Muslims, both Indian and foreign, Hindus, Christians and Jews.

Cherina Marakkar and Mammale Marakkar, who were the chief merchants of Cochin, belonging to the Muslim group, were taken in great confidence by the Portuguese. They gave 2,000 *crusados* in cash and 4,000 in kind to these merchants in 1504 with a view to getting 3,000 *bhars* of pepper at the time of loading the ships.[30] The King of Cochin took these merchants with him when he went to visit the Portuguese captain and the other persons of importance.[31] Even when the King made official visits to the viceroy these merchants accompanied him[32]—a fact which shows the importance of the position held by the merchants. They went all over Malabar to procure pepper as cheap as they could and delivered it to the Portuguese factories. Ali Apula, another Muslim merchant from Edappally, used to supply large quantity of pepper to the Portuguese every year and received special remuneration for the services.[33] Similarly, Khoja Mapilla and Abraham Mapilla Cunhavirey, both from Edappally and belonging to the Muslim community, sold the spices to the Portuguese at Cochin.[34] Mohammed Maçary was one of the principal muslim merchants of Calicut who helped the Portuguese in their trade in the second decade of the sixteenth century.[35] A certain Mammale was a great merchant who helped the Portuguese in the matter of trade in Cannanore. Similarly, Mohammed Aly and Pokkarachan were also merchants from Cannanore who extended considerable help to the

Portuguese.[36] Khoja Shams-ud-din was the most important merchant in the forties of the sixteenth century with whom the Portuguese had very cordial relations. The Governor with his retinue visited him at his palatial residence at Cannanore.[37] All these merchants were from the Muslim community. Khoja Bequy, a resident of Calicut, but hailing from Ormuz, was another Muslim merchant of substance who had close contacts with the Portuguese in their commercial activities.

The Portuguese King often instructed his officials to favour Christian merchants as against the Muslims.[38] In fact, special efforts were made by the governors and viceroys to encourage the Christian merchants. But only a few Christian merchants figure in the contemporary documents. Mathias and Bragaida Taquatome were the Christian merchants of Kayamkulam and Quilon who supplied commodities to the Portuguese.[39] Mathias with the co-operation of his colleagues delivered also cinnamon to them.[40] The Portuguese helped these merchants of South Malabar by giving them food material and cash for daily expenses. There was another Christian merchant by name Mathaimapila of Edappally who supplied pepper regularly to the Portuguese factory.[41] Apart from these stray cases of Christians taking part in the Indo-Portuguese trade there is no evidence to show that they rose to the expectation of the Portuguese. One of the reasons why they could not flourish was the utter lack of investment. They had very little to invest in trade as reported by the Portuguese officials.[42] Presumably the Christians considered trade as innovation to their traditional life and they were slow to take to trade.

In order to bring up a rival group to the Muslim merchants and to overthrow them, the Portuguese had made special efforts to encourage the Hindus in the matter of trade. Specific instructions were issued by the Portuguese King to this effect.[43] Though the desired effect was not achieved, a few Hindu merchants responded to the stimulus given by the Portuguese officials. Thus Ittikunju, a Nair merchant from Cranganore, supplied large quantity of pepper to the Portuguese factor.[44]

Jewish merchants too had their share in the Indo-Portuguese trade of the sixteenth century. They collected textiles from Cambay and took them to the Malabar coast which the

Portuguese exchanged for pepper and other commodities.[45]

In the light of the details furnished above, a few points could be raised. Why did the Portuguese fail to avoid the local merchants in general and enter into direct trade relations with the cultivators ? In spite of the earnest efforts made by the Portuguese, why could they not get rid of the Muslim merchants ?

It seems that on account of a number of problems inherent to the organisation of the Portuguese trade with India, it was impossible for them to avoid the local merchants. The officials in touch with the local conditions in India placed two suggestions in order to realise the target. One, the Portuguese merchants should go from cultivator to cultivator supplying rice, clothes and other things of daily need in exchange of pepper, ginger and so on. This would take a long time and had to be done before the arrival of the ships that could not afford to wait in the ports more than three to four months as the sailing depended on the monsoon winds.[46] But the Portuguese did not import these things to India and if at all they were to follow this, they should purchase them from various parts of India and take to those areas from where pepper and similar commodities were to be purchased directly from the cultivators. They brought mainly copper and cash to India and the mode of payment in copper and cash to the cultivators for the commodities they supplied was not at all welcome or profitable to the cultivators,[47] because they had no possibility to take copper to places like Cambay where it could be easily sold. Again they would fall prey to the local merchants. Therefore, the cultivators preferred local merchants who would supply goods of daily consumption in exchange for their products.

The other alternative would be the availability of cash to purchase the commodities at the harvesting time and also during the short time between the arrival of the ships and their departure. But the Portuguese did not bring that much cash necessary for quick transaction. The harvesting time did not coincide with the arrival of the ships from Portugal. If they had enough resources, they could purchase the commodities at the harvesting time and store them till the arrival of the ships. But the financial position and the other conditions were not favourable and so they depended on the local resourceful merchants who purchased the merchandise from the cultivators and stored them for the Portuguese. Another factor was the unreliability of the government officials of the Portuguese India who would take such stored commodities to Cambay and sell if the purchase and storing is done in advance. Thus they would be tempted to make private profit at the expense of the state.[48]

The inevitability of resorting to the local merchants springs from another source too. In certain cases the great merchants kept the cultivators and the retail merchants away from the direct contact with the Portuguese by spreading frightening rumours about the foreigners. They were told that the Portuguese officials would take extra weight while purchasing the commodities if they directly sold to them, and similarly they would pay very badly. It was also said that they would maltreat the cultivators and consider them slaves. These and several other rumours prevented the cultivators from being directly in touch with the Portuguese.[49] Since such a direct contact was rendered impossible, they had to rely on the local merchants.

As it is discussed elsewhere, the best and most trusted local merchants with whom the Portuguese had constant relations were the Muslim merchants of the west coast. The Portuguese King issued specific instructions to avoid them.[50] Though the officials in India had taken this instruction to heart, their attempts did not meet with success, on account of a variety of factors of which they were fully aware. In fact, the Christian merchants who had to be favoured in contrast to the Muslims, had very little to invest in trade nor could the Hindu merchants compete with the Muslims for lack of capital available in the matter of trade. The Muslim merchants, on the other hand, on account of their long-time involvement in trade had the wherewithal for the same and could challenge the others. As the contemporary Portuguese observer notes, the Muslim merchants had already inhabited the commercial centres in India and occupied prominent positions. Even the Hindu rulers and chieftains favoured the Muslim merchants on account of the great profit they reaped from the trade conducted by the Muslims.[51]

The mode of payment for the commodities, adopted by the Portuguese, was another ground for the growth of Muslim merchants in contrast to others. The payment for pepper was made partly in copper according to the contract concluded in the first decade of the sixteenth century. Except the Muslim merchants, nobody welcomed it. The Hindu as well as the Christian merchants immediately sold the copper to the Muslims and very reluctantly accepted this term.[52] The latter who owned and manned even the ships of the Hindus took this part payment to Cambay where it had a very good market and made much profit. The Hindus, who under some taboo, did not travel much in the sea could not welcome this mode of payment followed by the Portuguese. Hence the very structure of the Portuguese trade did not turn out to be conducive to the growth of the merchants other than the Muslims.

However, the induction of the Hindus, especially the Nairs and Christians into the field of trade brought about some considerable changes in the social structure on the west coast of India in general and of Malabar in particular. The Nairs in the past followed a martial life and remained as retainers of the Kings and chieftains. Now that new avenue was opened to them and encouragement was given by the Portuguese, some of them left their traditional profession and began activities connected with trade and commerce. A number of them were appointed in the various factories as accountants, interpreters and agents for the Portuguese. Similar change is effected in the case of the Christians too.

It may be concluded that the position of the local merchants did not suffer any lasting rebuff with the arrival of the Portuguese on the scene of Indian trade either in the internal or external trade. On the contrary they flourished by extending their commercial enterprises to a wider spectrum such as taking up trade in copper and other things imported by the Portuguese and sending commodities to various distant places under the security provided by the system of *cartazes*. Thus the non-producing elements got an opportunity to establish their sway between the two extremes of production, namely, the cultivator and the consumer, and finally exploit the producers. This situation was owing mainly to the very organisation of the Portuguese trade with India.

NOTES

1. Thomé Lopes, 'Navegação as India's Orientais', in *Collecção de Noticias para a Historia e Geografia das Nações ultramarinas que vivem nos Dominios Portugueses ou lhes são vizinhas*, tom ii. Nos. 1 & 2, Lisbon, 1812, pp. 181-82.
2. Antonio da Silva Rego, (ed) *Documentação para a Historia das Missões do Padroado Portugues do Oriente*, vol. I. Lisbon, 1947, pp. 22-24.
3. Thomé Lopes, *op. cit.*, pp. 199-200.
4. A.B. de Bragança Pereira, *Arquivo Português Oriental* tomo IV, volume I, Part I, Bastora, 1937, pp. 295-6.
5. Antonio da Silva Rego, *op. cit.*, vol. II, pp. 353-54.
6. Raymundo Antonio de Bulhão Pato (ed). *Cartas de Affonso de Albuquerque*, tom I, Lisboa, 1884, p. 268 (hereafter *Cartas*).
7. Archivo General de Simancas (MSS) Secretarias Provinciales Cod. 1571, fls 20-21.
8. Archivo Nacional da Torre Do Tombo (hereafter ANTT), Coll. de S. Lourenço (MSS) tom. II, fls 378-379.
9. Vide No. 6, *Cartas* tom III, (Lisboa, 1903), p. 397.
10. *ibid.*, p. 396.
11. Diogo de Couto, *Da Asia—Decada* V. part II, (Lisboa, 1780), p. 366.
12. ANTT. Coll. de S. Lourenço, fl. 128; ANTT. Corpo Chronologico. MSS, Part I, document 76-103, (hereafter ANTT CC).
13. Gaspar Correa, *Lendas da India* tom iv, part I, (Lisboa, 1864), p. 335.
14. Diogo de Couto, *op. cit.*, part II, pp. 387 ff.
15. ANTT. CC., I-76-103.
16. *Cartas* (supra), tom II, p. 378.
17. *ibid*, tom VII, p. 132.
18. *ibid*, tom VI, p. 31.
19. *ibid*, tom II, p. 378.
20. ANTT. Cartas dos Vicereis (MSS) No. 95.
21. ANTT. Col. de S. Lourenço, tom II, fls 378-9.
22. *Bhar* is a weight used in Malabar which is 166.3 kgs.
23. *Cartas* tom III, p. 257.
24. *ibid.*, tom. I. p. 49.
25. Gaspar Correa, *op. cit.*, tom iv, part 1, p. 341.
26. *As Gavetas da Torre do Tombo*, tom III, (Lisbon, 1963), p. 205.
27. F.C. Lane, 'The Mediterranean spice trade : its revival in the sixteenth century', in *Venice and History*, (Baltimore, 1966), p. 33.
28. ANTT. CC. I-78-108.
29. Gaspar Correa, *op. cit.*, p. 404.
30. *Cartas*, tom III, p. 257.
31. *Cronica do Descobrimento e a conquista da India pelos Portugueses*—codice anonimo, Museu Britanico, (Egerton 20901), Coimbra, p. 121.
32. *Cartas*, tom II, pp. 361, 368.

33. *Cartas*, tom V, pp. 503-4.
34. *Cartas*, tom VII, p. 174.
35. *Cartas*, tom I, p. 142, tom IV, p. 179.
36. *ibid.*, tom I, p. 125.
37. Gaspar Correa, *op. cit.*, tomo. IV, part I, p. 403.
38. *Cartas*, tom I, p. 306.
39. *Cartas*, tom II, p. 268, tom III, pp. 30, 258-59, tom VI, p. 114, 398-99 ; tom VII, p. 93. Barros, *Decada* I, Part I, p. 350.
40. *Cartas*, tom VII, pp. 93-94.
41. *ibid.*, tom VII, p. 174.
42. *ibid.*, tom I, p. 306.
43. *ibid.*
44. *Cartas*, tom VII, p. 174.
45. ANTT. Cartas dos Vicereis da India, No. 95.
46. *Cartas*, tom I, p. 330.
47. *ibid.*, tom I, *ibid.*
48. *ibid.*
49. A. Silva Rego, *op. cit.*, vol. II, pp. 352-53.
50. *Cartas*, tom I, p. 306.
51. *ibid.*
52. *ibid.* p. 330.

2

The Return Cargoes of the Carreira in the 16th and Early 17th Century

NIELS STEENSGAARD

IN SPITE of the historical importance of the carreira, our knowledge of the volume of commodities imported by the Portuguese carracks into Europe rests on a slender basis. Documentary sources such as bills of lading, invoices, cargo registers and so on have with few exceptions disappeared, and the representativity and completeness of contemporary reports is disputable.

On this background it is hardly surprising that historians have reached different conclusions regarding the volume of the return cargoes. The figures quoted most frequently are the estimates made by Frederic C. Lane and V. Magalhães-Godinho. Lane's primary aim was to determine the relative importance of the revived spice trade through the Levant after the middle of the 16th century. He based his estimate on various evidence, especially four entries in the famous Sanudo diaries from 1518, 1519, 1530 and 1531, reporting annual imports from 18.164 to 48.097 cantaras of pepper and spice.[1] He assumed that there was a falling off in Portuguese imports from the middle of the century, and with some reservations he quoted Bal Krishna's estimate of Portuguese imports by the end of the 16th century, a maximum of 30—40.000 quintals a year.[2]

Magalhães-Godinho made a much more thorough study of

the problem. He concluded that the return cargoes in the first third of the 16th century were not less than 40.000 quintals a year and possibly more than 50.000. Later in the century these figures increased by 50 percent, i.e., 60.000-75.000 quintals.[3] The evidence he builds upon is, besides the Sanudo diaries, a number of similar reports concerning the cargoes on returning fleets, six fleets from the years 1501-1506 and eleven fleets comprising 51 vessels from the years 1513-1548.

Only two or perhaps three of the documented cargoes are above 40.000 quintals,[4] but Magalhães-Godinho made two important assumptions, which made it necessary to increase the recorded figures, one that the volumes reported should be inflated by at least 25 per cent in order to compensate for unregistered commodities, the other that the average capacity of the carracks of the carreira increased by 50 per cent during the century.[5] Neither of these assumptions is entirely convincing.

The registration

Obviously, the problem of unregistered trade is crucial, because, as pointed out by C.H.H. Wake, the ultimate sources of the contemporary figures must be the cargo lists of the *escrivão da nao* or similar documents.[6] The question is, did the registers include all commodities brought on board or did all or part of the commodities carried according to the several liberties and privileges of the sailors, the officers and the merchants go unrecorded ? At our present state of knowledge the arguments are in favour of the former view. Firstly, because several travellers emphasize the strictness of registration. Linschoten gives a very detailed description of the procedure in stowing the ships in Goa or Cochin, and states that nothing could be brought on board the ships, before it was registered with the veador de fazenda; and that the stevedore did not let any chest on bale on board without having seen a certificate from the veador, specifying the contents.[7]

The same meticulous control with everything brought on board ship is emphasized by Pyrard de Laval, who, however, indicates that the *escrivão da nao* was the key figure.[8] Perhaps an analysis of the escrivão's instructions located by C.R.Boxer might reveal the procedure prescribed for the writer.[9] A third traveller, Mocquet, supplements the evidence concerning registration before departure in a most valuable way by his complaints over the trouble he had to get his chest after his arrival in Lisbon. Everything was brought to the *Casa da India,* he says, and nobody could get his chest, before it had been controlled and all dues were settled. Mocquet had to wait a month.[10]

The evidence of the travellers covering the 1580's and the first decade of the 17th century is conclusive as far as the principle is concerned: A complete registration including the liberty chests of the sailors and passengers was supposed to take place. But this does not prove that it always took place. Bribes and influence may have shielded the rich and the powerful against the strict control observed by the humble travellers. Corruption was, so to speak, a matter of routine in the Estado[11] and according to Linschoten the stevedores were not above receiving a bribe for finding a safe place for a bale or a chest. Mocquet tells us, that deplorable mistakes occurred in the *Casa*, some people had their chests returned neatly locked—but empty.[12] Neither of them intimates, however, that it should be possible to bribe one's way round the registration.

But in all probability smuggling did take place. According to Magalhães-Godinho a petition from the farmers of the customs—a biased source admittedly—indicates more than 25 per cent fraud on private imports before 1590. In 1601 the king ordered that the unloading of the carracks in Lisbon should be supervised by Castilian guards.[13] Still, I find it hard to believe that extensive smuggling in voluminous commodities took place. Control was easy, after all this was a matter of 3-5 ships a year, not the scores of vessels dodging the control of the Casa da Contratacion in Seville. Several bribes would have to be paid, in India, on board ship and in Lisbon. And finally, anyone smuggling on a ship of the carreira would have been very clumsy to choose voluminous goods, when pearls and precious stones were so much easier to hide and brought a profit of 2-300 per cent.[14]

So my conclusion is that the registers drawn up before the departure of the ships were fairly reliable and comprehensive so far as voluminous goods were concerned. So far we know of only two registers, from 1505 and 1518, published by Geneviève Bouchon. Both these registers have full details on the consignments carried in the name of officials and sailors.[15] Possibly more registers may be uncovered in the archives, but our main source of information remains at present second hand, summaries of the registers dispersed in various European archives and collections like the Sanudo diaries. Though it is impossible to give definite proof, the probability is that a summary of the register was prepared already in the port of embarkation and forwarded to the home authorities. At least one summary has been preserved with correspondence from Goa in the Provincial Secretaries' archive in Simancas. (See Table 2.1). There is also evidence indicating that the registers were amended after the unloading of the ship in Lisbon.

These summaries were of enormous interest to several parties. To the Portuguese and later to the Spanish authorities they would serve to indicate the resources available after the safe arrival of the fleet. To merchants dealing in spices and drugs they would reveal the probable development of the market. This was not a matter of idle curiosity, the recipients wanted complete and correct information. A sharp distinction should. therefore, be made between mere rumours and speculations and genuine summaries like those uncovered by Lane and Magalhães-Godinho in the Venetian diaries.

If the above line of reasoning is correct, the figures in the genuine summaries should not be inflated in order to account for unregistered goods. The registers and, therefore, the summaries would be minimal, but as far as voluminous commodities are concerned they may be expected to record fairly accurately the commodities carried by the *carreira* In support of this might be added, that complete information was what the recipients were looking for, and in no case, that I know of, has the informant offered any conjectures concerning unregistered goods.

The Fleet of 1587

The fleet which left India in 1587 is of special interest, because we are informed of its return cargo from several sides. The fleet originally consisted of four ships, but one of them, the Great Gonzo of the carreira, the *Reliquias*, capsized on leaving Cochin.[16] The *São Salvador* was damaged off the East African coast, part of the cargo had to be jettisoned, but she finally reached safely in Hormuz, where the remnant of the cargo was unloaded. The last two ships of the fleet, the *São Thomé* and the *Conceicão*, arrived in Lisbon in August 1587.

In the Provincial Secretary's archive in Simancas a summary of the cargo of the *São Salvador*, the *São Thomé* and the *Conceição* is preserved bound with original correspondence from India. In all probability, therefore, this summary was prepared in India after the foundering of the *Reliquias* but before the fate of the *São Salvador* was known.[17] This official summary may be compared to a report from an agent of the English crown, Hector Nunez, preserved in the Public Record Office. "The ladings of the ship called the Ste Thomas which came this year 1587 from Callacowth" and "The ladinge of the shipp called oure Ladie".[18] By and large this report corroborates the official summary, but some minor discrepancies together with the fact that only the cargoes of the *São Thomé* and the *Conceição* are registered indicate that Hector Nunez's informer had access to a list that was revised after the preparation of the first summary. The figures concerning pepper, cinnamon, and nutmeg are the same in the two lists but Hector Nunez' figures for indigo, cloves, nutmeg and mace are 2-5 quintals higher than the corresponding figures in the official summary. The assumption that Hector Nunez' informer had access to a later version of the register is supported by the fact that his list includes ebony, aloes socotrina and hard wax, presumably taken on board in Mozambique.

Two further sources offer information as far as the pepper cargo of 1587 is concerned. The Fuggers' representatives in Goa reported in 1587 that the pepper cargo of the *Reliquias* was 1,637 quintals; the *São Salvador* carried 2,586 quintals and the *São Thomé* and the *Conceição* together 10,368 quintals.[19] These are the same figures (except for the *Reliquias* which is only mentioned in the Fugger report) as in the two summaries referred to above. Figueiredo Falcão reports a cargo of 10,378 quintals of pepper on the *São Thomé* and the *Conceição*, the discrepancy of 10 quintals is probably only a copyist's error.[20]

The fifth source of information concerning the fleet of 1587 is rather a special case, the report of the Italian traveller Balbi, who watched the unloading of the damaged São Salvador in Hormuz and whose report often has been quoted as an example of the volume and value of the Portuguese return cargoes. A comparison between Balbi's estimate and the official summary referred to above is revealing.

TABLE 2.1 : **The cargo of the São Salvador according to Balbi compared to the official summary of the register.**

	Balbi[21]	*Off. Summary*
Pepper	4-5,000 cantaras	2,586 quintals
Indigo	1,500 bales	1,223 –
Cinnamon	500 cantaras	658 –
Ginger	100-150 cantaras	401 –
Chinese silk	40 chests	141 caixas
Various textiles	80 small chests	188 fardos
Nutmeg	200 cantaras	137 quintals
Cloves		137 –
Mace		50 –
Drugs etc.		87 –
Jettisoned	Goods to the value of 300.000 ducats.	

Balbi's estimate of the pepper cargo must be totally discarded, the 2,586 quintals of the official summary is confirmed by the fact that the same figure was quoted by the owners of the pepper when they claimed the insurance.[22] We cannot possibly imagine the smuggling of 2-3,000 quintals of the most closely supervised commodity in the India trade. Balbi may, however, have estimated the quantity of pepper to the best of his ability, pepper was stowed loosely, so that even for an eye-witness it would be difficult to determine the exact quantity.

The figures concerning indigo cannot be compared, as we do not know the weight of the bales. Normally, however, indigo was packed in bales of c. 2 quintals,[23] so the possibility that Balbi witnessed the unloading of contraband indigo cannot be excluded. All Balbi's other estimates are below the officially recorded quantities, his list is short by some 150 quintals cinnamon, 260-310 quintals ginger, 188 bales and 21 chests of textiles and more than 200 quintals of spices and drugs, in all c. 600-650 quintals, 200 bales and 20 chests.

Balbi's lower figures regarding quantities are accounted for by the fact that part of the cargo was jettisoned. He estimates the value of the jettisoned goods at 300.000 ducats. This figure should hardly be taken too seriously, a tendency among the individual owners to exaggerate the enormity of their losses is only to be expected. As we do not know the qualities of the textiles it is not possible to make an estimate of the value of the jettisoned goods, but the European sales value of 600 quintals of spices and drugs and 220 packs of textiles might easily be 100.000 ducats or more.

The character of the missing commodities is in harmony with our information concerning stowage of the carracks. The pepper was stowed on the two lower decks, it was poured in loosely from above in compartments which were sealed, when the stowing was completed. Only around the main mast a space was kept for water, provisions and firewood. On the third deck the ships' officials had their cabins, which they usually hired out to merchants, if they did not want to use them for transport themselves. On the fourth deck and in the superstructure the privately owned chests, bales and packs were stowed. Finally the ships, when departing from India, carried a considerable deck cargo, 7-8 chests on top of each other according to one informant, half-way up the main mast according to another.[24]

Part of the deck cargo consisted in privately owned provisions for the voyage, including hen coops. The king provided the returning sailors and soldiers with water and biscuit only, so that they had to bring their own provisions, if they felt they needed a more varied fare.[25] But probably the deck cargo also included the liberty chests of the more humble crew members and passengers. Pyrard de Laval tells us that the men started fighting among themselves and that several had to be clapped in iron, when part of the deck cargo had to be jettisoned during a storm off the Cape.[26] Linschoten adds another valuable piece of information: It was the apprentice sailors, the "grumetes", who were the first to lose, when part of the deck cargo had to be thrown overboard, because they could not afford to bribe the stevedores in order to secure a safe place for their chests.[27]

The last part of the cargo to go was the pepper, not only because of the strict rulings, but also because of its inaccessibility. An anecdote from the loss of the *Aguia* gives us a glimpse of the criteria that might be applied when goods were selected for jettisoning. When the crew were bringing out commodities to be thrown overboard, they came across a quantity of indigo, which the king had given to the monastery of Nossa Senhora da Graça in Lisbon. The captain was asked if it was to be jettisoned, but he refused "He added that if matters reached the stage that the only hope of salvation lay in jettisoning his own merchandise, then that should be thrown overboard, but that he himself was prepared to carry ashore on his shoulders the merchandise belonging to Our Lady, in whose favour he trusted for the salvation and preservation of that ship.[28]

So taking Balbi's figures at face value they rather confirm than invalidate the reliability of the official summary. The 600-1,000 quintals of spices, drugs and textiles missing in his list represent liberty chests and other easily accessible merchandise thrown overboard during the storm.

The varied information concerning the fleet of 1587 serves to strengthen the impression that a fairly complete registration of the cargoes took place before departure and that the genuine summaries in all essentials reflect the composition of the cargoes.

Register summaries 1588-1610

The cargo of 1588 is known through a summary sent to the Fugger consortium which held the pepper contract in these years by its representatives in India.[29] It may be considered a genuine summary, not only because the Fuggers certainly did not pay their factors to supply them with unreliable information, but also because the figures concerning pepper are confirmed by Falcão, who registers exactly the same quantity for the fleet of 1588 : 22963 quintals.[30]

The next preserved summary concerns the return fleet of 1600 and is located in a bundle of miscellaneous business papers of the Dandolo family, which was involved in the pepper import from Alexandria.[31] The two lists are headed : "Portata delle 5 nave d'India di Portogallo ene a Lisbona a 23 agosto 1600" and "Portata della nave che resta a dietro". These ships can be identified as the *São Rocque*, the *Conceicão*, the *Paz*, the *São Simão* and the *São Matheus*, which according to Falcão arrived in Lisbon on the 23rd of August 1600, and the *São Martinho*, which arrived in Brazil the same year.[32]

Similar summaries have been preserved in the Public Records Office bound with correspondence from Portugal and concerning 1602 and 1603. The two lists are headed respectively : "A nott of al shuch marchandises and comoditis which cam from the Easte India in these 2 shippes and now unladen hier in Lisbourne this august of a. 1602—the on of them caled the Sant Salvador and the other caled the sent Jhon" and "the lading of 4 shipps of the East India for Lisbone 1603".[33] The six ships may by means of Falcão be identified as the *São Salvador* and the *São João*, which arrived in Lisbon on 16th of August 1602, the *São Jacinto* and the *Nossa Senhora da Páz* arriving in Lisbon in June-July 1603 and the *São Rocque* and the *Conceição*, which made their port in Vigo, probably the same year.[34]

From the fleet of 1608 we know the summary of the cargo of one ship from a note appended to a letter from the Portugal council to the king and headed : "folha das fazendas que vão embarcadas nesta nao Jesus que desta barra de Goa parte este presente anno de 608 em 2 desenre delle".[35] As the letter to which the note is appended is dated the 23rd of September 1608 and the *Nossa Senhora de Jesus* according to Falcão arrived in Lisbon the 12th of September 1608[36] a slip in the dating of the note is most likely.

Finally two summaries from the Medici archive published by Braudel and Romano and placed by them among "problèmes sans solution"[37] may be identified as referring to Portuguese ships of the carreira. "Na Sa de Pieta venuta della India Orientale a di 14 di agosto 1610" can by means of Falcão be identified as the *Nossa Senhora de Piedade* arriving in Lisbon the 14th of August 1610, and "Nra Sa do monte del carmine", undated, can be identified as *Nossa Senhora do Monte do Carmo*, launched in 1608 and returning to Lisbon in 1610, in 1613 or 1614 and again in 1617.[38]

Average cargoes : Six samples

This survey has presented summaries of the cargoes of 23 ships returned between 1587 and 1610, which may be compared to the summaries concerning 51 ships returned between 1513 and 1548 published by Magalhães-Godinho and Wake.

TABLE **2.2 : Average cargo per ship distributed in samples 1513-1610 (bales and chests estimated at 2cw., small chests and bales at 1 cw.)**

	Number of ships	*Average cargo*	*Average pepper cargo*	*3 in % of 2*
	1	2	3	4
1513-19	24	6223 quint.	4978 quint.	80
1523-31	17	4345 —	3635 —	84
1547-48	10	6789 —	6023 —	89
1587-88	8	6638 —	4490 —	68
1600-03	12	7891 —	5519 —	65
1608-10	3	6110 —	4220 —	69

TABLE **2.3 : Average distribution of cargoes, sample as Table 2.2.**

	1513-19	*1523-31*	*1547-48*	*1587-88*	*1600-03*	*1608-10*
Pepper	80 %	84%	89%	68%	65%	69%
Ginger	7, 3%	6, 1%	4, 2%	3, 7%	2, 5%	1, 6%
Cinnamon	2, 1 —	3, 3 —	0, 9 —	6, 3 —	8, 7 —	9, 3 —
Moluccan spices	9, 0 —	6, 2 —	4, 5 —	1, 6 —	5, 0 —	0, 03 —
Textiles	0, 2 —	0 —	0 —	10, 5 —	12, 2 —	7, 8 —
Sundries	1, 4 —	0, 4 —	1, 4 —	1, 5 —	2, 2 —	4, 6 —
Indigo	0 —	0 —	0	8, 4 —	4, 4 —	7, 7 —
	100%	100%	100%	100%	100%	100%

The tables do not permit very definite conclusions concerning trends in the volume and composition of the return cargoes, the samples are very unevenly distributed and some of them, especially the last one, are too small to be considered representative. Nevertheless, some interesting features do emerge. The decline in the relative importance of the pepper which Glamann documented in the Dutch East India trade in the 17th century, apparently started already in the 16th century. The most important new commodities were textiles and indigo.

It is remarkable that four of the samples show an average cargo between 6,110 quintals and 6,789 quintals, this might suggest a very stable level of average cargoes. But the harmony is destroyed by the very high average of 1600-03-7891 quintals, the arbitrary composition of the samples may in fact hide a steady rise in the volume of average cargoes.

Even so, the lower figures of Lane's estimate must be preferred to the higher figures advocated by Magalhães-Godinho and Wake. Excepting the first 10-15 years the annual fleets send from India to Lisbon very rarely exceeded 5 ships. A shipment of 40.000 quintals must be a maximum rarely attained, the long term average must be between 25.000 and 30.000 quintals. The volume of goods safely arriving in Lisbon was further reduced by losses at sea, of course, an unpredictable factor but calculated by Magalhães-Godinho at 15 percent or more over the long term.[39]

Portuguese and English cargoes compared

The figures obtained may be compared to the scattered evidence concerning the return cargoes on North-West European company ships in the early 17th century. The Palsgrave and the Reformation departed from Bantam in January 1635 with the following cargo :[40]

In quintals of the *peso novo* the figures would be c. 7000 and 3400. The Reformation was a medium sized vessel, estimated at 4-500 tons in the English sources and at 200 lasts by the Dutch, while the Palsgrave was one of the largest English ships, estimated at 1000 or, with unusual precision, at 1083 tons by the English and at 400 lasts by the Dutch.[41]

TABLE 2.4 : **Cargo of the Palsgrave and the Reformation at Bantam 31st of January 1635.**

	Palsgrave	*Reformation*
Pepper	613541 lb. s	357540 lb. s
Cloves	225388 —	68330 —
Shells	4143 —	
Sugar	9702	
Ginger		4476 —
Textiles and silk	193 bales*	
Total	896,006 lb. s	430,346 lb. s

*Bales estimated at 2 cw. each.

Other company ships carried cargoes of the same magnitude. The Charles brought back in 1618 more than 8100 quintals of pepper, in 1621 more than 6400 quintals and in 1625 nearly 8000 quintals. Several other English East Indiamen carried cargoes of 6000-8000 quintals in the 1620's : The James, the Exchange, the Elizabeth, the Anne, the Mary, the Moon and the London.[42] The trouble is that the tonnage of these ships by contemporaries was estimated at 700-1000 tons, while their cargoes exceeded the highest Portuguese averages and approached the largest single Portuguese cargo on record, the São Thomé (1587) : 8675 quintals.

The Portuguese carracks were by the end of the 16th century considered the largest ships in the world. The travellers are unanimous on this point. According to Linschoten all the ships in the fleet on which he went out in 1583 were 7-800 lasts, corresponding to 14-1600 English shipping tons.[43]. Mocquet gives the tonnage of his ship the *Nossa Senhora do Monte do Carmo*, as 2000 tons and adds that it was one of the

the largest naos.[44] Pyrard de Laval tells us that the Portuguese East India men were the largest ships in the world with a tonnage of 1500-2000 tons.[45] We might discard these estimates as travellers' tales, if we did not have the evidence of the survey made of the *Madre de Deus* after it was brought into English harbour in 1592 and rated at 1600 tons.[46] How can we explain the discrepancy between the capacity and the registered cargo of the *naos* ?

The mystery of the missing monsters

Magalhães-Godinho considered the problem and reached the conclusion that the tonnage of the "normal" *nao* towards the end of the century was c. 600 tons, while the monsters, les mastodontes tardifs", "les monstrueuses de 1500 à 2000 tonneaux" were exceptions, with a capacity of 23000-30000 quintals besides contraband and liberty goods.[47] But this conclusion is hardly tenable in view of the fact that several of the notorious "monsters" are included in the samples presented above.

Wake argued that the "increase in the size of the carriers is a sure indication of the growth of the private trade of officials and mariners in the service of the Crown".[48] But, as I have shown above, an unregistered trade of such proportions is most unlikely.

In my opinion the key to the mystery is to be found in the description of the *Madre de Deus* :

> "The caracke being in burden by the estimation of the wise and experienced no lesse than 1600 tonnes, had full 900 of these stowed with the grosse bulke of marchandise, thc rest of the tunnage being allowed, partly to the ordinance which were 32 pieces of brasse of all sorts, partly to the passengers and victuals, which could not be any small quantity, considering the number of persons betwixt 6C0 and 700, and the length of the navigation...[49].

A ton of shipping allowed for each person sounds probable, L. Denoix has computed the weight of necessary provisions for an eight months overseas voyage at 850 kgs. or/nearly 15 quintals.[50]

This means that an ordinary crew of 120 men reduced the available hold capacity with c. H 1800 quintals. But the Portuguese carracks carried passengers as well as crew members. Several sources document the huge number of passengers on the outward voyage. In 1568 the *Chagas* left Lisbon with 830 persons on board.[51] A jesuit report of 1579 gives the figure of 500 plus 400 slaves taken aboard in Mozambique, he adds that mortality normally was low unless the ship was overcrowded, and refers to two cases where 500 out of 1140 and 300 out of 800 died during the voyage.[52] 500 is also the figure given by the Fugger employee Gabriel Holzschuher on his departure in 1579.[53] Sassetti allows 8-900 per ship as standard in the early 1580's.[54] Linschoten informs us that there were 4-500 persons on board each of the ships on departure from Lisbon.[55] *The São Jago*, which foundered on the outward voyage 1585/86 is said to have had 500 men on board.[56] Mocquet left Lisbon in 1608 on board the *Nossa Senhora do Monte do Carmo*, he states that the escrivão made a roll call after the departure and that they were 900 on board.[57] Pyrard de Laval tells us that outward bound ships often carried 7-800 soldiers besides sailors and passengers,[58] and about the fleet arriving in 1609 he tells us, that it consisted of four ships, each of 2000 tons, there had been 1000 men on board each on departure, but only 300 were alive on each ship when they arrived in Goa.[59] An English report from Lisbon about this particular fleet draws an even more sombre picture, there is said to have been 1500, mostly boys, on board each of the departing ships.[60]

The implications of these figures are obvious. 500 passengers would claim the hold capacity of a very large ship. Only a giant could carry 1000 passengers. The monsters were real.

We are less well-informed as far as the number of passengers on the homeward bound ships is concerned. Undoubtedly it was much below the figure for the outward bound sailings, when practically no cargo was carried. One Jesuit father informs us that the return voyage was the most comfortable, because those who travelled were richer and fewer, perhaps 20 Portuguese besides the sailors.[61] Nearly the same figure is repeated by Linschoten : 20-30 soldiers with their slaves.[62]

But the actual figures we have for the number of passengers on the return ships suggest, that these estimates are too conservative. The lowest figure on record concerns the ship on which Linschoten returned, the Indian built *Santa Cruz*, 200 persons in all, soldiers, sailors and slaves.[63] From the *Tragic History of the Sea* we know figures that are considerably higher. On the *Garça* and *Aguia* (1559) the total number of soldiers, sailors, slaves, women and children was 1037.[64] On the *São Alberto* (1593) 153 Portuguese and 194 slaves, 347 in all.[65] On the *São João Baptista* (1622) 279 persons survived on shore a month after the shipwreck.[66] Slaves were carried in large numbers. The *São Felipe* and the *Madre de Deus* carried 400 each.[67] In the ship on which Mocquet returned to Europe 300 slaves assisted by the pump.[68] The total number of crew and passengers on the *Madre de Deus* was 6-700, presumably including slaves.[69] Another carrack taken by the English, the *São Valentin*, had 600 persons on board.[70] Pyrard de Laval gives the total number of persons on board the *Nossa Senhora de Jesus* on departure from India as 800, including slaves and women.[71]

It was difficult for a soldier to obtain permission to return to Europe and he had to travel on his own cost. But the high officials of the Estado, the viceroy, the captain of the important captaincies, the members of the council and the archbishop were, of course, free to return and to return in state with family, slaves and retainers. "It must be noted that when a viceroy, archbishop or other great lord goes from Goa to Portugal all the poor soldiers and such others are exceedingly glad, for these grandees then promise to provide victuals for a certain number of men, a hundred or so."[72] In spite of all restrictions the number of homeward bound passengers might swell, especially on the largest and most prestigious ships.

So the mystery of the missing monsters can be explained not by assuming a grotesque amount of unregistered trade, but by taking the character of the empire into account. The Portuguese Estado depended for its survival not so much upon the quantity of spices and drugs annually transported to Europe as upon the strength and loyalty of the soldiers and gentlemen. Without the annual spectacle of the return of successful and prosperous and without the hope some day to be among the fortunate few the soldier would have had no incentive to serve and to distinguish himself.

NOTES

1. Frederic C. Lane, "The Mediterranean spice trade : Its revival in the sixteenth century", in *Venice and History*, The Collected Papers of Frederic C. Lane, (Baltimore, 1966), p. 31, n. 27. It is assumed that the *cantara* of the Italian sources represents the Portuguese *quintal.* The *quintal* used when drawing up the registers in India appears to have been the *peso novo, 1 quintal=4 arrobas=128 arrateis*=57-58 kgs. or c. 15 per cent more than the English cw. See Geneviève Bouchon, *Navires et cargaisons retour de l'Inde en 1518* (Société de l'historie de l'Orient, Paris 1977) p. IX, n. 28, cp. T. Bentley Duncan, *Atlantic Islands* (Chicago 1972), p. 259.
2. Bal Krishna, *Commercial Relations between India and England (1601-1757)* (London, 1924), p. 45 f.
3. V. Magalhães-Godinho, *L'Économie de l'empire portugais aux XVe et XVIe siècles* (Paris, 1969), p. 700.
4. *Ibid.*, pp. 701-4.
5. *Ibid* , pp. 674-77.
6. C.H.H. Wake, "The Changing Pattern of Europe's Pepper and Spice Imports, ca. 1400-1700", *The Journal of European Economic History* (Rome, 1979), p. 378.
7. *Het Itinerario van Jan Huygen van Linschoten*, Werken uitgegeven door de Linschoten-Vereeniging LX, (s'Gravenhage, 1957), p. 60 : "Men en mach gheen goet laden, het zy van wie het soude mogen wesen en ho weynich dat het is, ofte het moet gheregistreert wesen in het boeck ende registeren vande coningh, ende men moet een schrift hebben vande veador de fasenda, welcke is den oppersten besiender van des coninghs goet, waer in moet declareren van stuck tot stuck, wat datmen wil schepen ende in wat schip dat het sal wesen : sonder dat en sullen het die wachters en stouwers niet ontfanghen".
8. *The Voyage of François Pyrard of Laval*, vol. II : I, Works issued by the Hakluyt Society LXXVII (London, 1888), pp. 187-188.
9. C.R. Boxer (ed.), *The Tragic History of the Sea*, Works issued by the Hakluyt Society, 2nd series CXII (Cambridge, 1959), p. 287.

10. Jean Mocquet, *Voyages en Afrique, Asie, Indes Orientale et Occidentales* (Rouen, 1665), p. 361, cf. Linschoten. *loc. cit.*, p. 63.
11. M.N. Pearson, Corruption and corsairs in sixteenth century western India : A functional analysis, in Blair B. Kling & M.N. Pearson (eds.), *The Age of Partnership* (Honolulu, 1979), pp. 17-23.
12. Mocquet, *loc. cit.*
13. Magalhães-Godinho, *op. cit.*, pp. 697-98.
14. *Ibid.*, p. 707.
15. Geneviève Bouchen, "L'inventaire de la cargaison rapportée de l'Inde en 1505", in *Mare Luso-Indicum* III (Paris, 1976), pp. 101-125 ; *idem, op. cit.*, n. 1.
16. Friedrich Dobel Ueber einen Pfefferhandel der Fugger und Welser, 1586-91, *Zeitschrift des Historischen Veriens für Scwaben und Neuburg*, 13. Jahrg. (1886), p. 129 ; cp. Linschoten, *loc. cit.*, pp. 30-31.
17. Archivo general de Simancas, Secretarias Provinciales libro 1551, ff. 213-215, publ, in Niels Steensgaard, *The Asian Trade Revolution of the Seventeenth Century* (Chicago, 1974), p. 166.
18. Public Records Office, London, S.P. 12/204 f. 61 ; cp. G.V. Scammell, 'England, Portugal and the "Estado da India" c. 1500-1635', Paper presented to the *2nd International Seminar on Indo-Portuguese History* (Lisboa 1980). The full name of the *Conceição* was *Nossa Senhora da Conceicão* so the "shipp called oure Ladie" may safely be identified as Conceicão.
19. Dobel, *loc. cit.*, pp. 128-30 cp. Hermann Kellenbenz, 'Les frères Fugger et le marché international da pivre autour de 1600', *Annales E.S.C.*, 11 (1956), p. 3.
20. Luiz de Figueiredo Falcão, *Livro em que se contêm toda a fazenda e real patrimonio......* (Lisboa, 1859), pp. 61-62.
21. *Viaggi di C. Federici e G. Balbi alle Indie Orientale*, 11 Nuovo Ramusio IV (Roma, 1962), p. 220.
22. Dobel, *loc. cit.*, p. 129.
23. W.H. Moreland, *From Akbar to Aurangzeb* (London, 1923), p. 390.
24. Linschoten, *loc. cit.*, p. 60 : Mocquet, op. cit., p. 356.
25. Pyrard de Laval, *loc. cit.*, p. 285 ; Linschoten LVII, op. cit., p. 12-13.
26. Pyrard de Laval, *op. cit.*, II : 2, p. 292.
27. Linschoten, *op. cit.*, IX, p. 66.
28. C.R. Boxer, *Further Selections from the Tragic History of the Sea, 1559-1565.* Works issued by the Hakluyt Society, 2nd series CXXXII (Cambridge, 1968), p. 31.
29. Friedrich Dobel, *loc. cit.*, 132-33.
30. Falcão, *op. cit.*, p. 62.
31. Venezia Museo Civico-Correr, P.D. 988 ; cf. *The Asian Trade Revolution*, pp. 53, ff. and p. 166.
32. Falcão, p. 183.
33. Public Records Office, London, S.P. 89/3 ff. 39-40, cf. *The Asian Trade Revolution*, p. 166.

34. Falcão, p. 184.
35. Archivo general de Simancas, Secretarias Provinciales libro 1479, f. 280.
36. Falcão, p. 186.
37. Fernand Braudel & Ruggiero Romano, *Navires et marchandises à l'entrée du port de Livourne*, Ports Routes et trafics vol. I, pp. 68-69.
38. Falcão p. 187, Lisbon Arquivo Historico Ultramarino, papeis av. India CX 7 : Memoria das naos que vieram da India do A. 1612 endinate.
39. Magalhães-Godinho *op. cit.*, p. 671.
40. Commonwealth Relations Office, London, O.C. 1552.
41. Bal Krishna, *op. cit.*, pp. 339-40.
42. *Ibid.*, pp. 294 and 338-40.
43. Linschoten, *op. cit.*, LVII, p. 9.
44. Mocquet. *op. cit.*, p. 226.
45. Pyrard de Laval *op. cit.* II : I, p. 181.
46. Richard Hakluyt, *The Principal Navigations*, Vol. VII, p. 116.
47. Magalhães-Godinho, *op. cit.*, pp. 676-77.
48. Wake, *loc. cit.*, p. 380.
49. Hakluyt, *op. cit.*
50. L. Denoiz, "Caractéristiques des navires de l'époque des grandes découvertes", in Michel Mollat & Paul Adam (eds.). *Les aspects internationaux de la découverte océanique*, Artes du Ve colloque international d'histoire maritime, (Paris, 1966), p. 142.
51. *Documenta Indica*, vol. VII, p. 507.
52. *Documenta Indica*, vol. XI, pp. 353-54.
53. "Ein Brief des Gabriel Holzschuher aus Indien von Januar 1580" in *Anzeiger für Kunde der deutschen Vorzeit 30.* Jahrg. (Nürnberg, 1883), p. 158.
54. Ettore Manucci (ed.), *Lettere edite ed inedite di Filippo Sassetti* (1855), p. 280.
55. Linschoten *op. cit.*, LVII, p. 9.
56. *Ibid.* LX, p. 18.
57. Mocquet, *op. cit.*, p. 218.
58. Pyrard de Laval, *op. cit.* II : I, p. 193.
59. *Ibid.*, p. 272.
60. *Ibid.*, p. 119, n. 1.
61. *Documenta Indica*, vol. XI, p. 354.
62. Linschoten, *op. cit.*, IX, p. 63-64.
63. *Ibid.*, p. 62.
64. C.R. Boxer, *Further Selections*, p. 43.
65. C.R. Boxer, *The Tragic History of the Sea*, p. 115.
66. *Ibid.*, p. 199.
67. *Sir William Monson's Naval Tracts*, vol. I, Publications of the Navy Records Society XXII, pp. 150 & 291.

68. Mocquet, *op. cit.* p. 357. The ship came directly from India and made no call in Mozambique.
69. Hakluyt, *loc. cit.*
70. *Sir William Monson's Naval Tract* vol. II, Publications of the Navy Records Society XXIII, p. 163.
71. Pyrard de Laval, *op. cit.* II : 1, p. 284. Only 550 were alive when the ship arrived in Bahia after a long and arduous voyage. *Ibid.* II : 2, p. 307.
72. *Ibid.*, II : 1, p. 274.

3

Inauspicious Ambience :

The Historical Setting of Early Luso-Chinese Contacts

LEA E. WILLIAMS

IT IS generally and correctly deemed unprofessional for an historian to speculate on what might have been. Aware of the tolerance of the participants here, however, my present effort will be directed towards consideration of the origins of the climate of mutual mistrust and hostility that characterized Sino-Western relations throughout the age of imperialism and, by inference, to the possibility that a happier meeting of peoples might have been feasible at another time. Put most briefly the momentum of the *Carreira* brought Europeans to China in a most unfortunate period of Chinese xenophobia, in a century when the Ming dynasty sought to seal its sea frontier. It was an era when private traders became smugglers and pirates, and when pirates became virtual satraps. Given the distressing realities of early sixteenth century China and the commercial drive of the West, ruthlessness, corruption, crime and intransigence could not but dominate from the start and would continue to do so through long, ensuing centuries.

The Ming dynasty is known for imperial despotism, particularly in its early reigns, and for seeking to isolate China during the final two centuries of its tenure. Whether or not there are reasonable explanations for the heavy-handed treatment afforded the career officialdom by some Ming emperors is not of present concern. It is, however, appropriate here to attempt to understand middle and the late Ming anxiety over foreign contamination.

The perennial fiscal hunger of governments was, of course, a force in China as elsewhere. Levies on, or state monopoly control over foreign trade go far back in Chinese history and had figured prominently in the administration of the Sung dynasty,[1] the last indigenous Chinese imperial order before the Mongol conquest and the model for many features of Ming administration, including those in the area of international trade.

The tribute system was employed as the mechanism for state control. The ritualistic or diplomatic significance of the tribute missions often came to be eclipsed by their economic meaning. By limiting the size and frequency of the missions and through the enforcement of regulations setting itineraries, the imperial government sought to control international commerce. The motives were to be found in expectations of a manageable revenue base and in an endemic fear that the presence of outsiders would generate confusion and indiscipline among the general Chinese populace. Unfortunately, limitations on trade became more severe precisely when the Chinese economy attained growing levels of productivity. The Ming period saw the kind of expansion in both agriculture and the non-agrarian sectors that, along with increased urbanization and greater monetization of the economy, typify early modern economic development. That is, just when the demand for foreign goods and markets mounted, international trade was subjected to governmental restraints that were destined to be as ineffectual as they were ill-considered.

Although seemingly peripheral to the theme of this paper, the subject of Sino-Japanese trade is worth a look. For one thing, the Portuguese came to figure conspicuously and profitably in the commerce. (As is well-known, Macao's early prosperity was largely based on the colony's success as a Sino-Japanese entrepôt).[2] More important, the unhappy nature of Sino-Japanese relations in the fifteenth and sixteenth century greatly exacerbated Ming xenophobia and, thus, directly influenced Chinese attitudes toward the Portuguese. Finally, to be candid, it must be acknowledged that statistics on Japanese trade with China are conveniently accessible.

The volume and variety of trade is evidence of the scale of economic development on the eve of the Portuguese arrival. Official records provide invaluable data on the tribute trade. At the peak of its volume, tributary exchange with Japan was big business indeed. For example, in 1469 alone, Japanese swords worth 38,000 taels of silver were imported.[3] Ranging in price from three to 100 taels, some 200,000 swords were shipped prior to the cessation of tributary trade in 1511. Sulphur, in single shipments of up to 400,000 catties, was the next most valuable import from Japan. Copper was the third in rank, followed by a range of specialized consumer goods—Lacquer-ware, fans, screens and the like. Profits on a shipment could reach 400 per cent, as in the case of swords.[4]

In return, China sent Japan some goods but was essentially caught in an unfavourable balance of payments dilemma and obliged to pay the Japanese in cash. That is yet another explanation for Ming efforts to limit the import of foreign goods. The swords, sulphur and copper were needed but it was painful paying for them. Not incidentally, note must be taken of the fact that Sino-Japanese trade involved bulk cargoes of primary products and was not restricted to shipments of highly priced exotica. This is a measure of the state of shipping and of early modern East Asian economic development at the time of the appearance of the Portuguese.

Parallel to the tributary trade was that of private merchants. Believed to have been even more extensive than the commerce under tributary licensing, the independent trade was carried on over two routes. The northern reached Shantung ; the southern linked Japan, especially Kyushu, with the Chekiang and Fukien coasts. The latter was far more commonly used because the boisterous seas around the Shantung peninsula were intimidating and because the central and southern provinces had become the economic heartland of the empire.[5] Note should also be taken of the fact that the Portuguese of the early 16th century sought most earnestly to establish themselves in the Chekiang-Fukien commerce and in the carrying trade between the coastal area and southern Japan. The Europeans were thus not trail-blazers but, from an East Asian perspective, interlopers. Another source of hostility toward them is, therefore, apparent.

Trade with the countries of Southeast Asia and beyond was also bustling, although an examination of lists of the products shipped to China[6] indicates that the region was significantly less important than Japan in supplying essential commodities. The Ming dynasty had a clear military interest in importing swords and sulphur from Japan and cavalry remounts from Inner Asia, but the empire would not have been gravely weakened if Siamese ivory and cloves, Vietnamese coral and antelope horn, Javanese camphor and bronze drums were no longer available. In other words, although China earned needed gold and silver from Southeast Asia, the other items shipped north were intended primarily to appeal to the tastes of elite consumers. Good profits were made in the Sino-Southeast Asian trade, but it was not vital. Moreover, on the politico-diplomatic side, imperial Chinese involvement in trade with Japan was directly related to the long struggle against piracy on the China coast, a struggle in which the Portuguese were to become participants on both sides of the law.

It is presumably sound to assume that pirates had operated in Chinese waters from earliest times. However, in the Ming era seaborne crime grew to epidemic proportions unprecedented and unique in scale. The criminal depredations reached a magnitude that can best be described as warfare. The well-being, if not the survival, of the dynasty was endangered by a protracted struggle to maintain imperial authority over a wide and sometimes deep belt of coastal territory. Moreover, the conflict like more conventional war, had an international dimension.

Much has been written about piracy during Ming times.[7] It was formerly fashionable to lump all the criminals together under a single, unflattering label—*wo-k'ou* or *wakō*, pirates from the land of the dwarfs, that is, Japan. Now scholars recognize that the roving bands were multi-national forces in which Chinese were sometimes, perhaps usually, in the majority with Japanese warriors, often rōnin or leaderless samurai, forming special units of shock troops.

The role of Japanese in the conflict, nevertheless, was a

major source of the xenophobia to be encountered by the Portuguese. For one thing, China sought through trade restrictions to press Japan to keep lawless subjects at home. Exchanges of diplomatic correspondence on the subject went on through most of the Ming dynasty. Chinese efforts were often frustrated by the absence of an effectual Japanese central government in times of protracted internal turmoil and rivalry among the feudal lords, although the Ming court never understood the Japanese situation.[8]

In 1511, just as the *Carreira* was about to extend to China, Japanese relations had deteriorated to the point where the head of that year's tributary trading mission threatened a diplomatic rupture that, he warned, would lead to increased piracy. The next tributary trading year, 1523, brought even greater alarm when fighting among the Japanese envoys themselves touched off the pillaging of the port city of Ningpo.[9] Those events bracketed the disastrous tribute mission of Tomé Pires, whose imprisonment at Canton in 1521 and eventual death were products of Chinese fears of sea-going intruders.

In part as a tactic in the campaign against piracy, the Ming government instituted new prohibitions against maritime trade.[10] (The Chinese term, *haichin*, literally means *sea ban*). The goal was to cleanse the coastal seas of all international shipping except that authorized and regulated under the tribute system. Since Portugal had not been accepted as a tributary with trading rights, the prohibition, if enforceable, would have kept Portuguese ships out of the South China Sea. What the ban did produce was the proliferation of pirates.

Driven by the momentum of their global expansion and the conviction that right was on their side, the Portuguese challenged Chinese authority. (They also, as in the Tomé Pires mission, sought to accommodate themselves to Chinese ways). In 1522 and 1523, naval conflict broke out between the opposing forces on the Kwangtung coast. The Chinese claimed their fire-ships, a favoured weapon, achieved total defeat of the Portuguese at Tun-men in the former year ; a second victory was reported from Hsi-ts'ao wan in the latter. Thereafter, a prohibition on private trade with merchants from Southeast Asia, including the Portuguese who passed through there, was decreed.[11] Smuggling and piracy inevitably gained fresh recruits.

The lawlessness of the times dictated that all merchant vessels be armed, a circumstance that permitted immediate transformation from peaceful trader to coastal brigand and smuggler. The Portuguese fitted themselves into the pattern with relatively little effort and, presumably, with slight pangs of conscience. Thin in numbers and at the extreme end of their imperial lifeline, the Europeans were in no position to compel the reversal of Chinese policy. Yet, the goals of trade and profit had brought them eastward and could not be sacrificed.

For three decades, from 1518, the Portuguese maintained an illicit trade along the Chekiang and Fukien coasts, using temporary basis in Kwangtung such as Lampoco (*Lang-po-ku Lang-po-kao*) and St. John's island, or São João, (the name felicitously derived from the Chinese *Shan-ch'uan tao*).[12] It was a trying time for the Europeans. Commerce and navigation were made hazardous by the lawlessness of the seas and by the spasmodic efforts of the dynasty to seal the coasts.

As the century reached its mid-point, a more stable pattern took shape. The illicit trading posts at Shuang-hsü kang in Chekiang and at Tsou-ma ch'i in Fukien were destroyed by imperial attack in 1548 and 1549 respectively. On the latter occasion, a total of 206 captives, including "16 white barbarians, 46 black barbarians (and) 29 barbarian women" (ethnicity unspecified) were beheaded as pirates or accomplices.[13] The Portuguese retired southward, first to Lampoco and soon thereafter to Macao, where an *ad hoc* understanding was reached with Kwangtung authorities.[14] Regularized trade, even a role in the suppression of piracy, ensued ; but, those are developments beyond the scope of this brief survey.

The conclusion one may reach can be simply put and is far from revolutionary. In the early 16th century, the Portuguese were far too weak to force themselves on the Chinese government. They could neither kick open the door unilaterally nor ally themselves with others capable of doing so. On the Chinese side, another kind of weakness contributed to the climate of hostility in which the earliest modern meeting of East and West took place.

Dynastic vigour, although beginning to ebb, was still sufficient to support partial insulation of the empire ; however, there was not strength adequate for the maintenance of complete seclusion. Distracted by concerns over the security of the northern frontiers and by the endless tasks of ruling a vast land always threatened by the centrifugal forces of localism, geographical fragmentation and latent peasant rebelliousness, the dynasty regarded events on the sea coast as distressing rather than decisive. The golden age of Chinese sea power had ended almost a century earlier ; the Ming navy was a travesty. The official history of the dynasty contains a candid admission :

> In Chekiang and Fukien, the sea defense have deteriorated to the extent that there are only one or two warships and patrol boats and at the patrol stations...which in the past had a quota of 2500 archers each there are only about a thousand men left.[15]

Another contemporary work elaborated on the subject :

> On the pretext of keeping watch (warships) are anchored in harbors, some never going back to their stations, some used for private trade, trafficking in illegal salt, fishing or carrying fuel.[16]

It is not fanciful, then, to suggest that had China been secure against threats from the sea, the Portuguese could have been permitted to fit unobtrusively and comfortably into the tradition of tributary trade. Both sides could have been satisfied and Sino-Western interaction could have begun in a peaceful and congenial atmosphere.

NOTES

1. Lo Jung-pang, Maritime commerce and the relations to the Sung Navy, *Journal of the Economic and Social History of the Orient*, vol. XII, part I, (Leiden : E.J. Brill, 1969), pp. 66-69 ; Sun Pao, *T'ang*

Sung Yüan hai-shang shang-yeh cheng-ts'e, (Government policies on maritime commerce in T'ang, Sung and Yuan), Taipei : Cheng-chung shu-chü, 1969, *passim*.

2. The masterful study of C.R. Boxer, *The Great Ship from Amacon, Annals of Macao and the Old Japan Trade, 1555-1646*, (Lisbon : Centro de Estudos Historicos Ultramarinos, 1963) is the definitive source on this subject. Also most valuable is the book by Chang T'ien-tse, *Sino-Portuguese Trade from 1514 to 1644, A Synthesis of Portuguese and Chinese Sources* (Leiden : E. Brill, 1934).
3. Based on a memorial from the Board of Ceremonies contained in *Hsien-tsung Ch'eng-hua shih-lu, chüan 62*, (Veritable records of the Hsien-tsung Ch'eng-hua emperor), quoted in Chang Wei-hua, *Ming-tai hai-wai mao-i chien-lun*. A brief treatment of the overseas trade of the Ming dynasty, Shanghai : Jen-min ch'u-pan she, 1956, p. 89.
4. *Idem*.
5. *Ibid.*, p. 90.
6. *Ibid.*, pp. 58-72. See also : Feng Ch'eng-chün, *Chung-kuo Nan-yang chiao-t'ung shih*. (A history of Sino-Southeast Asian communication), 2nd edition (Taipei : Commercial Press, 1965) ; Chang Te-Ch'ang *Ming-tai kuo-chi mao-i*. (International trade in the Ming era), Taipei : Tai-wan hsüeh-sheng shu-chü, 1968.
7. See : Wang Yi-tung, *Official Relations between China and Japan, 1368-1549*, Cambridge : Harvard 1953 ; So Kwan-wae, *Japanese Piracy in Ming China during the 16th century* (East Lansing : Michigan State, 1975).
8. Chang Wei-hau, *op. cit.*, pp. 90-92, Wang Yi-tung, *op. cit., passim*.
9. Wang Yi-tung, *op. cit.*, pp. 76-77.
10. Pao Tsun-p'eng, *Chung-kuo hai-chün shih*, (A history of the Chinese navy), Taipei : Chung-hua tzu-shu pien-shen hua-yüan-hui, 1970, Vol. II, p. 461. See also : Ch'en Wen-shih. *Ming Hung-wu Chia-ching chien-ti hai-chin cheng-ts'e*. (The Ming maritime prohibitions of the Hung-wu and Chia-ching reigns), Taipei : History and Literature Series, no. 20 (Taiwan National University, 1966).
11. *Idem*.
12. *Ibid.*, p. 462.
13. L. Carrington Goodrich, Chaoyang Fang, *Dictionary of Ming Biography, 1368-1644*, (New York : Columbia, 1976), vol. I, pp. 374-375.
14. Pao Tsun-p'eng, *op. cit.*, p. 462.
15. *Ming Shih* (Ming history), 205 : 1, cited in untitled, unpublished manuscript of Lo Jung-pang.
16. *Ming ta-cheng tsuan-pao*. (A compendium from Ming government sources), cited in untitled, unpublished manuscript of Lo Jung-pang.

4

Glimpses of the Beginnings of the "Carreira Da India" (1500-1518)

GENEVIÈVE BOUCHON

THANKS to the sea route opened by the Portuguese sailors, direct and regular economic relations were established for the first time between Europe and South Asia. The *Carreira da India* was born at the time when the first exploration voyages to the Indian Ocean were organized. At once it established a link between India and Portugal. It enhances the steadfastness of the Portuguese fleets which never drew back from the dangers of the transoceanic voyages in order to purchase spices in the Malabar ports every year.

In spite of their importance for the history of the modern types, the origins of the *Carreira da India* are still in the dark. Nevertheless, they gradually come to light and enable to catch some glimpses of concrete facts. Everyone bears in mind the outstanding syntheses Drs. Nunes Dias and Magalhães Godinho[1] elaborated from the data available to them more than ten years ago. Since then, more research has been done and published. This throws light on this still unknown period and gives some clues for further research.

No doubt we shall have first to become aware of the reasons why these notions remained in the dark. The major cause is the scarcity of the original documents which, for the most part, must have been destroyed by the earthquake which swallowed up Lisbon in 1755. They may have disappeared before, because of the discretion generally prevailing on great enterprises that were still in the bud. We will not enter into the argument which formerly brought together the Portuguese historians and opposed the ones who were advocating "the policy of secrecy"—which would have been meant to keep the exploration of the Cape Route for the Portugese—against those who were denying it.[2] We cannot assert that a State secret was systematically imposed on the pioneers of the Portuguese expansion but we may guess that some pieces of information were not revealed, thanks to the seamen's and businessmen's well-known discretion. It is a fact that some of the letters written about those first voyages contain lots of sibylline allusions and that some few maps show deliberate inaccuracies.[3] It is also a fact that, except for a few official letters from King D. Manuel, no important text dealing with the activity of the Portuguese in India had been printed in Portugal before the second half of the sixteenth century. Nevertheless, in Flanders and more especially in Italy, much was written about those newly found lands—"Paesi nuovamente ritrovati". A few Portuguese reports came out under this title in Vicenza (1507),[4] and some more accounts were published by G.B. Ramusio in Venice (1550).[5] It is only after this date that the famous Portuguese chronicles, on which most of the works dealing with the first *Carreiras da India* were based, began to be published in Portugal, that is to say, about half a century after they took place.

The concern for researching and publishing manuscripts has only expressed itself during the last hundred and fifty years. Hence some original accounts of the expeditions of 1498, 1500 and of the following years were published, as well as a part of the correspondence sent from India by the Viceroys and Governors. At the same time were published collections of letters dating back to the early sixteenth century which had been gathered in Venice by Girolamo Priuli and Marino Sanuto.[6] Their Italian correspondents settled in Lisbon used to report the navigators' talks and to assess the cargoes they had brought back. However, their figures which have enabled to draw up several statistics and charts, particularly by Nunes Dias and Magalhães Godinho, take only the spices which arrived in Lisbon into account. One cannot reckon the ones which were actually loaded in the Indian ports. I should add that these figures do not take into account the different systems of weights which were in use at the time : the *peso velho* and the *peso novo*, for instance.[7]

The publication of those documents has provided us with a considerable amount of information about the naval, military and diplomatic operations, as well as the social and political context in the regions affected by the Portuguese expansion. But it only allows a fragmentary grasp of the first activities of the *Carreira da India.* Since the various data were very much scattered, no complete cargo could be built up again. One had to resort to apocryphal and erroneous *Livros das armadas*[8] so as to find out the fleets as well as the captains. The scarcity of the *regimentos* left the actual mission of the first *capitães mores* in the dark. Even if some noblemen and businessmen appeared in King D. Manuel's entourage, it was none too easy to guess their role and to determine what part they had actually played in the spice trade.

A new approach to the study of Portuguese expansion has extended the scope of the research area to the European basic archives and given greater importance to the economic documents scattered in some Portuguese collections. I would like to pay tribute to those who have left too early, having opened the way to such stimulating prospects, particularly Admiral Teixeira da Mota, who edited the sources published in the collections of the "Centro de Estudos de Cartografia Antiga" and whose colleague, Dr. Luís de Albuquerque, fortunately carries on the brilliant work. I would also like to honour the memory of Dr. António Banha de Andrade whose *Mundos novos do Mundo*[9] has become the guide of those who follow in the wake of the first Portuguese ships.

One cannot forget the late Virginia Rau[10] and Federigo Melis[11] whose investigations through the Italian archives reawakened the cosmopolitan society of the merchants of Lisbon and revealed the scope of the part they played in the armaments of ships and the exploitation of the Indian markets. Hence these scholars were able to be more accurate about the origins and parts played by the Italian businessmen settled in Portugal who had joined the great undertaking for the discovery of the Cape Route since the middle of the fifteenth century : the Palastrellis from Piacenza, the Passagnas from Genoa and the powerful Florentine group including the Marchionnis, the Sernigis, the Nardis and the Corbinellis. Those Italian people brought the Portuguese Crown not only a considerable financial help but also the experience of the Oriental markets they had reached since the fourteenth century after going through the Black Sea, Central Asia and the Persian Gulf.[12]

More research has been made in Europe on the organization of the early Indo-Portuguese trade, notably by J. Kieniewicz (Poland)[13] and H. Kellenbenz (W. Germany).[14] All those scholars and those who are carrying on their work enable us to cast a new look at the first years of the *Carreira da India*. I should add that accurate countable data have become available, thanks to the study of the economic documents, so far neglected, of the Torre do Tombo in Lisbon : orders and receipts of the ship captains and factors as well as notes scattered in the second part of the "*Corpo Cronologico*" and in the "*Fragmentos*". And mostly thanks to the patient restoration carried out by Dr. José Pereira da Costa who enabled the researchers to have access to the precious collection of the "*Núcleo Antigo*".

For a long time, the History of the Great Discoveries has been confined to specific geographical and cultural areas. The study of the Portuguese and Spanish expansion was carried on according to distinct fields of research. Therefore, the history of the discovery of America has been dissociated from that of the sea-route to Asia.

Such a conception of history is not in keeping with the ideas of the fifteenth and sixteenth centuries. It is true that at the time of the Treaty of Tordesillas, the Portuguese and the Castilian had come to an agreement and had potentially divided the world from the Atlantic meridian but they had warily kept silent about the Asian one. Such silence does not allow us to define the real geographic knowledge of the pilots since there was no account left. Nevertheless the documentation of the time shows that any layman or businessman, far from realizing the vastness of the Pacific Ocean, believed that America and Asia were close together. Indeed both continents are very close on the sketch maps drawn by the learned Venetian Alessandro Zorzi,[15] and in 1500, Girolamo Sernigi kept on mistaking the Maldive islands for the West Indies.[16]

As the proceedings of the "Coloquios Luso-espanholes de Historia Ultramarina" (Valladolid 1973/Lisbon 1974)[17] have confirmed, the discovery of America and of Asia was the outcome of the same enterprise. The fruitful meeting between the Spanish and the Portuguese historians leads us to regard the division of Tordesillas as irrelevant to the historical research. It is advisable to consider again the Iberian documentation as a whole. It shows, for instance, that the competition for the conquest of Malacca, Sumatra and Ceylon existed well before the one for the Moluccas.[18] In 1506, in order to get ahead of a Castilian fleet bound for Malacca, D. Manuel of Portugal ordered to explore the roundabouts in order to make sure the town was 'within our limits'.[19] It was to avoid to present themselves with a *fait accompli* that the Portuguese armadas had to outstrip the Castilian fleets, to find new markets and to go farther towards the East beyond the lands that had already been explored. Therefore, the first spice quests were showing some sort of empiricism. The fragments that have been found out from the *regimentos* of Pedro Alvares Cabral (1500) and Lopo Soares (1504) testify that nearly all initiative was left to the *capitães mores*. During those years of intense prospecting, the early *Carreiras da India* were fitted out to achieve much more than just a mercantile purpose ; they had to convey the spices from Malabar and explore new lands so as to extend the supremacy of Portugal as far as possible.

One can cast another look at those first voyages in the only light of the original sources, formerly or newly discovered. As there is no time for us to deal with all the aspects, we shall make do with some information about the beginnings of the Portuguese spice trade. Thanks to Alvaro Velho's logbook, a relevant source is available concerning the first call of Vasco da Gama's three ships at Calicut from where he only brought back a small number of spice samples.[20] Their origin was confirmed : out of the five well-known spices, two came from Malabar (pepper and ginger), one from Ceylon (cinnamon) and the other two from the Moluccas (clove and nutmeg). All of them were available in the Malabar ports and especially in Calicut where they could be exchanged for gold (as far as pepper was concerned) and for other western goods such as silver, copper, scarlet, coral and mercury. The Portuguese decided to set up a factory in Calicut until they were able to go to Ceylon and Insulindia by themselves.

Some original documents dating back to the voyages of Pedro Alvares Cabral (1500) remain.[21] Calicut had to be deserted because of serious incidents. The Portuguese were welcomed in Cochin where they could set up a factory and where they loaded spices. They called at Cannanore where they loaded 100 *bhars* of cinnamon of poor quality. This last piece of information is available, thanks to the anonymous account of a witness; but the other estimates of the cargo loaded by Cabral (about 4,000 *cantari*) had been made according to the Italian correspondents who only took what had actually reached Lisbon into account. What had been loaded onto the ships in the Indian ports remains unknown since five vessels were wrecked on the way back. It seems that profit-sharing was practised in favour of the sailors but we must be careful when dealing with the figures conveyed by Gaspar Correia.[22]

As there is no original document left from the third expedition (1501), commanded by João da Nova, there only remains second-hand data. Yet, those who witnessed the arrival in Lisbon are unanimous in stating the smallness of the cargo probably mainly composed of the loot plundered from the ships sailing on the Indian waters. All of them agree to enhance that the four caravels—two of which had been fitted out by the king and the other two by private individuals—had not carried along the quantity of gold necessary to obtain pepper. However, a factory was set up in Cannanore. João da Nova's expedition must have included an exploratory mission to the Indian Ocean about which only surmises can be made.[23]

This brief appraisal of the first three voyages underlines not only the scarcity of original documents stemming from economic sources, but also the affluence of second-hand and apocryphal pieces of information which enable only a questionable assessment of the first cargoes of the *Carreira da India.*

The shadows clear up, thanks to the accounts of witnesses

taking part in Vasco da Gama's second voyage (1502). Tomé Lopes's account, published by Ramusio, is well-known[24] It relates how the *Almirante*, commanding a squadron of twenty ships, confirmed the split with Calicut and managed to set the prices of the spices in agreement with the kings and merchants of Cochin and Cananor. A second account by an anonymous Flemish man is more confused and less reliable.[25] A third account is so unknown that economic historians have never mentioned it. It was written by Matteo da Bergamo, an agent of the Affaitati from Cremona, who had gone on board a ship of '*mercadores*' commanded by Giovanni Buonagrazia. The fact that such an account had been overlooked is all the more surprising since it is the only genuine testimony in which the terms of the agreement between Vasco da Gama and the kings of Malabar are mentioned. It is much more detailed than what had been recorded by António Nunes more than fifty years later.[26] Hence it deserves to be quoted here.[27]

More numerous are the original documents which throw light on the voyage undertaken by Afonso de Albuquerque and his cousin Francisco in 1503/1504. The account of a witness (the Tuscan Giovanni da Empoli) some letters from Cochin and some notes from Cananor enable to grasp some more features of the *Carreira*. The partnership between the king and the merchants is confirmed : out of ten ships, two were fitted out by the Florentine Girolamo Sernigi, and one by Catarina Dias, a businesswoman of Lisbon, whom we meet again later on.

When he reached India in late August 1503, Francisco de Albuquerque found Malabar at war. The presence of the Portuguese in Cochin had rekindled the secular conflict between the Raja of Cochin and the Zamorin of Calicut. The latter had invaded his rival's kingdom at the beginning of 1503 ; but instead of handing the forty Portuguese entrusted to his safe-keeping over to his conqueror, the Raja had taken refuge in Vaipin island with them. After a few dazzling raids, Francisco de Albuquerque gave his rights and territories back to the Raja of Cochin. It enabled the captain to obtain 12,000 *cantari* of pepper ; but he refused to share the cargo with Afonso de Albuquerque who had arrived later, so that the latter had to purchase spices elsewhere. On Christmas of 1503 his squadron went to Kollam where plenty of pepper was loaded and a factory set up with the Prince's agreement. While the forces of Calicut were blockading the backwaters of Cochin and were diverting the pepper boats towards Cranganor, a few Portuguese managed to contact the merchants of the town and obtained at least 200 *bhars* of pepper.

The original sources are too incomplete to allow us to assess the whole cargo loaded in India, since most of it was destroyed in the shipwrecks on the way back. But a few short notes from Cananor give important information. The captain's *mandados* and the ship factor's *conhecimentos* reveal the dates of the various calls as well as the names of the ships. For instance, those notes help to establish the identity of the ships lost on the way back : the *São Miguel* known as *Rainha Nova* with her captain Francisco de Albuquerque and the *Santa Maria de Fayal* with her captain Nicolau Coelho. The *conhecimentos* also reveal the role played by the *factory* of Cananor, the first and the last port of call for the *armadas* in India. This was the place where fresh supplies were provided and the ships repaired. A variety of goods were loaded there such as rice, dry fish, sails, masts and tar, oil for the lamps and medicines for the doctor of the ship. An order signed by Alfonso de Albuquerque to recruit a pilot ready 'to go to the island' shows that a reconnaissance mission to the Laquedive or the Maldive islands had perhaps been carried out or at least planned.[28] Such are the details given by the archives they allow some glimpses of a reality that cannot be grasped throroughly, and they open new horizons for further research.

One can summarize the principal features of the early *Carreiras da India* on the eve of the establishment of the *Estado da India* (1505), thanks to the documents dating back to the Lopo Soares' voyage (1504/1505).[29] Two reliable accounts were recently published : the anonymous *Crónica*[30] of the British Library edited by Dr. Luís de Albuquerque, which presents a slightly different interpretation from that of the other chronicles ; and an anonymous Florentine account, edited by A. Teixeira da Mota, which was written by a sailor belonging to António de Saldanha's armada (1503/1505).[31] In addition to these two texts, there are sixteen documents that I have found scattered through the collections of the Torre do Tombo. Among them there is a major piece, namely, the oldest account of the *Carreira da India* which assesses the cargo of each ship, (including the wrecked ones) and counts up the profits of the King, private persons and sailors.[32] The whole documentation enables to find out some reliable pieces of information.

About the regulations of the overseas trade :

In 1503 already, some merchants were entitled to fit out ships provided they unloaded their cargoes at the *Casa de Mina* in Lisbon and paid a fee (a quarter and a twentieth) on the goods they brought back from the East. The same fee was enforced for those who loaded goods on the King's vessels. In 1504, D. Manuel equipped all the ships of Lopo Soares's fleet, except the one of Catarina Dias who fitted her own ship by herself. Private persons and sailors were entitled to share the profits of the voyage if they imported a certain quantity of spices. The *quintaladas*—or importation licences—allowed anyone who sailed to India to import into Portugal, but at one's own expense, a certain quantity of pepper or, in particular instances, of other spices which were to be sold as a profit.

The system used to work as follows : The participants had to give the royal *feitor* a certain amount of cash which had been determined according to the status of each person : the captains were allowed to give from 300 to 1300 *cruzados*, the doctor 200, the *mestre* 150, the *feitor* and the *escrivão* 30, and so on. The men-at-arms could also participate, but the conditions are unfortunately not mentioned. The *feitor* was entrusted with the purchases in India—the quantity corresponding to the sum paid by each of the participants. Such a deal was profitable for the Crown for the participants had to give the King a quarter and a twentieth fee, (*quarto e vintena*) or half their share (*partidos do meio*). Through our document, it appears that some of them could not invest the whole of the value of their license and had to sell a part of their *quintalada* to other people.

About the participants' identity.

Among the business people in Lisbon and the nobility of the

Court : Bartclomeo Marchionni, Girolamo Sernigi, Catarina Dias, Pantalião Dias, the Baron of Alvito, D. Alvaro, D. Nuno Manuel, D. Manuel Pereira, Henrique da Silveira's wife and so on.

About the ships

For the first time in 1504, the names as well as the complete list of the ships sailing on the routes there and back could be established. Such information shows that the lists that had previously been made out according to the apocryphal *Livros das armadas* were more or less erroneous.

About the navigation regulations.

For the first time as well, Lopo Soares's *regimento* mentioned the navigation laws of the sea-route to India. It includes the order of the ships, the instructions of the round-up, the signals and the disciplinary regulations of the crew.

About the conditions of the loading in India

The documentation mentioned above confirms that Lopo Soares inflicted two severe defeats on the forces of Calicut : one on land by conquering Cranganor again in favour of the Raja of Cochin, and another at sea by wiping out, in the port of Kappatt; the Calicut fleet that had been fitted out for the Red Sea. Such military successes provided him with an exceptional cargo, yet gathered under difficult circumstances since the networks for the supplies with pepper had been disrupted by the Cochin wars and by the conflict opposing Kollam to Vijayanagar.

For the first time, the names of some Malabari merchants appear : the Mappilla Cherian and Mammali Marakkar from Cochin, who had at first been reluctant to supply the Portuguese fleet because of the debts run up by a few captains of the previous expedition, but who yielded to the order of the Raja of Cochin ; and the Christian Matias who gathered up the cargo of two Portuguese ships in Kayankullam.

About the nature and the volume of the cargo

Whereas the only countable documents of the time (the *Cartas de quitação do Rey D. Manuel*)[33] only draw up the list of the stocks of the factories and give a partial account of the movement of the goods, the account-book 1505 assesses, ship after ship, the cargo of pepper and makes out the list of the other products loaded by Lopo Soares's armada.

Cargo loaded in India

1504/1505	*Quintals*	*Arrobas*	*Arrateis*
Pepper	20 895	1	17
Pepper (long)	1	2	18
Ginger	554		
Cinnamon	171	17	17
Cloves	139	3	30
Cardamon	4		14
Nutmeg mace	1	1	8
Tamarinds	6		
Myrrh	10		
Camphor	3	1	12
Galbanum	4	1	4
Artemisia indica	2	2	
Socotra aloes	2	1	
Lac	8		
Indigo	29	3	13

Lisbon, *Torre do Tombo* : *Cartas Missivas* 3/337 & 367[34]

The biography by António Banha de Andrade of Tristão da Cunha[35] provides more information about the system of the *Carreira da India*, soon after the creation of Portuguese State in India. The author shows that, at the time, the Crown wished to give the Portuguese expansion an essentially mercantile character. Thanks to the documentation he gathered, including unpublished pay-books, he was able to present an unquestionable study of the armada of 1506. Through a series of clear charts, he reveals the formation of the fleet, and an almost complete list of the crew and men taken on board, with their birthplace, the duration of their duty, their pay, the value and quantity of spices brought back, thanks to the *quintaladas*, as well as an assessment of the death-rate among the crews. Exclusively based on original data, his study introduces us into the business circles of Lisbon. It shows the variety of interpretations the people of the time made about the voyage to India, and this on the eve of Albuquerque's government which was to give the Portuguese expansion another nature and a wider scale.

A study which would enable us to follow the evolution of the *Carreira da India* at the time of Afonso de Albuquerque had not been made yet because there remains a considerable and difficult palaeographic work to be undertaken in the collection of the *Núcleo Antigo* But a major document from the same collection allows to assess the situation two years after the famous captain's death. The *Caderno dos officiais da India*[36] gives an account of the loading of six ships which was begun in Cochin in November 1517, carried on in Kollam and achieved in Cochin on the 11th of January 1518. Besides the nature and the tonnage of the cargo of the Crown and of the merchants—*peso velho* and *peso novo*—this document gives a detailed list of the spices loaded as *quintaladas* and other *liberdades*. Nearly 300 people are registered—captains, gunners, pilots, factors and men-at-arms with their names, duties, service records and transfers from one vessel to another. More than forty ships are also mentioned, each with the name of her *capitão mor*, which enables to assess the fleets of India as a whole or in part during the period 1505-1518. But the movement of those ships cannot be grasped correctly since different ships were often given the same name. However, the data given by the *Caderno* complete and correct at several points the apocryphal lists of fleets to which the historians had referred so far. This document is also the last testimony of the *quintaladas* system which was superseded, right from the following year, by annual instalments in cash so as to avoid the excesses and speculations begotten by the previous system.

The few works and texts that I have just presented contribute greatly to the elaboration of the history of the *Carreira da India* but they are not at all exhaustive. Other research works are carried on, the results of which must be taken into account at each of our ISIPH so as to bring our knowledge up to date. None the less we have already a much more complete image of the beginnings of the *Carreira da India*—an image more precise and sometimes very different from the one that had been popularized so far by the numerous history handbooks and the various chronicles. It is necessary to spread these essential new data, which must not be overlooked by the specialists of social and economic history of the great oceanic voyages which opened the way to the modern times.

NOTES

1. Dias (Nunes). *O capitalismo monárquico português*, (Coimbra, 1964), 2 vols. ; Godinho (V. Magalhães), *L'Économic de l'Empire portugais aux XVe et XVIe siècles*, Paris, 1969 ; *Os Descobrimentos e a economia mundial* (Lisbon, 1963) 2 vol.
2. Cortessão (A.), sums up the matter in *The Mystery of Vasco da Gama*, Centro de Estudos de Cartografia Antiga, 12 (Coimbra, 1973).
3. Mota (A. Teixeira da), *Reflexos do tratado de Tordesilhas na cartografia nautica do século XVI*, Centro de Estudos de Cartografia Antiga, 80, (Coimbra, 1973).
4. Montalboddo (F. da), *Paesi novamente ritrovati et novo mondo de Alberico Vespucci intitulato*, (Vicenza, 1507).
5. Ramusio (Gianbattista), *Delle Navigatione e Viaggi*, Venice, 1550, vol. I.
6. Priuli (Girolamo), *Diarri (1494-1512)* dans Muratori, *Raccolta degli storici italiani*, Bologna, 1937, vol. 24/3 (1) ; Sanuto (M.), *I Diarii di Marino Sanuto* (Venice, 1879-1903) 58 vol.
7. 1 quintal (peso velho) = 51,405 kg.
   „ „ (peso novo) = 58,752 kg.
   cf. G. Bouchon, *Navires et cargaisons retour de l'Inde en 1518* (Paris, 1977) p. IX-X.
8. Quirino da Fonseca, *Os Portugueses no Mar, Memórias históricas e arqueológicas das naus de Portugal* (Lisbon, 1926).
9. Andrade (A. Banha de), *Mundos novos do mundo* (Lisbon, 1972) 2 vols.
10. Rau (Virginia), *Affari e mercanti in Portogallo dal XIV al XVI secolo, Rivista italiana di storia economica e sociale*, vol. 14 (1967) ; *Francisco Corbinelli feitor de Goa, Memórias do Centro de Estudos de Marinha*, vol. 4 (1974), pp. 107-141 ; *Um grande mercador banqueiro italianos em Portugal : Lucas Giraldi, Estudos italianos em Portugal*, n°. 24 (1956), pp. 3-35 ; *Uma familia de mercadores em Portugal no século XV : os Lomellini, Revista da Faculdade de Letras*, Lisbon vol. 22 : 2nd series, n°. 2 (1956), pp. 56-83.
11. Melis (Federigo), *Di alcune figure di operatori economici fiorentini attivi nel Portogallo nel XV secolo*, in Kellenbenz (H.), *Fremde Kaufleute auf der iberischen Halbinsel*, (Köln/Wien, 1970), p . 56-73 : *Documenti per la storia economica dei secoli XIII-XVI*, (Florence 1972).
12. Ballard (M.), *Precursori di Cristoforo Colombo. I Genovesi in Estremo Oriente, in XIV secolo, Atti del Convegno internazionale di studi colombani* (13/14 Ottobre 1973), (Genova, 1974).

13. Kiniewicz (Jan), *Factoria e farteca (Handel pilprzemma oceanic Indyjk im i ekspansja portugalska w XVI wicku)*, (Warszawa, 1970) ; *The Portuguese factory and trade in pepper in Malabar during the 16th century, The Indian Economic and Social History Review*, vol. 6 (1969), pp. 61-84.
14. Kellenbenz (Hermann), *La participation des capitaux de l'Allemagne méridionale aux entreprises portugaises d'outre-mer au tournant du XVe siècle*, dans *Les Aspects internationaux de la découverte océanique aux XVe et XVIe siècles, 7e Colloque international d'Histoire maritime*, ed. M. Mollat du Jourdin, Paris, 1966 ; *Fremde Kaufleute auf der iberischen Halbinsel* (Koln/Wien, 1970).
15. Crinó (S.), *Schizzi cartografici inediti dei primi anni della scoperta dell'America, Rivista marittima*, nov. 1930, supplemento.
16. G. Sern'i i. de Lisboa, 10, VII, 1499, trad. in Ravenstein, *A Journal of the First Voyage of Vasco da Gama, 1497-1499*, (London, 1898).
17. *El Tratado de Tordesillas y su proyeccion* (Segundas jornadas americanistas de la Universidad de Valladolid, Primer Coloquio Luso-espanhol de História de Ultramar) Seminario de História de America, Universidad de Valladolid, t. I (1973)—II, (1974) ; *A viagem de Fernão de Magalhães e a questão das Molucas*, Actas do II Colóquio luso-espanhol de História ultramarina, ed. A. Teixeira da Mota, Lisbon, Centro de Estudos de Cartografia Anti~a, 16, 1975. C. f. also Mahn-Lot (M.), *Conceptions géographiques et découverte : la question des Moluques jusqu'en 1521, Archipel*, vol. 22 (1981), pp. 75-86.
18. G. Bouchon, *A propos de l'inscription de Colombo (1501). Quelques observations sur le premier voyage de João da Nova dans l'Océan Indien*, Centro de Estudos de Cartografia Antiga, 139 (Coimbra, 1980).
19. Albuquerque, *Cartas*, ed. Bulhão Pato, vol. 3, p. 270.
20. Velho (A.), *Roteiro da primeira viagem de Vasco da Gama (1497-1499)*, ed. Fontoura da Costa (Lisbon, 1969) ; Ravenstein (E.G.). *A Journal*, o.c. ;
21. Cortessão (J.), *A expedição de Pedro Alvares Cabral* (Lisbon, 1922) ; Brooks-Greenlee (W.), *The voyage of Pedro Alvares Cabral to Brazil and India from contemporary documents and narratives* (London 1937) ; Pereira (Moacir Soares) *Capitães, naus e caravelas da armada de Cabral*, Centro de Estudos de Cartografia Antiga, 11- (1979).
22. Correia (G.), *Lendas da India* (Lisbon, 1860-1866). vol. I/1, p. 147.
23. Bouchon (G.), *A propos de l'inscription de Colombo (1501), o.c.*
24. Tomé Lopes in Ramusio, *o.c.*, f. 143 b-156 a.
25. *Calcoen, a Dutch narrative of the second voyage of Vasco da Gama to Calicut printed at Antwerp circa 1504.* Ed. J.P. Berjeau, London, 1871 ; Polisensky (J.) & Ratkos (P.), *Eine new Quelle zur zweiten Indienfahrt Vasco da Gamas, Historica*, vol. 9 (1964), pp. 53-67.
26. Nunes (A.), *Livro dos pesos e moedas da India, 1554*, pp. 33-34 in *Subsídios para a História da India portugueza*, ed. R.J. da Lima Felner (Lisbon, 1868).

27. Peragallo (P.). *Viaggio di Matteo da Bergamo in India nella flotta di Vasco da Gama (1502-1503), Studi bibliografici e biografici sulla storia de la geografia in Italia*, (Roma, 1875), cf. Appendix.
28. Bouchon (G.), *Les Albuquerque au Malabar (1503-1504) selon des sources inédites* Universidade de Coimbra (forthcoming).
29. Bouchon (G.), *Le premier voyage de Lopo Soares en Inde (1504-1505), Mare Lusoindicum*, vol. 3 (1976), pp. 57-84.
30. *Crónica do descobrimento e conquista da India pelos Portugueses* (codice anónimo Egerton 20901). Introdução e notas de Luís de Albuquerque. Centro de Estudos de Cartografia Antiga, 86 (Cóimbra, 1974) ; Aubin (J.), *Un nouveau classique, l'Anonyme du British Museum, Mare Luso-indicum*, vol. 3 (1976), pp. 183-188.
31. Mota (A. Teixeira da), *A viagem de Antonio de Saldanha em 1503 e a rota de Vasco da Gama no Atlântico Sul*, Centro de Estudos de Cartografia Antiga, 64 (Lisbon, 1971) ; Lobato (A.), *António de Saldanha, his time and his achievements*, (Lisbon, 1962).
32. Bouchon (G.), *L'inventaire de la cargaison rapportée de l'Inde en 1505, Mare Luso-indicum*, vol. 3 (1976), pp. 101-136.
33. Braamcamp Freire (A.), *Cartas de quitação de D. Manuel, Archivo Historico português*, (Lisbon, 1903-1917/1923-1925), passim.
34. Bouchon (G.), *L'inventaire... o.c.*
35. Andrade (A. Banha de), *História de um fidalgo quinhentista português, Tristão da Cunha*, (Lisbon, 1974) ; Aubin (J.), *Pour une biographie de Tristão da Cunha, Mare Lusco-indicum*, vol. 3 (1976), pp. 188-193.
36. Bouchon (G.), *Navires et Cargaisons retour de l'Inde en 1518, Caderno dos oficiaes da India da carreguaçam das naos que vieram o anno de b^c xii j* (Tdt. Núcleo Antigo, 705), Paris, Société d'Histoire de l'Orient, 1977.

Price set in Cochin & Cananor (March 1503)

from Matteo da Bergamo (ed. Peragallo, *Viaggio de Matteo da Bergamo in India...*)

COCHIN

Pepper :*	150½	*fanam* + duties :	9% per *bahar*
Cinnamon :	245	*fanam* + duties :	15 *fanam* per *bahar*
Camphor :	100	*fanam* + duties :	6½% per *bahar*
Aloes wood :	1000	*fanam* + duties :	6½% per *bahar*
Cloves :	400	*fanam* + duties :	15 *fanam* per *bahar*
Nutmeg :	145	*fanam* + duties :	8 *fanam* per *bahar*
Benzoin :	500	*fanam* + duties :	6½% per *bahar*

* 20% per *bahar* was to be paid with copper (Price of copper : 720 *fanam* per *bahar*)

CANANOR

Pepper :	210	*fanam* + duties :	2 *fanam* per *bahar*
Ginger :	55	*fanam* + duties :	6% per *bahar*
Indigo :	50	*fanam* per *farazola***	
Mirobolans :	7	*fanam* per *farazola*	

** 1 *bahar* = 20 *farazolas*

5

The Indian Merchant Communities in Malacca under the Portuguese Rule

LUIS FILIPE FERREIRA REIS THOMAZ

SINCE its origins at the beginning of the 15th century Malacca has been a mercantile city-state, where the ruling class, the Sultan and the State itself, were concerned with seafaring and trade.[1]

Its role was not that of a regional center, but that of an essential knot of a large maritime network, embracing most of the Indian Ocean shores, from the Straits of Hormuz and Bab-el-Mandeb till the Molucas and South China. Its character—as even its urban lay-out testifies - was, therefore, quite different from the medieval agrarian towns of South East Asia.[2] Its population was of very mixed origin : a large part of it was formed by foreign mercantile colonies, such as Chinese, Javanese, Luzonese and chiefly, Indian communities.[3] Most of the long distance trade was conducted by these communities. As in many other states with the same characteristics - one can think of the famous *metoikoi* of Athens in ancient times—the official policy in Malacca was to welcome foreign traders and to attract them to settle in the town.

This policy appears to be inspired by two orders of reasons. First, a technical one, their know-how—since their experience and their knowledge of their own countries enabled them to act as middlemen between Malacca and those areas, ensuring so the expansion of the trade centered in the town. Second, a purely economic one, their financial capacity—since the development of Malacca as a great trading centre has been too quick to be fo lowed by the weak capacity of investment of the native population, formed mainly by descendants of poor sailors and fishermen. This is, in short, a question of economies of scale : their presence, conferring to the enterprise an optimal dimension, appeared thus as a general advantage. As long as the system was in expansion, the foreign merchant communities were, therefore, welcome.[4]

Amongst them two Indian communities—the Tamil-speaking Hindus, called *keling* in Malay, and the Gujarati Muslims—were the most powerful, rich and influential.

The presence of Indian merchants (chiefly Dravidians from Coromandel Coast) in South Asia goes back to the earlier centuries of the Christian era ; their role in the indianization of the whole area is well known. It is even possible to talk about a Dravidian thalassocracy around the Bay of Bengal during the Middle Ages. The campaigns of Rajendrachola I in Malaya Peninsula and Sumatra represent probably a swift attempt to create a kind of colonial empire in these indianized regions. Anyway, the Chola intervention is undoubtedly related with the expansion of the Dravidian maritime network. When, at the beginning of the XV century, the Malacca Sultanate suddenly emerged, this network was already suffering the strong competition of the Arab and Muslim network ; but it still continued to exist—and, naturally many Tamil traders came to settle in the new seaborne emporium.[5] According to Malay traditions collected by the Portuguese chroniclers, they got a priviliged position and became specially influential under the region of Mudhafar Shah (1446-1459), third sovereign and first Sultan of Malacca, who was the son of a *keling* princess.[6]

On the eve of the arrival of the Portuguese the Hindu merchants living in Malacca were more than 1,000. As the other foreign colonies, they were settled in a special quarter, called *Kampong Keling*, along the seashore in the suburb of Upeh, on the right bank of the Malacca river.[7]

As well as the Chinese, the Javanese and the Gujaratis, the Kelings had their own *shahbandar*, entrusted with the reception, accommodation and presentation to the Malay authorities of all the seamen and traders coming from the countries around the Bay of Bengal.

Apparently the Tamil merchants were specially concerned with the spice trade in the Archipelago ; they virtually monopolized the relations of Malacca with the islands of Maluku and Banda, sharing with the merchants of Geresik and Panarukan, in East Java, the control of the cloves and nutmeg trade.

The Gujaratis, on the other hand, appeared to be specially concerned with the commerce between Malacca and the Red Sea, providing by this way Indonesian and Southeast Asian spices to the markets of the Mediterranean basin.[8] In this trade, in a rather triangular system, India, and particularly Gujarat, played an active role, since all over the Southeast Asian coasts the spices and drugs were bartered against Indian cotton textiles.[9]

Although ruled by Muslims since its conquest by the Sultans of Delhi in 1305, Gujarat had a majority of Hindu population and many Hindus amongst its trading classes.[10] Nevertheless we find no Hindu merchants among the Gujaratis settled in Malacca and other South-East Asia ports. It appears that the different groups of the Gujarat mercantile class were specialized in different kinds of trade and in the relations with special zones. Perhaps, owing to the fact that most of the commodities purchased in Malacca were directly exported to Aden and other Muslim ports, the Muslim merchant communities of Gujarat were particularly engaged in this trade. Perhaps also, because of their traditional taboos and prejudices against seafaring, the Hindus preferred the overland commerce. In fact, the Portuguese records refer to many Gujarati ships reaching South-East Asia and belonging to Hindu merchants, who preferred to remain ashore in the centre of their business, and to send in their vessels, Muslim factors and Muslim crews.[11] Anyway, the Muslim Gujaratis played an essential role in the Islamization of North Sumatra and, later on, of Malacca.[12]

According to Tomé Pires the Gujarati merchants settled in Malacca were roughly as numerous as the Kelings : more than 1,000.[13] Like their rivals, they also had their own *shahbandar*, entrusted with all the vessels coming from the countries west from Ceylon.

The balance of influence between them and the Kelings appears to have been quite delicate ; therefore, a muffled rivalry did exist between both communities. With Mudhafar Shah, the son of a Keling princess, who came to the throne murdering the crown prince, his cousin a kind of *coup d'etat* perhaps supported by the Keling community – the Hindus had become more influential. But on the eve of the arrival of the Portuguese the Gujaratis, supported by the powerful *bendaharas*, or prime-ministers of the Sultan, had already overthrown their rivals and become the favourite of the ruling powers.

In 1509 the first Portuguese fleet arrived at Malacca, under the command of Diogo Lopes de Sequeira, looking for trading facilities in the port. The Gujaratis, closely linked with the interests of the main rivals of the Portuguese in the west half of the Indian Ocean, the Arabs, tried to excite the authorities against them. The Javanese did the same, while the Chinese immediately fraternized with the new comers, and the Hindus, apparently, kept in wise wait-and-see attitude.[14] But, as soon as the troubles started, one of them, Nina Chatu, appears, trying to act as a mediator between the *bendahara* and the Portuguese. We can assume that, at least tacitly, he was supported by his community, as well as the Gujarati and Javanese *shahbandars*, who led the opposition to Portuguese pretensions. Anyway, his role becomes suddenly very active, conveying messages between the Portuguese fleet and some Portuguese caught ashore by the *bendahara*, and, later on, after the departure of the fleet, providing messengers to carry them to Afonso de Albuquerque in India. When, two years later, this one came with a second expedition, determined to obtain by peaceful or forced means the liberation of the prisoners as well as the desired trading facilities, Nina Chatu tried again to act as a mediator between Albuquerque and the Sultan—while the richest Hindu merchants endeavoured to persuade the sovereign that it was better to accept the Portuguese conditions and to idemnify them with money for the losses they had suffered.[15]

When it became clear that war was unavoidable, most of the Hindu merchants, including Nina Chatu, left the town, retiring to the sanction of the jungle. The Gujaratis, naturally, decided to join the Sultan against the Portuguese, while the Chinese supported them, providing them boats for the landings, and the Javanese *shahbandar* sent secret messages promising to co-operate – trying so to ensure his position if the fortune of weapons moved to the Portuguese side.

After the conquest—which appears so partly as the result of the rivalries between different merchant communities inside the Sultanate—Nina Chatu, leading the whole Keling community came back to the town, while most of the Gujaratis followed the Sultan to his exile at Pagoh, and afterwards in Bintan island.[16]

So, the Hindu colony became the most powerful and influential merchant community of Malacca, while the Gujaratis disappeared from the town.[17] Nina Chatu, who actively co-operated with Albuquerque in coining money, building a stronghold and reorganizing the city life, was granted by the Governor the dignity and the rents of the former *bendahara*, with jurisdiction over all the *kafir* (i.e. neither Christian nor Muslim) people. A Muslim from Luzon – significantly neither a Gujarati, a Malay, or a Javanese – received the title of *temenggong* with the jurisdiction over all the Muslim communities. These grants were, afterwards, confirmed by the King, who, in addition, made the functions of *bendahara* hereditary in the lineage of Nina Chatu.[18]

He was a very rich merchant indeed. Insofar as we know, in 1513-14 he sent two junks to Siam, one to Bengal and one *pangajava* to Palembang, in Sumatra, fitted out at his own expenses;[19] in partnership with the Portuguese Crown, a junk to Pegu, another to China[20]—the first Portuguese ship to reach China—and a third to the Coromandel Coast.[21] A little earlier he had sent a junk to Banda and Ternate, fitted out in partnership with his friend Rui de Araujo, the first factor of Malacca.[22]

The richest merchant of Malacca we are aware of was also a Hindu : Nina Suryadeva. According to Tomé Pires, under the Sultanate he shared with a merchant of Geresik, in East Java, called Pate Cuçuf (i.e. probably Patih Yusuf), the monopoly of the trade of Banda and Maluku. Usually he sent there every year eight junks, while the Javanese fitted out just three or four.[23] Under the Portuguese rule he continued to do so, at least until 1527. He also sent junks to China and other spots.[24] As Nina

Chatu he often appears associated with the mercantile activities of the Portuguese Crown: we found, for instance, among the records of the *almazem* (arsenal) of Malacca receipts of loans of artillery to protect his vessels, since he carried spices and other commodities belonging to His Highness' factories.[25]

Yet the importance of the Hindu colony of Malacca was not merely commercial. It also had a political and social role. Very often the Hindu merchants acted as economic advisers of the captains of the fortress. Rui de Brito Potalim, the first captain, always took counsel with Nina Chatu in commercial matters before taking his decision—as he confessed in a letter to Albuquerque.[26] Certainly the ease and rapidity of the Portuguese adaptation to the economic conditions of South-East Asia cannot be understood without the experience and know-how of these native co-operators, and perhaps specially Nina Chatu. Later on we find a few written advices given by other Hindu merchants about prices of commodities, and so on.[27]

Their role is equally noteworthy as money lenders to the Portuguese Crown—chronically insolvent due to permanent wars, piracy and shipwrecks, imperfect financial organization, bad administration, corruption and, perhaps chiefly, because of the asymmetry of the trade between Europe and India, which caused most of the coinable metal to run into the pockets of the pepper producers. One of the worst accusations produced before the King against certain captains of Malacca was, therefore, that of tyrannic behaviour towards the merchants—since "without the loans of the Kelings, Malacca and His Highness cannot live.[28]

They also played a curious social role. According to the Malay customary law[29], which the Portuguese tacitly accepted in matters such as naval organisation and commerce—it was possible to entrust money to the owner of a ship, before a voyage, receiving on the return the same amount increased by a certain percentage, fixed in advance according to the port of destination. This kind of contract—one of the rare form of usury not condemned by the Koran—was very popular in Malacca under the Sultanate, and continued so during the Portuguese rule. The profits were usually between 35 and 50 per cent in voyages inside the Archipelago, but they rose to 80 or 90 per cent in the case of those to India and 200 per cent in the case of China.[30] This procedure ensured a large investment by collecting the small savings, and at once, enabled even the poor people to participate in long distance trade. In fact, we find receipts passed by sailors, soldiers, even illiterate people like a certain "black man native of Santarém", who had so entrusted large sums to the local merchants.[31]

As early as 1515 we find Portuguese—even noblemen—embarked in ships belonging to the richest *keling* merchants, sometimes at their service as seamen or commercial agents.[32]

There are also cases of association between Hindu and Portuguese traders, such as the company formed in 1527 by the *bendahara* (probably the son of Nina Chatu), Francisco de Brito and the captain of Malacca, Jorge Cabral, to send junks to the tin-mining regions of Perak and Kedah in North Malaya.[33]

So, the Hindu community which formed the b ckbone of the local bourgeoisie appears to have close ties with the State, the Portuguese aristocracy and the common people. Apparently the prosperity of trade had created a symbiosis of interests—which, of course, did not prevent occasional shocks, but contributed to the social stability of the town. In fact, Malacca, after a few seditions in favour of the former Sultan, led by the Javanese community during the first two years of Portuguese rule, has a very quiet internal life, despite the tyrannic behaviour of many captains and of the continuous assaults of the Malays from Bintan and the Achinese. The contrast is marked with, for instance, the Moluccas, constantly agitated by quarrels with the Sultans, the captains and the Portuguese merchants.

As in the times cf the Sultans, and probably for the same reasons, the new settlers were welcome at Malacca. In 1521 the captain, Garcia de Sá, sent a messenger to persuade secretly the merchants living in Pahang, on the Malay Peninsula East Coast, to come over to Malacca.[34] In the next year the new captain, Jorge de Albuquerque, proclaimed in the ports of the Coromandel Coast that "great liberties" should be granted to every merchant who decides to settle in Malacca.[35] To attract further merchants to the town, Pero de Faria announced in

1537 that they should be allowed to participate in the fleet which was being prepared to sail to China.[36]

We must also note that with the number of merchants increased the revenue of the customs, and the customs were the sole revenue of the State in Malacca. It was already so in the times of the Sultanate and it continued to be so under the Portuguese, who, as everywhere in Asia kept in Malacca the native tax system.[37]

Curiously, the Hindu and Muslim merchants paid in the Malacca custom-house just 6 per cent as customs duties, while the Christians paid 10 per cent. Probably the crown wished by this measure to prevent the Portuguese from becoming merchants, thinking that one more merchant meant one less soldier [38]

Unfortunately, we are not able to accompany the historical evolution of the Hindu community of Malacca during the second half of the XVI century-since after 1545 very few records are kept.

We can nevertheless presume that they were in less favour than during the first half of the century, for three reasons. First, an economic one : the Portuguese commercial network was no more in expansion, and, thus, the competition inside it tended probably to be stronger. Second, a social reason : the number of Portuguese private merchants had increased, and the Crown had given up, on their behalf, most of its trading activities ; the social weight of the new bourgeoise, formed by Portuguese, half-caste and converts, ought, therefore, to be stronger, while the need of the *keling* know-how and capital ought to be less felt. Third, an ideological reason, the mental atmosphere of the Counter, Reformation, more suspicious towards every kind of heathen-although its effects were less felt in spots such as Malacca, Diu, Macao etc., which essentially remained trade centers, than in Goa, which was intended to become the political, cultural and religious center of a Christian empire.[39]

As sign of this change, by the end of the century, the rates paid at the Malacca custom-house were inverted : since then the Christians paid 6 per cent, the Muslims and the Hindus 10 per cent[40]

Yet we have reasons to suppose that the Hindu community of Malacca was diminishing, as, since the middle of the century, a considerable part of it became Christian. Some of them had become converts as a result of the great fervour of proselytism generated by the Council of Trent and the coming of the main religious orders to Malacca : the Jesuits in 1549, the Blackfriars in 1554, the Greyfriars in 1582, the Augustinians in 1587.

The *bendahara*—probably a grand son of Nina Chatu—became a convert in 1564, yielding to the pleas of the Viceroy Dom Constantino de Bragança.[41] He entrusted then his son to the Jesuits to be educated in their college. Probably that was him the *bendahara* D. João killed in 1573, fighting against the Chinese, who had besieged the stronghold.[42] Apparently, the Nina Chatu's dynasty ended with him—since in the next year, during a new siege, the chronicles mention already another *bendahara*, Dom Henrique. He was an uncle of the King of Tidore, in the Molucas, converted to Christianity, called Cachil Labuzaza when still a Muslim.[43] Perhaps the choice was dictated by a desire to fall in favour with his nephew, whose friendship had become essential after the revolt of Ternate against the Portuguese in 1570. Anyway, the choice of a Muslim converted to Christianity to become chief of a Hindu community shows clearly that something had changed since the days of Albuquerque.

Later on this *bendahara* D. Henrique was appointed knight of the Military Order of Christ, rewarding so his services, probably during the siege.[44] Apparently he is the ancestor of the subsequent *bendaharas* till the end of the Portuguese rule in 1641. The chronicles often talk about them, almost always as to the successive sieges of the fortress-where they fought first against the Achinese, later on against the Dutch, commanding their subjects, the Kelings.

In fact, in peacetime, the role of the *bendaharas* appears to have been mainly judicial ; but in wartime they also had military functions, gathering their subjects and leading them during the sieges. Usually the merchants served in war with their own servants and slaves ; often, in critical situations, they also spared them to man the Portuguese war vessels. The Portuguese settlers—the *casados*—did the same ; at the beginning of the

XVII century they owned a total of 2,000 slaves, employed mainly for military purposes. So, the Portuguese themselves reproduced the model of the traditional armies in Southeast Asia towns, generally formed by the assembled clienteles of the different *orang kaya* who constituted the ruling class.[45]

If we can use the list of salaries of the budgets as a scale of social importance, then the *bendaharas* held in the Malacca hierarchy the fourth place, beside the judge, after the bishop, the captain and the factor. In fact he earned annually 100$000rs, while the bishop earned 800$000, the captain 600$000 and the factor 200$000 ; on the other hand the secretaries (escrivães) had 50$000 and the canons of the cathedral 20$000.[46]

After their conversion to Christianity th. *bendaharas* used their title (under the Portuguese form "bendara", sometimes in the chronicles "Bandarra") as a family name. As also, for instance, the noblemen of Flores and Timor, they always used the Portuguese title of *dom*.

Since the Muslims in Malacca as everywhere revealed themselves quite refractory to conversion, most of the Malacca Christians—7,400 at the beginning of the XVII century, according to Manuel Godinho de Herédia were from Chinese, and chiefly, Indian origin.[47]

So, curiously, these Indian converts must be the ancestors of a large part of the present Portuguese-speaking Catholic community of Malacca—as their physical appearance seems to show.

NOTES

1. Meinlink-Roelofsz, *Asian Trade and European Influence in the Indonesian Archipelago between 1500 and about 1630* (The Hague, 1962).
2. Denys Lombard, Pour une histoire des villes du Sud-Est Asiatique, *Annales* E.S.C. 4, juillet-août 1970, pp. 842-856.
3. *Cf.* our study "Malacca - The town and the society during the first century of Portuguese rule", paper presented to the *VIII Conference of the International Association of Historians of Asia* (Kuala Lumpur, Malaysia, August 1980).

4. *Cf.* John Hicks, *A Theory of Economic History* (Oxford University Press), 1969.
5. These traditions were collected specially by Tomé Pires (see Armando Cortesão, *The 'Suma Oriental' of Tomé Pires and the Book of Francisco Rodrigues,* ... Hakluyt Society, London, 1941—sixth book, English translation, pp. 229 & seq.) ; they are also quoted by João de Barros (Asia, Decada II, livro VI, cap. I) and by Afonso (Brás) de Albuquerque, *Comentários do Grande Afonso de Albuquerque*, Part III, ch. XVII (5th edition, reimpression of the 2nd, 1576, by Joaquim Veríssimo Serrão, Imprensa Nacional - Casa da Moeda (Lisbon, 1973) vol. II). They roughly agree with the Malay written tradition, preserved chiefly by the *Sejarah Melayu* or *Malay Annals* (editions by Shellabear, *Malay Literature Series,* 9, 1909 (p. I), 1930 (p. II) and by Sir Richard Winsted, *Journal of the Malay Branch of the Royal Asiatic Society* (*JMBRAS*), 16, pt. 3, 1938 ; English translation by C.C. Brown, *Sejarah Melayu or Malay Annals,* a translation of Raffles MS 18 in the Library of the R.A.S., London, with commentary by..., *JMBRAS,* vol. 25, pt. 2 & 3, n. 159 (Singapore, 1952-53).
6. For the history of Malacca before the Portuguese conquest see: Meilink-Roelofz, *op. cit.* ; J.C. Var Leur, *Indonesian Trade and Society: Essays in Asian Social and Economic History,* The Hague - Bandung, 1955 ; Haji Buyong Adil, *The History of Malacca during the period of the Malay Sultanate,* Dewan Bahasa dan Pustaka, Kuala Lumpur, 1974 ; Sir Richard Winstedt, *Malaya and Its History,* 7th ed., 1966, Hutchinson University Library, London ; D.G.E. Hall, *A History of South-East Asia,* 3rd, St. Martin Press (New York, 1970).
7. *Kampong* means in Malay "village", but it is also used in the sense of "suburb, quarter of a town", *Keling* (from the name of the well-known ancient Indian kingdom of *Kaliṅga*) is a generic name for Tamil or Telugu speaking people. *Benua Keling,* "continent or region of the Kelings" is the Malay name for the Coromandel Coast or even for India in general. These names passed into Portuguese under the form *quelim* and Bonua *Quelim.* Some of the richest Hindu merchants from Benua Keling were also landed proprietors ; they lived in their *dusun* (orchards, farms), cultivated by slaves, around Malacca, having in the town their commercial agencies and stores. It was still so under the Portuguese rule. *Cf.* the letter of Francisco Faria quoted belew, n. 24.
8. Our main source of information about the trade as well as about the organization of Malacca is Tomé Pires, (*Cf.* note 5). Duarde Barbosa also provides us interesting elements : see *Livro em que dá relação do que viu e ouviu no Oriente Duarte Barbosa,* several editions, v.g., by Augusto Reis Machado, Agência Geral das Colónias (Lisboa, 1964).
9. Even in the treaties of commerce between the Portuguese and some Indonesian rulers, such as the Sultans of Ternate, the price of spices is fixed in terms of Indian textiles instead of money. For further details see our study, Maluco e Malaca, in *A Viagem de Fernão de Magalhães*

e a Questão das Molucas, Actas do II Colóquio Luso-Espanhol de História Ultramarina, J.I.C.U. (Lisbon, 1975).

10. See M.N. Pearson, *Merchants and Rulers in Gujarat*, Munshiram Manoharlal, (New Delhi, 1976).
11. Tomé Pires, *op. cit.*, p. 369 (Portuguese text).
12. See H.J. de Graaf, South-East Asian Islam to the eighteenth century, in *The Cambridge History of Islam*, Vol. 2-A (Cambridge University Press, 1977) ; also W. Stöhr & P. Zoetmulder, *Les Religions d'Indonésié*, Payot, Paris, 1968. The beginnings of Islam in Sumatra are recounted in a half-legendary form by the earliest Malay chronicle, the *Hikayat Raja - Pasai*, edited with English translation by A.H. Mill in *JMBRAS*, vol. XXXIII, pt. 2, n. 190 (Singapore 1960). The thesis of Slamet Muljana giving to the Chinese converts a central role in the spread of Islam does not seem well founded ; see his *Runtuhnja Keradjaan Hindu-Djawa dan Timbulnja Negara Islam di Nusantara*, Bhratara (Djakarta, 1968).
13. He also calculates the number of Gujaratis coming every year to Malacca for trading purposes and going back to their country in the next monsoon, as four or five thousands ; but there is, perhaps, a certain exaggeration in these figures. See *op. cit.*, p. 369.
14. The coming of the first Portuguese fleet to Malacca in 1509 is related from the Portuguese side by Barros, *Asia*, Década II, Bk. 4, chs. III-IV ; Fernão Lopes de Castanheda, *Historia do Descobrimento e Conquista da India pelos Portugueses*, Bk. 2, chs. CX-CXVI (last edition, Coimbra, Imprensa da Universidade, 1928) ; Gaspar Correia, *Lendas da India*, Bk. 2, Lendas de Afonso de Albuquerque, ch. V. From the Malay side, quite shortly, in the *Sejarah Melayu*, ch. XXI of the Winstedt-Brown edition.
15. For further details about the attitudes of Nina Chatu during this crucial period, see our study, Nina Chatu e o comércio português em Malaca, in *Memórias do Centro de Estudos de Marinha*, vol. V (Lisboa, 1975).
16. The fall of Malacca is briefly told from the Malay side in the *Sejarah Melayu* (ch. XXIII of the Winstedt-Brown edition, ch. XXXIV of the Shellabear edition). From the Portuguese side we have Barros, *Asia*, Década II, Bk. VI, chs. I-VII ; Castanheda, *op. cit.*, Bk. 3, chs, L-LXIII ; Gaspar Correia, *op. cit.*, Bk. 2, Lenda de Afonso de Albuquerque, chs. XXVII-XXXII ; Afonso de Albuquerque, *Comentários...*, Bk. 3, chs. XIX-XXXIX. The letters of Afonso de Albuquerque himself, together with many related documents, are published by R.A. Bulhão Pato & Henrique Lopes de Mendonça, *Cartas de Afonso de Albuquerque seguidas de documentos que as elucidem*, 7 vols., Academia Real das Sciencias de Lisboa, 1892-1935. A critical survey of all these historical sources can be seen in our thesis *Os Portugueses em Malaca, 1511-1580*, 2 vols. (cyclostyled), Faculdade de Letras de Lisboa, 1964.
17. The vanishing of the Gujarati community put, nevertheless, a new problem to the Portuguese, since the whole commercial economy of

South-East Asia – as well as that of Africa East Coast—was based on the importation of Indian textiles, coming largely from Gujarat. To secure this essential input the Portuguese tried to resort to different means. In former times they obtained Gujarati textiles through their factories in Malabar ports, which kept close relations with the Gulf of Cambay. For instance, in 1512 João Piteira, sent as a factor to North Sumatra and Malacca, received from Lourenço Moreno, factor of Cochin, 8,058 pieces of cloth from Cambay (see the order of Afonso de Albuquerque issued at Cochin, 14th August 1512, ANTT, *Corpo Cronológico*, II-33-195, and the receipt of the factor, *ibidem*, II-33-192). Later on, they obtained the textiles in their own settlements in the North, specially Diu and Chaul. For instance, in 1526 Antonio da Silva, captain and factor of the carrack "Conceição" received in Diu and afterwards in Chaul 732$060 rs, then 440 pardaus and finally 2,000 *pardaus em tangas* to buy clothese for Malacca. The Portuguese also used the services of other merchants of Malacca, keeping ties with Gujarat, such as the Luzonese Muslim Suryadiraja, who sent a junk to Cambay in 1520, carrying some commodities belonging to His Highness, with a Portuguese *escrivão* (secretary) ; for this reason he received a loan of artillery and ammunitions from the *almazem* (royal arsenal) to protect the vessel (see its receipt, written in Malacca, 13th January 1520, ANTT, *Corpo Cronológico*, II-93-120). Also we have notice of a few attempts to attract Gujarati merchants to settle again in Malacca – as Jorge de Albuquerque tried to do in 1520 (see the letter of Garcia Chainho, factor of Malacca to the King, Malacca, 31st August 1521, ANTT, *Corpo Cronológico*, III-7-15). Apparently these attempts did not prove successful since virtually no trace of Gujarati merchants settled in Malacca are found after 1511 in Portuguese records. Perhaps the decline of the links with Gujarat was compensated by an increasing importation of textiles from Coromandel and Bengal. As to the importance of Gujarat in Portuguese policy, see Jean Aubin "Albuquerque et les négotiations de Cambaye" in *Mare Luso-Indicum*, tome I, Genève - Paris, 1971 ; also Geneviève Bouchon, *Mamale de Cananor - un adversaire de l'Inde Portugaise (1507-1528)* (Genève-Paris, 1975).

18. For further details see our *Nina Chatu e o comércio português ...* (*Cf* super note 15), where the full text of the Royal Charters can be seen

19. Letter of Rui de Brito Patalim, first captain of Malacca to Afonso de Albuquerque, Malacca, 6 January 1514, ANTT, *Corpo Cronológico*, I-14-52, pub. in *Cartas de Afonso de Albuquerque*, vol. III, pp. 216-231. The *pangajava* sent to Palembang carried commodities worth 5,000 *calains* (=150 *cruzados*) belonging to the defunct factor Pero Pessoa, killed in a sedition a little earlier. See the receipt of the procurator of the dead (*provedor dos defuntos*), Duarte Coelho, Malacca, 4th July 1514, ANTT, *Corpo Cronológico*, II-49-24, pub. *ibidem*, vol. VII, p. 128.

20. The full account-book of the junk sent to Pegu (includin ; the accounts of the purchase of the other, bought in Pegu to be sent to China in the next monsoon) is amongst the rare Portuguese account-books of this period. We published it in our study *De Malaca a Pegu – Viagens de um feitor português*, Centro de Estudos Históricos anexo à Faculdade de Letras de Lisboa, 1966.
21. Letter of the clerks of Malacca factory to the King, Malacca, 7th January 15·4, ANTT, *Corpo Cronológico*, I-14-51 ; pub. in *Cartas de Afonso de Albuquerque*, vol. III, p. 89.
22. João de Barros, *Ásia*, Década II, Bk. 6, ch. VII.
23. Tomé Pires, *Suma Oriental*, p.447 (Portuguese text).
24. Letter of Francisco Faría to the King, Malacca, 14th August 1517, ANTT, *Corpo Cronológico*, I-22-62, transcribed in our *Os Portugueses em Malacca*, Vol. II, doc. 9 ; see also the two letters of the factor of Malacca, Pero Barriga, to the King, Malacca, 3rd August 1527 and Cochin, 31st December 1527, ANTT, *Corpo Cronológico*, III-9-94 and II-145-173, transcribed *ibidem*, doc. 35.
25. See, e.g., the receipt of Gonçalo Correia, captain of his junk "Paleão" (probably in Malay *pelayang*, "flyer") sent to Banda. Malacca, 13th January 1521, ANTT, *Corpo Cronológico*, II-93-119.
26. See the letter quoted above, note 19.
27. See, e.g., the documents issued at Malacca 4th July 1513, ANTT, *Corpo Cronológico*. II-39-134 and 21st December 1519, *ibidem*, II-83-48. According to the latter a *chetti* called Beirame used to serve officially as "tier of metals in the stronghold and town of Malacca".
28. See the letter of Pero Barriga from Malacca, quoted above, note 24. Writing to the King to expose to him their main problems, needs and aspirations, the *keling* merchants of Malacca complain that many loans are not yet paid : Malacca, 10th September 1527, ANTT, *Corpo Cronológico*, I-37-84, transcrided in *Os Portugueses em Malacca*, Vol. II, doc. 40.
29. *Cf.* Liaw Yock Fang, *Undang-undang Melaka – The laws of Malacca* (introduction, Malay text and English translation), Bibliotheca Indonesica, (The Hague, 1976).
30. These figures are given by Tomé Pires, *Suma Oriental* (p. 507 Portuguese text, fl. 177 of the Ms.) Another means often used of getting a share in a voyage was to hire a *pitaca* (Malay *pĕtak*, from Sanskrit *piṭaka*) or compartment of a junk ; but this procedure was only accessible to rich people. The Portuguese Crown used it very frequently, sending its merchandise in junks belonging to *keling* merchants (*Cf.* note 32); some noblemen (chiefly captains and civil servants of the stronghold) did the same ; but the first procedure remained, of course, more popular.
31. See for instance the *post mortem* inventory of João Freire's goods, received by the procurator of the dead by Garcia Chainho, Malacca, 5th June 1513, ANTT, *Corpo Cronológico*, II-39-59. He had invested money and Indian textiles in five different voyages, four of them

conducted by Tamil merchants. See also the receipt of Lourenço Moreno, the "black man native of Santarém", Malacca, 11th March 1513, ANTT, *Corpo Cronológico*, II-37-218.

32. Alvaro do Cocho sailed to Banda in 1515 in a junk belonging to Nina Suryadeva, to purchase mace by order of the 2nd captain of Malacca, Jorge de Albuquerque ; the next year his successor Jorge de Brito sent him again to the Moluccas, entrusted with some *pitacas* of a junk loaded with commodities belonging to His Highness. During the regency of Dona Catarina (1557-62) a certain Baltasar do Prado was captain and factor of a vessel belonging to Coje Mercar, coming from China to Malacca and Goa ; in this vessel, a certain Jorge Fernandes, who died during the voyage, had loaded 14,000 *pardaus* of silk, porcelains and other merchandise from China. After his death the captain sold, at Negapatam, the goods of the defunct (who had paid the freight till Goa) and went to Pegu. Because of this, a Queen's injunction (ANTT, *Colecção S. Vicente*, vol. X, fl. 128) withheld the Coje Mercar's *cartazes*.
33. See the second letter of Pero Barriga quoted above, note 24.
34. See the instructions given by Garcia de Sá to Martim da Rocha, ambassador to Pahang, Malacca, 15th April 1520, ANTT, *Corpo Cronológico*, I-27-88, transcribed in *Os Portuguese em Malaca*, vol. II, doc. 15.
35. See the letter of Garcis Chainho to the King quoted above, note 17.
36. Letter of Pero de Faria, appointed captain of Malacca, to the King, Goa, 18th November 1537, ANNT, *Corpo Cronológico*, I-60-17, fl. 8, transcribed in *Os Portugueses em Malaca*, doc. 112. The traditional idea that the Portuguese policy in the Indian Ocean was to monopolize the whole maritime trade, excluding the native merchants from it, must be, therefore, completely given up. Van Leur and specially Meilink Roelofsz (*cf.* notes 1 and 2) had shown that the Portuguese never succeeded in destroying the native maritime networks, but we can now go farther : It appears quite clearly from the preserved records that the official policy was rather to ensure for the Portuguese Crown, the largest participation in Asian trade possible with the means at its disposal, and to cause the rest of it to turn around the Portuguese positions, in order to control it politically and to get share in its revenue through the custom-taxes. The *cartaz* system appears to have also a tax-hunting scope, since it compelled the Asian vessels to pass through the ports ruled by the Portuguese to get their safe-conducts. Already the instructions of D. Manuel to the first factor of Malacca, Rui de Araújo urge him "to work for the sake of peace and justice in Malacca, in order to prevent the foreign merchants from leaving it, and trade from diminishing", Almeirim, 2nd March 1514, ANTT, *Corpo Cronológico*, II-42-260, pub. in *Cartas de Afonso de Albuquerque*, vol. VII, p. 116.
37. See our paper "Estrutura Politica e Administrativa do Estado da India no século XVI", presented to the II International Seminar on Indo-

Portuguese History in its proceedings under print ; also Vitorino de Magalhães Godinho, *Les Finances de l'Etat Portugais des Indes Orientales* (Paris, Centro Cultural Português, F.C.G., 1982).

38. See the Simão Botelho's *Tombo da India*, published by Rodrigo de Lima Felner, *Subsídios para a História da India Portuguesa*, Academia Real das Sciencias (Lisboa, 1848).

39. In fact, unlike those of Goa, the Hindus and Muslims of Diu, for instance, always kept their religious freedom and their own temples and mosques ; they asked and they received in 1707 the confirmation of their liberties. *Cf.* Goa Historical Archives, *Livro de Monções*, n. 69, fl. 65, pub. by J.H. Cunha Rivara, *Archivo Portuguêse Oriental, vol. 6, supplement, p. 178-181, (Goa, 1866).* In Malacca between 1562 and 1580 just eight people were judged by the Inquisition ; two of them were absolved, and one was admonished, four abjured, and only one, a Jewish woman, was "released to the secular justice" ; see *Repertorio Geral de três mil oitocentos processos que sam todos os despachados neste Santo Officio de Goa e mais partes da India do ano de 1571 que começou o dito Santo Oficio até o anno de 1627*, Biblioteca Nacional de Lisboa, *Fundo Geral*, cod. 203 ; we transcribed the parts concerning Malacca in *Os Portugueses em Malaca*, vol. II, n. 273.

40. See "Alvará em forma de Regimento do Vice Rei Matias de Albuquerque para a cidade de Malaca sobre o rendimento da alfandega e outras coisas do serviço de S.M.", Goa, 14 de Abril de 1595, pub. por Panduronga S.S. Pissurlencar, *Regimentos das Fortalezas da India*, (Bastorà, Goa, 1951).

41. Letter of Fr. Baltasar Dias, S.J., to his confreres in Portugal, Malacca, 31st December 1564, Biblioteca da Academia das Ciências de Lisboa, *Cartas do Japão*, vol. III, fl. 85v-86v ; pub. by Artur Basilio de Sá, *Documentacão para a História das Missõess do Padroado Português do Oriente*, Insulinda, vol. III, n. 12, p. 103, A.G.C. (Lisboa, 1945).

42. Diogo do Couto, *Ásia*, Década IX, ch. XVII.

43. António Bocarro, "História de Maluco no tempo de Gonçalo Pereira Marramaque e Sancho de Vasconcelos", B.N.L., *Fundo Geral*, n. 474, pub. by A. Basílio de Sá, *Documentação...*, vol. IV, (Lisbon, 1956), doc. 37 ; Cf. Couto, *Asia*, Década X, Bk. 3, ch. 2, and Bk. 8, ch. 4.

44. Information given by Fr. Manuel Teixeira, *The Portuguese Missions in Malacca and Singapore (1511-1958)*, Vol. I - Malacca - p. 131, A.G.U., (Lisboa, 1961).

45. António Bocarro, *Livro das Plantas de todas as fortalezas, cidades e povoações do Estado da India Oriental*, ed. A.B. Bragança Pereira, *Arquivo Português Oriental* (nova série) tomo IV, vol. II, parte II, Bastorá (Goa, 1938).

46. See the *Tombo da India* (*cf.* note 38) ; the *Regimentos das Fortalezas da India* (*cf.* note 40) ; the budget of 1574, pub. by Dr. Águedo de Oliveira, *Orçamento do Estado da India (1574) feito por mando de Diogo Velho, Vedor da Fazenda da India*, Lisboa, 1960 ; and the budgets of 1581 and 1588 in Artur Teodore de Matos, *O Estado da India nos anos*

de 1581-1588 - estrutura administrative e económica : Alguns elementos para o seu estudo, Universidade dos Açores (Ponta Delgada, 1982).

47. See Manuel Godinho de Erédia, *Declaraçam de Malaca*, pub. by Lear Janssen under the title *Malaca, l'Inde Méridionale et le Cathay* (Bruxelles, 1881), ch. 1. Under the Portuguese rule most of the Kelings of Malacca remained in their quarter, Kampong Keling, which formed with the Chinese Quarter, Kampong China, and their environments, the populous suburb of Upeh, on the right bank of the Malacca, river. It was the economic centre of the town, while the central district on the left bank, with the stronghold, the town hall (*câmara*), the Cathedral, the *Misericordia* and the main convents and churches, was the political and ecclesiastic centre. The central district was surrounded by a palissade since the days of Albuquerque - reinforced with bastions about 1520, replaced by a mud-wall by 1539 and finally, about 1569, by a stone bulwark. While the poor quarters, Ilher and Sabak, did not undergo noteworthy transformation, the rich quarter of Upeh, owing to its economic importance, was fortified with a palissade (in Portuguese *tranqueira*, whence the present name of the quarter, Trankerh). The original palissade was by 1539 replaced by a mud-wall with a bastion (called *baluarte do Bendara*) built at the expenses of the Keling merchants, with a small allowance from the Royal Treasury. Owing to the christianization of most of the inhabitants, two parish churches were built, one in Kampong Keling, near the seaside, the other in Kampong China, along the river bank ; both of them were built during the second half of the XVI century. See details in *Os Portugueses em Malaca*, vol. I, ch. 4, and also in the paper quoted above, n. 3.

6

The Origin and Rhythm of Dutch Aggression against the Estado da India, 1601-1661

LEONARD BLUSSÉ & GEORGE WINIUS

IT IS a commonplace that the VOC, or Dutch East India Company, reduced the Estado da India Oriental to a minor entity between 1602, the year of its formation, and 1661, but it is surprising that neither Dutch nor Portuguese historians have taken an especially close look at precisely how this rivalry began and what strategic pattern the Dutch attackers followed.

Our paper will address itself to precisely these two questions, and we believe they, or rather, the answers to them, provide some very useful reference points for anyone working in the Indo-Portuguese history of the XVII century—if only because the Dutch menace was the skeleton at every Goan feast. The first topic involved when and how the Dutch turned from friends into bitter enemies of the Portuguese ; the second addresses itself to why the Dutch scarcely bothered to penetrate the core of the Estado da India, that is, the west coast of the subcontinent itself, until around 1636—and then all but demolished it within a few years. It seems almost as of old friends suddenly became mortal enemies, then waited a generation before their showdown fight in these Goan parts.

The friendly Dutch become unfriendly

Practically everybody in our field knows that the Dutch and the Portuguese enjoyed friendly commercial relations during the XVI century ; the role of Dutch ships in the transport of spices and other Asian goods between Lisbon and Northern Europe from the reign of Dom Joao III is well appreciated. Moreover, the stories of Dirk Gerritsen Pomp and Jan Huyghen van Linschoten,[1] both of whom apprenticed in Portugal and then travelled to India in Portuguese employment, illustrate that relations between the nationals were easy and cordial, that is, until well after Philip II's takeover of the Portuguese throne.

To assume that this act automatically turned Dutchmen against the Portuguese would be far from true. The most active pretender to the Portuguese throne beside Philip himself, was Dom António, Prior do Crato, who happened to be the father of Prince Maurice of Orange's brother-in-law, Dom Manuel. To all but a few Portuguese of the ruling classes, Dom Antonio *was* their king, at least in preference to Philip, and no matter what his faults. If this had not been so, then the Spaniards could easily have caught him as he traipsed around the north of Portugal after losing the battle of Alcântara in 1580. The Dutch Republic, of course, recognized him, not Philip,[2] and this gave them a bond with the Portuguese people. Even when Philip seized over fifty Dutch ships trading in the Tagus in 1592, there ensued no wave of anti-Portuguese feeling in Holland ; in fact Spanish authorities continued to complain of Portuguese and Dutch collusion in the Acores in favour of Dom António. And even the Dutch carrying trade between Lisbon and the North soon resumed.[3]

At the same time, there can be little doubt that the unwilling Spanish connection of the Portuguese worked to the detriment of the Estado da India. The Spice Islands, the Moluccas, lay much closer to the Spanish Philippines than they did to Goa, and after Philip's takeover of Portugal, there could have seemed no compelling reason to stay out of Asia, if only because, according to *Inter Caetera* and the Tordesillas treaty, the whole world outside Europe and the Mediterranean was in Spanish hands. Hence, while there would seem very little anti-Portuguese motivation in the first Dutch passage to Asia in 1595, any clash between the Netherlanders and the Portuguese acting on orders of the Spanish king might alter the equation completely. The Dutch did not go out of their way to challenge the Luso-Hispanic claims to the Orient, incidentally, but focused much of their initial effort upon the discovery of a Northeast passage, partly because they feared retribution and partly because they rather fancifully hoped that finding a new way to the East would more fully legitimize their presence.[4] Even when they did take the Cape route around Africa, they made certain that they did not intrude into the Strait of Malacca, but chose the other passage, the Sunda Strait, and made for the Javanese port of Banten, which Linschoten had said not to be visited by the Portuguese. Only on arrival did they find that this was incorrect.

All of this would tend to explain why Dutch navigators between 1595 and 1601 assumed that they could make friendly contact with the Portuguese in outlying places—just as they were continuing to do in the Atlantic islands. In any case, they certainly did not look for trouble. In 1601, however, the trouble came. On two separate occasions in two separate places the crews of Dutch ships were treated with brutality. Quickly, public opinion turned as anti-Portuguese as it had earlier been pro-Portuguese. Or, perhaps, it would be even truer if one said that the Dutch were already highly anti-Spanish and that all they did was to stop differentiating between the two nationalities and simply think of them as common subjects of the Spanish monarch.

By 1601, there had been several independent Dutch voyages to the Moluccas, by both the Cape of Good Hope and the Magellan Straits, including one highly successful one by Captain Jacob van Neck, of the Amsterdam Oude-Compagnie, a forerunner of the VOC. Van Neck's second voyage in that year, however, was less than a triumph.[5] For on sailing into Ternate, he learned that the crew of a Dutch ship had recently been massacred by the Portuguese garrison while visiting nearby Tidore. This vessel, the *Trouw* had been part of an expedition which had set out from Rotterdam in 1598 to privateer against the Spanish in South America, but had suffered little save disaster. Beaten off in Chile, it then set off across the Pacific and strayed into the Moluccas, which it thought in friendly hands, arriving with but twenty-four survivors. All these had at first been welcomed by Portuguese of the Tidore garrison, but then captured by surprise, tortured and executed. (Portuguese sources are silent on the matter, incidentally, at least the one we would find, including the chroniclers, printed sources of the C.E.H.U. and the *Documentos Remetidos* ; we would welcome any additional documentary information from the Portuguese side). Van Neck then attacked Tidore to exact revenge, but he had only two ships to three Portuguese ones, plus two galleys. His ships were not only beaten off, but he lost several fingers in the bargain.

He then sailed off toward Patani, for his directors had charged him to reconnoitre for markets there. But on the way, the two vessels ran into a typhoon, lost direction and finally ended up in Macau, only lightly damaged but in need of provisions.

It is curious, but revealing that Van Neck still did not fully regard the Portuguese as enemies, but sent a boat ashore with eleven sailors and a factor, one Martinus Apius, to see if the Dutch might be permitted to trade. All twelve were immediately taken prisoner ; moreover, at about the same time, Van Neck sent another boat with his mate aboard to look for a better anchorage. Once again, the Portuguese took them all prisoners, this time after approaching the boat with a white flag. All Van Neck's subsequent attempts to make contact with the Portuguese failed, and likewise, directly with the Chinese. With rations short and ships in danger of running aground, Van Neck thereupon departed for Patani.

Upon his return in Holland, he made his story public, with explosive results. It provided Jacob Van Heemskerk with an immediate pretext to attack the homeward-bound Portuguese carrack *Santa Catarina* in June 1603. Then the whole matter was revived a few years later, when the factor, Apius, returned to Europe via Goa. In a sworn statement, Apius revealed that all crew members, save himself and two seventeen-year-olds, had been executed.[6] Coming as these two reports did soon after foundation of the United East India Company, or V.O.C., the effect was to launch its ships into a quest for revenge. The young company lawyer, Hugo de Groot, for example, was given these very documents, "tracterende van de wrede, verradische ende hostile proceduren van de Portuguesen in Oostindien" "about the cruel, treacherous en hostile deeds of the Portuguese in East India"—and he used them as background material for this tract *De Jure Praedae* (1604) to justify Dutch acts of retribution, especially in the *Santa Catarina* affair.[7] The real point is that the Dutch were in high dudgeon : Portuguese henceforth were identified in documents as "the enemy" and were lumped together with the Spaniards as if undifferentiable. Thereafter, the Dutch applied to their East India dealings exactly the same formula applied to the Spaniards : "The vijand soo veel afbreuk mogelijk doen"—do the enemy as much damage as possible.

In the generation following this hostile beginning, though, the Dutch and the Portuguese had minimal contact in the Indian Ocean. To be sure, there was the unsuccessful attack of Paulus van Caerden on Moçambique in 1607, and there was some naval skirmishing outside Masulipatam and Pulicat on the Coromandel Coast, where the Dutch had established factories. These actions, however, did not add up to either a cohesive V.O.C. attack plan or to a Portuguese defensive strategy. Nor did the Twelve Years Truce of 1609-1621 appear to have affected matters much either, in spite of the freedom granted by King Philip III and II for Dutch ships to visit places outside Europe where local rulers permitted it. It even appears that the Spanish did not make these articles of the truce (IV and V) known to their commanders overseas, and that these continued on the attack, as did the Hollanders.[8]

About all that happened in Asia during the truce was a series of actions between Spanish naval forces operating out of the Philippines and V.O.C. fleets in the Moluccas. The Spanish might have pressed the Dutch sorely for a time, but the Portuguese did not take much part in the operations—and there is little reason to believe that the Spanish actions bound up the Dutch and kept them from moving in on the Portuguese in India, either. Any way one views it, it would appear that the Dutch simply were not interested in carrying out extensive anti-Portuguese operations in waters around the Indian subcontinent.

In the years between the first V.O.C. visits to Ceylon in 1602 and its decisive intervention in 1638, the Company merely sought to maintain a certain degree of pressure on the Indian theatre by blockading Goa and sometimes Cochin during the monsoon sailing season to Portugal. It thereby hoped to disrupt the Portuguese pepper shipments to Europe. In November, 1623, during the time Jan Pietersz Coen was on business leave in the Netherlands, he prepared what one might call a white paper for the Heren XVII, the seventeen board members, in Amsterdam, giving an overview of V.O.C. activities against Iberian possessions in Asia. Though it names Moçambique and Goa along with Manila and Macao, it indicates that the Dutch were not really about to enter into actions there with the same hostile intensity as they displayed in the China Seas. Unexpectedly, Coen found an ally in the person of one David Nuyts, who represented a mutinous faction among shareholders in the Company which maintained that too much money was being spent in expensive raiding and blockading in Indian waters, money which could better be paid out to shareholders.[9]

Events were working from another direction to limit Dutch blockading activity as well. In 1629, during an intensive V.O.C. patrol against Portuguese shipping on the Coromandel coast, loud complaints were heard from friendly Indian princes that what was designed to hurt the Portuguese was hurting them, too. The Company thereupon took a leaf from the Portuguese book and began selling *laissez-passer* documents to friendly merchants, exactly like the long-standing *cartazes*. In this way the blockade became less costly because the income involved could partly defray the costs of maintaining them.[10] But by the same token, they became routinized and less prone to aggressive follow-up.

Prior to 1636, the commanders of the V.O.C. factories in "Westerse Quartieren", as the administrative region was called, repeatedly urged a more active Company presence in India, as did a V.O.C. emissary to Ceylon Marcellus Boschouwer. Yet these were constantly rebuffed. One can only wonder that the Company which later crushed are Estado da India decisively so long remained totally uninterested in what its agents *in situ* regarded as such a promising opportunity. Had the V.O.C. simply decided, like a Malayan Tiger, to take a long siesta between meals ?

The V.O.C. strategic plan

A siesta for the V.O.C. was hardly the case. In truth, it had other, more ambitious plans which had nothing at all to do with either napping or patriotic wars to weaken the Iberian foe. Tigers, even big tigers, can only stalk one prey at a time, and this prey was the Far Eastern trade. It was only when it had secured as much as it could of the riches of China and Japan that India began to look like a reasonably attractive proposition. This quest for the riches of the China Seas occupied a score of years after the truce expired in 1621, and it required an uninterrupted and highly expensive military effort.

As it is claimed repeatedly in Dutch records, the necessary capital for the Portuguese pepper trade in Asia was provided by commerce with China and Japan.[11] It was the goal of the Dutch to get into their hands this lucrative commerce, which would enable them to do without the large amounts of silver that had to be brought from Europe.

First, there was the outright attack on Macao in 1622, which as everyone knows, failed. Then the Dutch ensconced themselves on the Pescadores Archipelago, directly in front of the Amoy Bay area, from which the profitable Chinese junk trade to Manila was conducted. Within two years, in August 1624, the provincial governor of Fukien, Nan-Chü-i, forced the Dutch to withdraw to nearby Formosa, which at the time did not fall within the Chinese sphere of influence.[12]

Only eight years later, in 1633, did a regular trade come into existence between China and Japan, via Formosa. In the meantime, there had been a long rivalry with the Chinese authorities, including ferocious naval battles. Oddly, it was only after they had suffered a decisive defeat at the hands of Iquan, a pirate turned Imperial admiral, that the Hollanders got their trade on Chinese conditions. It seems that after their victory, the Chinese feared the Dutch would try to revenge themselves by bringing in a large fleet to seal off the entire Chinese southeast coast. To avoid this, they made the V.O.C. an offer it could not refuse.[13]

Meanwhile, the Japanese had discovered that the V.O.C. was capable of satisfying their demands for foreign goods and sales and without becoming involved in Japanese politics,[14] only then did they begin to think of limiting their trade with the Portuguese but also native shipping to Indo-China. Finally, at the Shimabara uprising (1637), in which the Portuguese were implicated, they ended it altogether. This left the V.O.C. supreme in the Japanese market.

Of course, as Pieter van Dam, the first historian of the Company, has remarked, the dream of unbounded profits turned into something like a nightmare when civil war in China and the restricted policies of the *Bakufu* in Japan (that is, the limitation of the Company to one island, Deshima) eventually reduced the China-Japan trade to a shadow of its former extent.[15]

By 1636, the Heren XVII, the V.O.C. directors, could turn their attention to other theatres and they sent a large fleet of sixteen ships, manned by 1743 sailors and 691 soldiers for a new offensive. One can perceive that the Dutch now attacked the Estado da India in stages, beginning at its periphery, and that only after they had mastered the China trade, (or what they could of it) did they move into its heartland and divest it of its cinnamon and pepper.

The new Governor-General Van Diemen, who had been groomed by the great Coen himself, turned out to be as much of an empire-builder as his former tutor. The affairs of the Far East, having been arranged by his direct predecessors Specx and Brouwer (who, by the way, were both old Japan hands), he could not at last embark on the effective sealing off of the China Seas by blockading and ultimately capturing Malacca. All the previous attempts in 1606, 1608, 1623 and 1627—had only succeeded in temporarily deregulating Portuguese shipping, but not in any territorial gains.[16] In 1636, however, the Dutch not only blockaded Malacca, but soon laid siege to it.

Two years later, Van Diemen affirmed that "the time is born to help the Portuguese out of India". From captured letters, it had come to him that the Portuguese were now despairing of Malacca unless they received immediate and substantial aid from Portugal.[17] But, as the Dutch commander of the blockading forces was warned in a dispatch, Malacca was "no cat to be taken without gloves".[18] Not until 14 January 1941 was the city forced to capitulate. With its loss, not only was the Far East and the Indonesian Archipelago cordoned off, but Portuguese India itself lay open to conquest. Or, as Van Diemen himself put it : "Among the captured Portuguese, the fall of Malacca has worked enormous discouragement. They openly declare that they have no India any longer now that Malacca is gone. And it is for certain, with God's help and the sending of the necessary troops by Your Lordships (the Heren XVII) we can soon force the Portuguese out of all India."[19]

A tight blockade of Goa had been applied in the same year 1636—as that of Malacca, and as a supporting move, so that no further aid could be sent. By 1638, this twin blockading in fact had succeeded so well that the Company felt able to move into Ceylon and take Batticaloa, an east coast port, in preparation for farther penetration towards the spicelands on the west coast. In doing so, it also established an alliance with the local potentate. The story of Ceylon's fall and the later capture of Cochin and the other Malabar ports is well known and need not be repeated here. Suffice it that it has never been seen as the outcome of a much grander strategy by the Company which was hardly apparent to writers of the time, especially the Portuguese ones. Prior to 1621 it concentrated on the Moluccan spice trade and cut off Malacca from its main source of income. Then, starting in 1622, it went for the China-Japan trade that provided the Portuguese operation in India with its necessary capital to buy pepper. Then the Dutch neutralized Malacca itself—and from that moment onwards could direct their sole attention to the Indian Ocean. Incidentally, Macao, with its regional trade no longer formed a threat to Company interests and eventually even was fitted into general Dutch trade strategy, with *casado* and *burgher* ships plying between there and Batavia. And after 1636, as just remarked, came the massive blow against the Portuguese stations in India—a full forty years after the first Dutch vessel had turned the Cape of Good Hope—ironically enough, almost in a spirit of fellowship.

NOTES

1. J.W. IJzerman, *Dirck Gerritsz. Pomp*, Linschoten-Vereeniging Vol. IX. The Hague 1915. J.H. van Linschoten, *Itinerario, Voyage ofte schipvaert van Jan Huyghen van Linschoten naar Oost ofte Portugaels Indien 1579-1592*, H. Terpstra, (ed.) Linschoten Vereeniging Vols. II, LVII, LVIII, III, IV and V, (The Hague 1910-1939).
2. Pedro de Frias, *Crónica del Rei D. António*, Coimbra (Coimbra, U.P.), 1955, pp. 94-98.
3. J.W. IJzerman, "Amsterdamsche bevrachtingscontracten, 1591-1602. I. De vaart op Spanje en Portugal", *Economisch-Historisch Jaarboek* 17 (1931), pp. 163-291.
4. I. Commelin (ed.) *Begin ende Voortgangh van de Vereenighde Nederlandsche Geoctroyeerde Oost-Indische Compagnie*, 4 vols. (Amsterdam 1645), Vol. I : 1.
5. H.A. van Foreest, A. de Booy (eds.) *De vierde Schipvaart der Nederlanders near Oost-Indië onder Jacob Wilkens en Jacob van Neck (1599-1604)*. Linschoten Vereeniging LXXXII (The Hague 1980).
6. W. Ph. Coolhaas, "Een bron van het historische gedeelte van Hugo de Groot's De Jure Praedae", *Bijdragen en Mededelingen van het Historisch Genootschap* 79, 1965, pp. 415-540.
7. R. Fruin, "Een onuitgegeven werk van Hugo de Groot" in *Verspreide Geschriften*, Vol. II (The Hague 1901), pp. 367-445.
8. Albert Hyma, *The Dutch in the Far East*, Ann Arbor (George Wahr), 1953, p. 76.
9. See Collectie van Hilten, "Brieven van David Nuyts aan v. Hilten, betreffende de belangen van de Oost - en West-Indische Compagnie, 1623", in : *Kronijk van het Historisch Genootschap te Utrecht*, 30 vols., (Utrecht 1846-1876), XXV (1869), Letters of 30 March and 29 November.
10. N. Mac Leod, *De Oostindische Compagnie als Zeemogendheid in Azië, 1602-1650*, 2 vols. (Rijswijk, 1927), I, pp. 488-489.
11. See for example Pieter van Dam, *Beschrijvinge van de Oostindische Compagnie*, F.W. Stapel (ed.) vol. II, part I, p. 676.
12. L. Blussé, "The Dutch Occupation of the Pescadores, 1622-1624", *Transactions of the International Conference of Orientalists in Japan*, 18, 1973, pp. 28-44.
13. L. Blussé, "The VOC as Sorcerer's Apprentice, Stereotypes and Social Engineering on the China Coast", in : W.L. Idema (ed.) *Leyden Studies in Sinology* (Leiden 1981), p. 103.
14. E. Kato, "Unification and Adaptation. The Early Shogunate and Dutch Trade Politics" in : L. Blussé and F.S. Gaastra eds. *Companies and Trade*, (Leiden U.P., 1981), p. 2?8.
15. Pieter van Dam, *Opus Citandi*, Vol. II, part I, p. 698.

16. J.K.J. de Jonge, *De Opkomst van het Nederlandsch Gezag in Oost-Indië*, 13 vols. (The Hague, 1862-1888), III, p. 50.
17. P.A. Tiele and J.E. Heeres, *Bouwstoffen voor de Geschiedenis der Nederlanden in den Maleischen Archipel*, 3 vols. (The Hague), II, p. 358.
18. P.A. Leupe, "Stukken betrekkelijk het beleg en de verovering van Malakka op de Portugezen in 1640-1641", in : *Berigten van het Historisch Genootschap te Utrecht*, 2e serie, vol. II, p. 1 (1861), p. 162.
19. MacLeod, *Oostindische Compagnie*, II, p. 215.

7

Manuel Godinho's Alternatives to the Carreira da India

JOHN CORREIA-AFONSO

MUCH has been said and written—and much more will be said and written in the course of this international seminar—about the *Carreira da India*, the sea route from Europe to the Indies. Less talked is the *caminho da India por terra*, the land route to the East, much older than the sea route, and not altogether abondoned because of it.

The land route was not just one clearly traced itinerary. "Between Marco Polo's day and Vasco da Gama's discovery of the way around Africa, there had been six major routes connecting Asia and the Mediterranean", writes George Winius.[1] Of these, he tells us, two were in use only during the Mongol Peace, roughly between 1268 and 1340 ; they were the northerly route from the mouth of the Don River at the top of the Black Sea that led eastward above the Caspian and a medial route that began at Trebizond on the south shore of the Black Sea and led through Tabriz to Central Asia. A third of minor importance was from Ayas in the Gulf of Alexandretta to Tabriz. It was the other routes, making use of the Persian Gulf and the Red Sea, which bore the lion's share of the traffic, silks going principally through the former, and spices through the latter.

It is with the Persian Gulf and Red Sea routes that our author, Fr. Manual Godinho, is chiefly concerned.

Manuel Godinho needs no introduction to this audience. Having come out to India from Portugal in 1655 as a young Jesuit priest, he did good work here, and was sent back to Portugal in 1662 by the Viceroy Antonio de Mello e Castro, on an important and arduous mission. The character of that mission is well known to those who have studied the decline of the Portuguese power in India. In 1661, Portugal, threatened at home by the Spanish armies, and hard-pressed overseas by the rising power of the Dutch, concluded a treaty of alliance with England. But English help was only to be obtained at a price, and part of the price was "the Port and Island of Bombay in the East Indies, with all its rights, profits, territories and appurtenances whatsoever thereunto belonging".

The Viceroy was firmly convinced of the great value of the port of Bombay, "with which that of Lisbon is not to be compared", and of the bad faith of the English who had rendered him none of the promised help. He accordingly refused to hand over Bombay to them on a number of grounds which are set forth in an extant letter of his to the King of Portugal, of December 1662.[2] Fr. Godinho was at that time already on his way to Portugal, probably with a similar letter.

It is with the account of this journey to Portugal, first published as early as 1665 in Lisbon, that we are now concerned. The *Relação do novo caminho que fez per terra e mar vindo da India para Portugal no anno de 1663, o Padre Manuel Godinho*[3] is a very methodical and precise work, opening with a brilliant essay in the grand style on the actual state of the Portuguese power in India, and neatly divided into chapters filled with historical notes and personal observations.

The Dutch and the Arabs having made the sea route to Persia unsafe for Portuguese ships, it was thought best that Fr. Godinho should embark at Surat, then under Mughal sovereignty. How he got there, and proceeded to Lisbon by sea and land is a most fascinating and instructive story. It is on the basis of his experience and investigations that Godinho wrote Chapter XXIV of his book, about various itineraries by land "that may be availed of between India and Europe, some easier than others ; some shorter, others longer ; some safer, others riskier." We propose to outline these adventuresome itineraries, for each of which Godinho gives practical and detailed advice, which does not lack in humour.

The first and shortest route, according to Godinho, is by way of the Strait of Mecca or the Red Sea. Arriving at Mecca by ship from India, the traveller sails again for Suez, thence he goes by land to Cairo and down the Nile to Alexandria, where he embarks for Europe. The danger along this route is from the Turks, who will not allow Christians near Medina.

The second route is through Persia. Arriving at Bandar Abbas, the traveller proceeds through Lar to Shiraz. Thence he either goes to Romus, and along several rivers to Lasah, Babylon and Aleppo or Damascus ; or he moves to Isfahan and thence to Tabriz and Smyrna or Babylon or Aleppo. These itineraries are relatively long and safe, due to stringent security measures taken by the state.

The third and most frequently used route is via Basra and up the Euphrates to Hait and Babylon. This is a long and tedious journey, with danger from the desert Arabs, on account of which Godinho sets down a number of precautions which should be taken. He also proposes some alternatives for the Basra-Babylon stage of the journey and explains how one may go from Babylon to Damascus or Aleppo. A variety of stratagems is suggested in view of the attacks on the caravans : "The diamonds can go into the sausages, which are abhorred both by the Hebrews and the Turks...Never say that you are coming from India but from Persia, as otherwise they will think that you are loaded with diamonds and pearls".

The fourth route is, starting from the West, from Hamburg through Lubeck and Riga to Moscow. Thence by the rivers Moskva, Oka and Volga to Astrakhan, and across the Caspian to Rasht, Tabriz and Isfahan in Persia, and on to India. It is also possible to travel from Moscow to India via China.

"The overland route from Angola to India," says Godinho as he concludes his chapter, "has not yet been discovered, but it is known nonetheless, and it will afford easy passage."

A very interesting postscript to this chapter, and indeed to Godinho's entire book, is a neatly-written five-page document to be found in the Biblioteca Nacional, Lisbon (Fundo Geral). An entry concerning this Ms had appeared in the *Fontes para a História do Antigo Ultramar Português*,[4] and according to it Ms. 30, No. 14 was "Papel sobre se mandarem por terra os avisos a India, Pelo Pe. Manuel Godinho (sec. XVII)." After a couple of unsuccessful attempts to locate this Ms—No. 14 was an entirely different document—I had the good luck last year to find, after careful search, that the Ms had a new number, 231, and I now possess a photocopy of the same.

The Ms carries neither date nor signature, but it bears the name of Manuel Godinho at the end, and appears to be a copy of a letter addressed by him to the Portuguese king. It does not seem to have been ever published, and only a relevant extract is given below. Godinho describes how a royal courier could travel to India.

> As soon as any of these usual couriers receives Y.M.'s letter, he starts on his journey by taking the first ship that sails from this port (Lisbon) to Marseilles or Lyons. At these ports he looks out for a ship to proceed to Syria. If the does not find one immediately, he waits until there is one and, if the first one available is not strong enough, he waits in the hope that soon there will be another which will carry him with greater personal safety and, perhaps, also without delays due to mercantile activity. He has departed and reached (as I presume) Alexandretta directly, as touching another port such as Smyrna, Beirut, Sayda or Jaffa would have greatly extended the journey. From Alexandretta it is a three days' journey to Aleppo where he halts for rest, sells goods, if he carries any, and awaits a caravan wherein to travel overland, but in a very leisurely manner to Babylon or to the river which flows by it and is three days' journey away from Aleppo. Once in Babylon he tries to find a *daineca* (a boat of the Tigris and the Euphrates) one of the bigger variety, which can carry enough people capable of defending themselves against assaults by the Arabs at night and, after finding one, he boards it and lands at Basra. At this point he makes arrangements to pursue his journey to the Persian Congo (Kangun) but does not rely on any other *terrada* (boat plying in that strait) besides those from the Congo proper, avoiding all others belonging to Arabs who are subjects of or friendly to the

> Imam of Muscat. And, in view of these precautions, there may be a few days' delay at Basra until he finally lands at the Congo. Either here or at Bandar Abbas he seeks a British or a Dutch ship bound for India, thereby avoiding the risk of Muscat Arabs. However, these ships come from India to Persia only during two seasons in a year, that is, earlier in the months of January and February, and later in April and May, and if the courier does not reach in time to find these ships when they arrive, it becomes necessary to await them for some months. And although this is the shortest possible route, it involves so many waits for favourable season, shipping and safety, reasons which make it so prolonged, that often ships reach India before the overland couriers who have left months earlier, especially if there are wars between the Arabs and the Perasins, or if the routes are closed or become particularly difficult. And, also, if the courier dies or is robbed by the Arabs of the Desert, the messenger is lost along with the letter, as we have experienced sometimes.

Godinho goes on to suggest that if the Portuguese king wished to save on the expenses of a courier, he could use the services of one of the three European consuls (French, English and Dutch) at Aleppo, or of one if the religious orders there, for onward transmission. And he adds, "In order that this proposal of mine may not seem to be mere speculation, I offer to go personally to Aleppo to put it into practice and at at my own cost..."

Two points come to mind after this brief review of Manuel Godinho's alternatives to the *Carreira da India*.

The first is that the *caminho da India* was by no means an easy one. "The difficulties of the *Carreira da India* in the terms of the hazards and the great distances it represented have been mentioned," writes Winius. "What usually escapes notice is that the Middle Eastern routes were almost equally disadvantageous in spite of their vastly shorter traverse."[5] Godinho's account of the Middle Eastern routes is very succint, yet it is sufficient to make one realise the dangers these routes involved, to which there should be added the heavy expenses of transfers and portages, and the risks of navigation in the Red Sea.

The second refers to Godinho's own narrative. Even when he is merely outlining an itinerary, Godinho has the gift of making things come to life, of making his reader share his adventures and dangers. It has been said that he is an excellent reporter who at times disappears before the objective realities which he relates in detail, and at others allows his personality to shine through his work.

The *Carreira da India* is one of the most important themes in Indo-Portuguese history. It has been and will continue to be studied for long, throwing light on many scientific and social aspects of the Age of Discovery. But much before the *Carreira da India* was established, Europeans had reached India travelling overland for the most part, along several routes which were not abandoned after 1498, and which also merit study.

NOTES

1. Bailey Diffey and George Winius, *Foundations of the Portuguese Empire, 1415-1580* (Minneapolis 1974), p. 203.
2. Cf. M.D. David, *History of Bombay*, 1661-1708 (Bombay 1973), pp. 41-44.
3. 4th edition, with introduction and notes by A. Machado Guerreiro (Lisbon 1974).
4. Vol. I, *Estado da India*, Tomo I (Lisbon 1978).
5. *loc. cit.*

8

The Financial Situation of the State of India During the Philippine Period (1581-1635)

ARTUR TEODORO DE MATOS

THERE are various sources and abundant studies about the economic evolution of the State of India during the sixteenth and seventeenth centuries, and even about its financial situation.[1] However, that reading has not always been done taking into account essential sources for the study of that theme, such as the *Livros de Receita e Despesa*, also known as *Orçamentos*.

As a rule, these sources, besides informing about the value of the ordinary income of each fortification during one year and its provenance, they also register the extraordinary receipts, according to the average of the previous years. The current expenses are mentioned according to the "regimentos" and "provisões", completing them or correcting them, whenever it is opportune. The extraordinary expenses are, for the most part, calculated in accordance with the average of the two preceding years.

The Philippine period is particularly rich in sources of this kind.[2] One knows the budgets of 1581[3], 1588[4], 1588-90[5], 1607[6], 1609-12[7], 1620[8] and 1635[9], which include all the possessions of the State of India, whose jurisdiction extended, as it is known, from Sofala to Ormuz on the West, and included the Molucas and Macau in the East. However, there are other budgets of fortifications, concerning the same period, also denominated *tombos*,[10] as the one of Chaul (1591-92), Damão (1592), Diu (1592), Baçaim (1595), and Goa (1595 and 1623-27), most of them already published.

What is the credibility of such sources? Unlike what happens nowadays, these budgets were real detailed accounts. Therefore, they were called, in some cases, *Rendimento e despesa do Estado da India*, *Relação do Rendimento e despesas de todo o Estado da India e despesas ordinarias*, or even, *Livro da receita a despesa de todas as fortalezas que S. Mage tem neste Estado da India.* They always refer to the financial situation of former years and the overseer of the public finances of India or the "vedor da fazenda dos contos" was liable for them. They were prepared by an experienced book-keeper.

In the act of composing them, the "regimento" (rule) of the fortification is considered as the judicial and financial document that stipulates the ordinary expenses. So also the charters and leases, the accounts of the respective administrators and those of the book-keepers of the "Casa dos Contos" in Goa determine the preparation.[11] The elaboration of these general accounts was irregular, as one may conclude from the known ones, and they were always called for by the crown or the viceroy.

We shall try to analyse the financial situation of this State using the general "orçamentos" (budgets) from 1581 to 1635 since they are very detailed accounts and constitute preferential documents for such an analysis. First of all, however, we shall see, although at a glance, some of the structural aspects of the "Fazenda Real" (Royal Treasury) in the Orient.

The financial administration practised in the Portuguese Oriental Empire during the period that interests us (which was continued from the former times) had a decentralized pattern, marked by financial autonomy regarding the Portuguese Crown, although locally placed in Goa. The "Vedor da Fazenda de Goa" (Overseer of the public finances of Goa) was liable for the financial execution. This office was exercised jointly with that of "Vedor da Fazenda dos Contos". The *Casa dos Contos* existed as an Audit Office of the State.[12]

Reorganized in 1589 through an Act of 23rd March of that year, the Casa dos Contos of Goa was an instrument of fiscal control, regulator of various administrative and financial services, in order to effect "boa arrecadação da fazenda".[13] In each of the fortifications the financial management was in the hands of the "feitor" (factor), according to the "regimento" and rules imposed by the Royal Treasury of Goa. As a top organism, we may distinguish the *Conselho da Fazenda* (Treasury Council) created in the beginning of the seventeenth century. It had consultative attributions, and was presided by the governor or viceroy, and included the intendant and the scrivener of the treasury.[14]

Some years before the beginning of the Philippine administration in Portugal, the most important document revealing the financial situation of India, the *Orçamento do Estado da India*, of 1574, was elaborated in that territory by the book-keeper António de Abreu. It was ordered by Diogo Velho, intendant of the Treasury of India.[15] A financial reorganization had started in 1546 under Simão Botelho who had prepared the *Tombo Geral do Estado da India*, finished in 1554.[16]

In this process of administrative and financial improvement, D. Antão de Noronha played an important role. His reformist attitude—solicitated by the Crown—originated the promulgation of the new rules in 1568 for many fortifications on the coast of the Indian Ocean. This interest in the uniformization of the economic and financial laws originated the compilation of various rules, done by Diogo Velho in 1574, known as *Regimentos das fortalezas da India*, although other legislation was registered subsequently, till 1612.[17]

The budget of Diogo Velho is extremely useful for diagnosis of the financial situation of the State of India in the end of the third quarter of the sixteenth century. As a matter of fact, according to him, the receipts totalled 275,290$380 réis, the expenses amounted to 231,795$162 réis : therefore there was a credit balance of 43,495$218 réis at the end of 1574. How the situation will develop ? In what way do the general accounts of this State attest the economic and financial decadence during the decades of the Philippine government ?

Let us see, in short, the balance of some accounts between the years 1581 and 1635.[18]

Ano	*Receita*	*Despesa*	*Saldo*
1581	263 036$953	242 784$701	(+) 20 252$252
1588	303 051$620	259 949$854	(+) 43 101$766
1607	355 530$600	235 677$600	(+) 120 153$000
1609	249 780$000	156 627$088	(+) 93 152$912
1620	326 089$600	318 370$600	(+) 7 719$000
1635	355 579$234	334 636$773	(+) 20 942$461

The results are evident : in every studied year the State of India shows a significant financial solvency. How can we interpret this fact ? How can we compare these new elements with the traditional denunciation of an increasing deficit worsened year after year, creating, according to some writers, very critical situations in the fourth decade of the seventeenth century ? How can we explain the dependence on the credit, so often needed by the Government of India, or the subsidies sent by Lisbon mainly in the second quarter of the seventeenth century ? [19]

If it is right that the global balance of the general account of the State of India is positive, this does not mean that the same happened in each fortification. So, there are fortifications such as Cranganor, Coulão, Cananor, Onor, that have never had any income although they were strategically important to the Portuguese commerce in the Indian Ocean. Others, like Goa during some years, or Barcelor, had a yearly debit balance.

According to the available sources, the receipts of the State of India are enough to meet the normal expenses which covered the staff, social assistance, education, regular and secular clergy, army, pensions and defence. One must remark, however, that the expenses with the fortifications were not usually registered, being supported by the 1 per cent tax that, for the same reason, could not be added to the receipts.

In some cases, it happened that the amount of salaries and provisions for the totality of people established by the "regimento" was debited in the account, when in fact only a part of it existed. Thus it happened in Mozambique in 1629. Having permission to command three hundred soldiers, Pero Barreto de Resende verified that there were less than a hundred, while three hundred figured on the rolls [20] The same author would say the following about this subject :

> On checking the accounts of the factors in various fortresses during six years I have found that the muster roll never had a fixed number of soldiers on it. About a third was always missing.[21]

Both, Barreto de Resende in 1635, and Francisco Pais before him, two men with great geographic knowledge of the State of India and a prodigious administrative and financial experience in the same State—reveal the anomalies committed in the general register (*Matricola Geral*), with the consequent dishonest aggravation of the expenses. And when the income of the customs of Goa and Cochin doubled and became 20 000 pardaus,[22] the 1 per cent tax gathered in all the customs[23] with the tributes of Bacaim and Damão amounted to 100 000 pardaus, the third part of the copper contract—recently made with China sent yearly 50 000 pds and the receipts of the customs of Malacca and Diu had an increment of 50 000 pds, the Fazenda Real of India required still more. Francisco Pais, the Superintendent of Accounts, explained this :

> Even if more and fresh sources of revenue were to be tapped, the viceroys and captains of fortresses would continue spending on their relations and friends as if the public exchequer was entrusted to their care for this purpose. Hence, it is essential that the standing orders and instructions for revenue administration be strictly enforced.[24]

The general register, the non-performance of the rules stipulated by D. Antão de Noronha and the compilation of Diogo Velho were named by the same Superintendent of Accounts as the main causes of such anomalies. About the first he says : "Chief drainage canal of the public exchequer and a cover for many abuses.[25] And if rules were not observed, it was because the viceroys and captains observed those they liked and interpreted others to suit their intentions." If only the expenses approved by D. Antão de Noronha and Diogo de Noronha were permitted, the overhead charges could be reduced by more than 100 000 cruzados[26] in salaries and provisions "a homens de ymaginação que não ha has fortalezas" (to imaginary men in the fortresses).[27]

If such a situation can help to explain some of the financial difficulties by the Oriental Empire, it represents, above all, a normal economic development in the end of the century. On the other hand, one may conclude that despite the corruption of the public administration, the salaries could reach higher amounts than the ones showed in the general accounts, since the expenses seemed to be falsified. Later Francisco Pais, in 1612, in *Lembranças do serviço de S. Mag.* ^de^ together with the budget of 1609, provides a lucid analysis of the financial situation of the State of India and so valid it is because its author had fine knowledge of the financial management of the region, having occupied a high position in it during nearly half a century.[28] "He was convinced that all financial difficulties resulted from administrative abuses, and there would be enough funds even to sustain extraordinary wars if there was more competence zeal and honesty in the men in service."[29]

He reminds us that the governments of D. Antão de Noronha, D. Luis de Ataide, Matias de Albuquerque, D. Frei Aleixo de Meneses e André Furtado de Mendonça, had faced very difficult war situations, but would build fleets and fortifications, after having inherited empty coffers. They could do it all with the public revenue and without imposing new taxes. It could be concluded from these instances that India yields more than it spends. If the revenue is not sufficient now, it is due to the disorderly capacity of the officials.[30]

Also P. Barreto de Resende finishing the general accounts of the State of India for 1635 states "that when India is well governed there is always surplus revenue."[31] Concluding his accounts, he says that the balance could be more than thirty-one "contos"[32] since nothing more was to be spent with the fortifications of the strait of Ormuz or with the patriarch and clergy of Ethiopia, despite the disappearance of the receipts of the fortification of Malacca and Gale and those of the voyages from China to Manila. And in the years wherein all the fleets were not organized, if these were formed by less ships and the building of other ships was avoided, the income could be still more.[33]

From the totals showed in each budget and from the testimony of qualified persons, with responsibility in the financial management of the State of India, one may conclude that the receipts were enough to pay the normal expenses of the administration of the territory. The extraordinary charges, such as those motivated by the war or investment on building of fortifications could be payed from the receipts of the "Fazenda Real" (Royal Treasury) of Goa. We believe, however, that the situations of insolvency, eventually verified, were provoked by crisis, bad management, nepotism,[34] and above all, by great corruption that existed in the administration of Goa. Francisco Pais, who very often revealed these irregularities, did not conceal from the king the main causes :

> I repeat that it is important for Your Majesty to bring to book the viceroys and captains who do not fulfill the terms of your standing orders and instructions in the administration of public treasury, which needs to be carefully administered to provide for war needs.[35]

The non-observance of the rules seems to be one of the causes of the defalcation of the public revenue. In 1608 the king complained about the expenses in India : "There is no order, the standing orders are not kept. Only customs are observed and these too to suit private interests."[36] Twenty years later a report was requested from the Conde de Linhares about the use of the revenue of this State so that one could investigate if the rules had been observed or if, on the contrary, illegality had been practised.[37]

But how could the State of India solve its financial duties considering all the political and military problems of the Portuguese in the Orient, since the end of the sixteenth century ?

It is not the object of this study to analyse the economic situation of the State of India during the Philippine administration. However, it may be interesting to refer to some aspects for better understanding of the situation of the treasury in the East.

As it is known the economic structure of the Portuguese Empire in Asia depended on the commerce. One must distinguish the regional coastal trade, from the traffic of products among the various ports of India, East Africa, Arabic Peninsula, Middle East, and the commerce between India and Portugal.[38] From the first, the Royal Treasury of Goa received the revenue of the customs and the taxes on certain products (spices, cloth, betelnuts, horses, and so on), which represented its main sources of revenue during some time. The commerce with Lisbon did not affect the Treasury of Goa, as the organization, duties and rights of that commerce belonged to the sphere of the *Casa da India* in Lisbon. And, if it is true that the fleet supply on the return was done in Goa or Cochin, we have have never seen these expenses debited to the Royal Treasury or those done with the building of some ship required for such voyages. Therefore, the success or failure of this "carreira" cannot be interpreted as an economic indicator of the financial situation of Portuguese India.

However, let us see, the origin (in percentage) of the receipts of the "Fazenda" (Treasury) in the Orient, based on the general statements of accounts.[39]

Year	*Customs*	*Quit Rents "Foros"*	*Tributes "páreas"*	*Duties on horses*
1581	58	24.8	12.3	4
1588	59.8	24.5	13.6	2.1
1607	58.9	25.1	13.8	2.2
1609	62.4	16.3	15.3	6.0
1620	63.1	19	17.8	0.2
1635	23	18.1	58.8	0.1

As one verifies the receipts that came from the Commerce were for long, the main source of revenue of the Royal Treasury in Goa. And when the Portuguese lost the control of various routes and markets, on account of the military vicissitudes, they were obliged to impose taxes on various products—nearly all collected in Goa—to establish the financial solvency of the State. The budget of 1635, made by Barreto de Resende, distinguishes the various taxes and their sources.

It is also important to verify the geographic origin of the receipts : Goa, Hurmuz, Baçaim and Diu contribute with 80 per cent of the total income ; the rest came mainly from Malacca, Damão, Chaul and Manar. Follow a table of profits (also in percentage) of each fortification of the Orient :

Fortification	*1581*	*1588*	*1607*	*1609*	*1620*	*1635*
Goa	26.3	28.5	34.2	34.3	34.7	56.4
Hurmuz	21.3	18.2	16.6	17.9	18.5	
Baçaim	17.9	14.1	10.4	9.8	11.8	10.3
Diu	15	17.5	18.1	19	18.8	3.8
Malacca	7	8.3	7.4	7	5.5	3.1
Damão	6.5	6.5	5	4.3	3.6	5
Chaul	3.8	5.1	2.6	3.1	2.8	4.5
Manar	1.6	1.3	2.1	1.8		0.1
Ceylon	0.3	0.2		0.8		6(42)
Maluco	0.1					
Mangalore	0.1	0.2	0.2			0.3
Barcelor	0.1	0.1				
Mascate			0.1		0.1	6
Mombaça			0.5		0.6	1
Mozambique			2.8		3.6	3.5
Cochin	3.8	5.1	2.6	3.1	2.8	4.5

The loss of Hurmuz in 1622 had a great repercussion in the profits of the State of India, as its income was about 20 per cent. The imposition of taxes and the receipts of Jafanapatam, Colombo and Gale in the island of Ceylon compensated the loss of the profits of Hurmuz and its decrease in Diu.

From the elements we have been analysing, we conclude that the Portuguese Empire in the Orient, during the period we studied, showed a balanced financial situation, showing always a a credit balance. The receipts of the customs are till late the main source of revenue of the State and when it decreased, other ways were sought to maintain financial solvency.

Some crisis may have occurred, worsened by bad management of some viceroy and carelessness of the employees, and mainly by the corruption that tormented the public administration. However, the difficulties were solved either by requesting the credit of corporations and of individuals, or by imposing new taxes. The sending of subsidies to India in gold and silver to be applied exclusively to military needs was another method of solving difficulties.[40] Such conjectures, however, must have been limited in place and time, because they seem to refer only to Goa and in a time of conflict, more than in a situation of permanent economic crisis extended to the entire State of India. It seems to us that the consumption and misemployment of the receipts could justify certain moments of economic difficulties. Besides, in 1629 one asked what was the use given by the viceroys to the six hundred thousand pardaus of credit balance "pois el Rey nunca no thesouro tem hum real" (because the king never has a dime in his treasury).[41]

The interpretation of the available sources for the study of the financial situation during the period of 1581-1635, that corresponds more or less to the period of Philippine administration, leads us to the conclusion that the State of India, far from being a burden to Portugal, maintained a profitable commerce with Lisbon, and had enough resources for its economic survival and even registered a favourable balance.

NOTES

1. Jaime Cortesão, "O Império Português do Oriente", in *História de Portugal*, ed. Damião Peres, vol. V, Barcelos, Portucalense Editora, 1933, pp. 319-389 ; Lúcio de Azevedo, *Épocas de Portugal Económico*, 3rd ed., Lisboa, Clássica Editora, 1973, pp. 131 ff., V.M. Godinho, *Os Descobrimentos e a Economia Mundial*, vol. II, Lisboa, Arcádia, 1965, pp. 78, 131 ff. ; A.R. Disney, *A Decadência do Império da Pimenta. Comercio Português na India no Século XVII*, Lisboa, Edições 70, 1981. A.H. de Oliveira Marques, *História de Portugal*, vol. I, (Lisboa, Agona, 1972), pp. 467-469 ; states for the first time that the Portuguese State of India was solvent under the Philips.
2. *Cf.* V.M. Godinho, *Les Finances de l'Etat Portuguais des Indes Orientales (1517-1635). (Materiaux pour une étude structurale et conjuncturelle)*, Paris, Fundação Calouste Gulbenkian, Centro Cultural Português, 1982, pp. 16-39 ; A.T. de Matos, *O Estado da India nos anos de 1581-1588 : estrutura administrativa e económica. Alguns elementos para o seu estudo*, Ponta Delgada, Universidade dos Açores, 1982.
3. Arquivo Nacional da Torre do Tombo, *Fundo Antigo*, p. 845.
4. Arquivo Histórica Ultramarino, cód. 500. Cf. V. Magalhães Godinho, *Les Finances* [..], pp. 24 ff.
5. British Library, *Additional*, 28, 433, fls. 75-157.
6. Biblioteca da Ajuda, 51-VI-54, fls. 271v-293, published by José-Gentil da Silva, "Une image de *l'Estado da India* au debut du XVIIe siècle et ses enseignements", in *Arquivos do Centro Cultural Português*, Paris, F.G. Gulbenkian, 1977, pp. 242-287.
7. Biblioteca Públíca e Arquivo Distrital de Évora, CXVI/1 - 18, fls. 5v-52 e Real Academia de la História (Madrid), K - 61, fls. 44-70.

8. B.P.A.D.E., CV/2 - 7.
9. Biblioteca Nacional (Lisboa), cód. 1783 e Biblioteca da Sociedade de Geografia da Lisboa, Res. 2 - maço 3-4.
10. These *tombos* exist in Goa Historical Archives (Panjim) excepting the budget for 1623-27 which is in the A.H.U., cód, 219. Most of these sources were edited by Jerónimo Quadros in *Oriente Português* (1914) XI, (1915) XIII, (1932) 4, (1935) 11, (1937) 18, and by P.S.S. Pissurlencar in *Boletim do Instituto Vasco da Gama* (1945-52), 62, 66 e 68.
11. Cf. *Budget of 1581*, fl. 65v ; *Budget of 1588*, fl. 52v ; *Budget of 1588*, fl. 70 ; *Budget of 1607*, fl. 276v ; *Budget of 1609*, fl. 25 ; *Budget of 1635*, fl. 1.
12. Cf. A.N.T.T., *F.A.*, 845, fl. 40.
13. J.H. da Cunha Rivara, *Archivo Portuguez Oriental* (1866) v. 3 ; Virginia Rau, *Revista do Centro de Estudos Económicos*, (1949), 9.
14. J.B. Amâncio Gracias, *Subsidios para a história económica-financeira da India Portugueza*, Nova Goa, Imprensa Nacional, 1909, pp. 84-86.
15. A.N.T.T., *Livraria*, N^{O}. 32. Jean Aubin, *Studia*, (1959) IV ; Águedo de Oliveira, *Orçamento do Estado da India (1574) feito por mandado de Diogo Velho, Vedor da Fazenda dá India*, Lisboa, Tribunal de Contas, 1960. Best version with good annotations by V. Magalhães Godinho, *Les Finances* [...], pp. 157 ff.
16. José de Lima Felner in *Subsidios para a História da India Portugueza*, Lisboa, Academia Real das Sciencias, 1868, pp. 5 ff.
17. Goa Historical Archives, *Fundo Geral*, 4470, ed. Panduronga S.S. Pissurlencar, *Regimentos das Fortalezas da India*, Bastorá, 1951. B. da Ajuda, cód. 51-VIII-21 ; A.H.U., cód. 217.
18. The budget of 1588-90 (B.L., *Add.* 28433) has not been used for the analysis because of several errors we have detected in it.
19. Cf. A.R. Disney, *A decadência do império da pimenta* [...], pp. 67 ff.
20. B.N.L., Cód. 1783, fl. 112.
21. Id., *ibid.*, fl. 112.
22. Pardau had 300 réis.
23. Ordered by D. Luís de Ataide (1578-81).
24. Archivo General de Simancas, *Secretarias Provinciales*, cód., 1551, fl. 491, letter of Francisco Pais to the king, Goa, 10 November 1588.
25. *Ibid.*, fl. 491.
26. Equivalent to 40,000 réis.
27. *Ibid.*, fl. 324, letter of F. Pais to the King, Goa, 15 November 1589.
28. On Francisco Pais his *Lembranças* [...], cf. V.M. Godinho, *Les Finances* [...], pp. 34-35.
29. Real Academia de la História (Madrid), K-61, fl. 63.
30. *Ibid.*, fl. 63v.
31. B.N.L., cód. 1783, fl. 112v.
32. Exactly 31 318$834 réis (Cf. *Ibid.*, fl. 113).
33. Cód. 1783, fls. 113-113v.

34. Cf. A.G. Simancas, S.P. cód. 1551, fl. 634, letter of Francisco Pais to the king, Goa, 15 November 1589.
35. *Ibid.*, fl. 634.
36. A.N.T.T., *Livro das Monções*, N°. 2, fl. 65, published by Raymundo Antonio Bulhão Pato, in *Documentos remetidôs da India* ou *Livro das Monções* [ ], vol. I, Lisboa, Academia Real das Sciencias, 1880, p. 232.
37. Arquivo das Indias (Panjim), *Livro das Monções*, N°. 13A, fl. 98, letter of the king to the Count of Linhares, Lisboa, 22 February 1629.
38. Cf. Our study on *O Estado da India* [...] part VI and the bibliography in it.
39. It is difficult to present the income of Portuguese India during the period of our study because the revenue accounts have not been recorded sufficiently accurately and in some cases there are so many data available that it becomes difficult to organize them. In the present table we have taken into account six budgets when the income data were presented more systematically. Whenever necessary, we sought clarification in the standing orders of the settlement concerned. Cf. A.N.T.T., *F.A.*, 845 ; A.H.U., cód. 500 ; B.A., 51-VI-54, fls. 271v-293 ; B.P.A.D.E., CX VI/1-18 fls. 5v-52 e CV/2-7 ; R.A.H.M., K-61, fls. 44-70, B.N.L., cód. 1783.
40. A.R. Disney, *A decadência do império do pimenta* [..], pp. 79-80.
41. B.N. Madrid, Ms. 3015, fl. 129 in *Documentação Ultramarina Portuguesa*, II, Lisboa, Centro de Estudos Históricos Ultramariños, 1962, p. 147.

9

Capital Input in Goa's Freedom Struggle : The Bombay Connection

TEOTONIO R. DE SOUZA

IT IS undoubtedly true that nationalist movements or struggles for freedom have been exercises in selfless dedication to a cause on the part of some individuals. However, it would be naive to believe that the success of such movements and struggles resulted exclusively from the inspiration and drive of such persons. There are always other personal and less noble factors that also play their role and make their contribution. Such private and selfish interests often coincide with the march of the Spirit towards freedom, as Hegel has explained it metaphysically and called it "the cunning of reason". However, less metaphysically inclined minds can also see such sinking of differences with the motivation of reaping a hundredfold after a new dispensation is brought into existence under grateful leaders who could reward the enlightened self-interest.

Any freedom struggle needs to be seen as a web woven with many threads of many hues. Anil Seal's *The Emergence of Indian Nationalism* is one model of such a welcome approach.[1] There are many other similar and laudable studies as regards the Indian nationalism and struggle for freedom.[2] A cool historical analysis of this nature, exposing the saints and the knaves in Goa's freedom struggle, has not yet been undertaken, and it will not be possible to do so satisfactorily until most of the relevant records, including the archive of the Portuguese military tribunal in Goa, are released for research in another decade of years or so. Such an analysis is likely to be hazardous also to one who ventures into such a task by inviting the wrath of the knaves, and perhaps of the saints also who may still be around.

Given the reasons and the difficulties for a research undertaking that we consider desirable, the present essay seeks to perform a model exercise on a very modest scale permitted by a seminar like this. The international composition of the seminar and the varied interests of the participants have been kept in mind. A theme of Goan history which has found treatment at the micro-level is sought to be projected on a broader canvas in order to draw more than regional interest. "The Bombay Connection" is brought in to shift the focus from local incidents in Goa's liberal-constitutional struggle of 1820's-30's to extra-regional vested interests. We start with a quick survey of the existing studies with a two-fold purpose, namely, to provide the necessary context and to point out to the shadowy figure of the Bombay Connection looming in the background of the developments taking place in Goa. This is followed up with the shift that we are proposing. Published and new archival evidence is used to unravel the Bombay Connection. It is hoped that this model exercise will encourage younger people to re-write the regional history of Goa with new perspectives and with new evidence.

GOA'S FREEDOM STRUGGLE AND THE GHOST OF ROGERIO DE FARIA

Goan authors of late 19th century, like Miguel Vicente d' Abreu, J.C. Barreto Miranda, and A.A. Bruto da Costa, have written scholarly works in Portuguese, analysing the political developments of the century with almost a nationalist slant.[3] We need to make concessions to the constraints in which they wrote, and also to their time-bound vision. Still we find in their works much matter that can enable us today to attempt a shift in perspective. A.F. Moniz wrote at the beginning of the 20th century and may be classified as a reactionary as compared with the earlier writers, but his *Noticias e Documentos para a Hostória de Damão* contains many pointed references to the "Bombay Connection". They are documents that refer to the administration of the Prefect Bernardo Peres da Silva in Daman (1835-37) and were published by the author to uphold the honesty of his grandfather, who was an old hand in Daman administration, but was unceremoniously dismissed and disgraced by the Prefect. Whatever the intentions of the author, he has done excellent service to history by editing many important documents.[4]

Marquis of Pombal had already utilized press very skilfully to malign his clerical enemies ("os denominados Jesuitas"), but at the turn of the century the influence of Jacobinism and the masonic clubs in Portugal saw a flourishing gutter-press that sustained partisan interests. The spill-over of the Portuguese liberalism into Goa brought to Goa a committed official press and much underground pamphleteering. It provides for the historian much material to be critically used.[5] It is stated, for instance, that the first rumblings of the liberal discontent in Goa in 1821 followed the arrival of a copy of the royal decree accepting constitutionalism in Portugal. This copy of the decree was sent to Bernardo Peres da Silva by Rogerio de Faria from Bombay.[6] The liberal coup on 16th September 1821 deposed the viceroy count of Rio Pardo and established a Junta rule. It was the beginning of a long political turmoil, reflecting the instability that reigned in Portugal. The Goan natives were growing in political maturity, and they could see more and more clearly that all the noise and liberal proclamations by the Portuguese and the white settlers of Goa did not coincide with their native self-respect and their desire for self-rule. There were, of course, a few enlightened white sympathisers. Among these stood boldly the friar Archbishop of Goa, D. Manoel de S. Galdino. For voicing boldly the discontended feeling of the natives against the oppressive rule of the Junta and its white supporters, this spiritual leader was forced to shift his residence to Sunkery, across the southern border of Goa. We know from a few published extracts of Archbishop's correspondence, intercepted by this political enemies, that he was in contact with Rogerio de Faria of Bombay.[7]

The liberal- constitutional regime had brought to the Goans the opportunity of sending their elected representatives to the

House of Representatives in Portugal. The system actually favoured the Portuguese-educated landed gentry, but still one can notice wide popular support to the elected representatives. This was obviously generated by people's anti-colonial feelings that had no other viable outlet. In spite of the efforts of the white settlers to manoeuvre the elections with their political power and military intimidation, they could find no popular support for their candidates. Bernardo Peres da Silva, a Goan native and trained in Medicine, was elected in every election held from 1822 till 1842. Once, in 1836, when he was in exile (to which we shall turn our attention soon) the Portuguese forced an election in which only two European-controlled constituencies participated, while the remaining four stayed away.[8]

Bernardo Peres da Silva had fought actively on the side of the liberals in Portugal. His son, serving in the military in Portugal, had also been actively involved in defending the cause of Prince Regent Pedro, and was in the expeditionary force that landed in Portugal from Terceira island and won a decisive victory for the liberals in 1834. It was then that Prince Pedro appointed Bernardo Peres da Silva Prefect of the Portuguese State of India.[9] It was a new post that replaced the viceroy or governor of earlier times. The arrival of the Prefect in Goa on 10th January 1835 created panic and anxiety among the beneficiaries of the erstwhile regime. The administrative changes and fresh appointments in the Departments of Justice and Finance, undertaken by the Prefect within a week from taking office, led to a coup by the old guard and the Prefect was forced to leave Goa on 1st February, that is, just after a fortnight in power. His many native supporters and some white sympathisers could do nothing against the military opposition to protect the Prefect. They themselves were soon forced to seek security outside Goa, all along the coast from Malvan to Daman. It should be noticed that the administration in Daman and Diu remained loyal to the Prefect as the legitimate authority until a substitute was officially sent from Portugal in 1837.[10]

Bernardo Peres da Silva was solemnly received in Daman in July 1835. Till then, for nearly five months after his deposition, he was in Bombay. He spent those months preparing an expeditionary force to recapture Goa by force. Perhaps the memory of the expeditionary force that gained Portugal for the liberals in 1834 was the source of inspiration to his plans. The undertaking had the active support of Rogerio de Faria, who was also hosting the Prefect in Bombay. The papers in Bombay were reporting the progress of the plans. For instance, *The Bombay Courier* of 26th May 1835 describes the composition of the expeditionary crew : "Sr Peres semms is determined to follow the example of Don Pedro in this country, and for this purpose has collected out of the Bazar a body of nearly three hundred as ragged looking fellows as ever were seen". The reporter continues : "The quantity of opium smuggled this year into Damaun, over the revenues of which he possesses some control, having been much greater than usual, unexpected resources were placed at his disposal, and everything has since gone smoothly up to the present moment." He concludes: "It only remains to be seen whether fortune will continue to smile and as a few days will now settle this momentous question, we shall not venture to hazard an opinion regarding it."[11] The liberals do not seem to have learned from the repeated mistakes of the old regime in matters of Portuguese shipping. Late departures and consequent running into stormy weather had caused greater damage to Portuguese shipping since they arrived in the East than did the Dutch or the pirates.[12] The expeditionary force of the Prefect had left Bombay on 27th May, disregarding public warnings of the advancing monsoon that had set in since some days at Cochin. Right enough, the expeditionary fleet that had embarked in two lumber-boats converted into gun-boats, a ketch and a corvette, was wrecked by a thunderstorm and was back in Bombay on the fifth day in a wretched condition and with heavy casualties. *The Bombay Courier* had the following editorial comment on 6th June 1835 : "The Portuguese corvette with Sr. Peres, returned yesterday, after an unavailing attempt to contend against the southwest monsoon, which appears to have been totally forgotten in fitting out the expedition against Goa. The rest of the small craft which accompanied her arrived here a day or two previously, and are now scattered about the harbour in a disabled state. Thus, we presume, a stop has been put to the efforts against Goa for some months at least, if not for ever. What will become of the motley crowd of Sindians, Cutchees, Moguls and people without any designation whatever, who composed the exepedition remains to be seen. But come what may, we trust for the security of private property that measures will be adopted to prevent them from congregating in Bombay." I have not followed the worries of the Bombayites, but the Prefect had left Bombay and entrenched himself in Daman as we have already mentioned earlier. Once there, a son-in-law and partner of Sir Rogerio de Faria submitted a bill for Rs. 67,957 to the Prefect. It was meant to recover expenditure on arms supplied for the defence of Daman and Diu, as well as the expenses of the expedition that had failed.[13]

THE BOMBAY CONNECTION INTO FOCUS : ROGERIO DE FARIA AND CIA.

All the above sources of information do not take us further than we have reached in knowing the activities or the personality of Rogerio de Faria. We are left with the impression that he was a silent operator. The CIA after his name has nothing to do with the modern equivalent of it. It was the Portuguese abbreviation for *Company* because Rogerio de Faria had registered himself as Portuguese national domiciled in Bombay.

My interest in Rogerio de Faria was aroused when a part of his business correspondence, dating from 1789 to 1830, with the Mhamai Kamat Agency House in Goa came into my hands a couple of years back. This correspondence includes business reports, balance-sheets, lading-bills, bills of exchange, receipts, and even just friendly letters. Surprisingly, there is no reference in this correspondence to the political development in Goa. This may be explained by the fact that this correspondence is reduced to a trickle after 1817. Whatever correspondence followed was more to seek closure of accounts, because in 1818 the Mhamai House was charged with heavy indebtedness to the State Exchequer in connection with tax-farming and it nearly declared itself insolvent.[14] The papers prior to 1818 contain much interesting information that can help us to correct and supplement whatever we know about Rogerio de Faria from a few contemporary published sources and from a few late and sketchy biographies.

The earliest published reference to Rogerio de Faria occurs in Lady West's Journal. Sir Edward West, the Chief Justice of the Supreme Court of Judicature of the Bombay Presidency, and his wife had been on a visit to Goa from 7th to 23rd December 1824. It appears from the correspondence of Rogerio de Faria that he was instrumental in making arrangements for their stay in Goa through the agency of the Mhamai House.[15] However, Lady West Journal has no mention of Rogerio de Faria in this connection. She has two insteresting entries on him though : "Sir Roger de Taria (sic) has sent me 2 sheep and a keg of humps, tongues, and so on. As he is a great Portuguese merchant I thought I could not refuse all, and, therefore, accepted of the dead stock (Sept. 12, 1825)", and "Even Portuguese Merchants are not to be depended upon, for yesterday a Cause came on in Court in which Sir Roger de Taria (sic) was interested. It taught me not to put any trust in man" (Sept. 13,1825).[16]

The only other contemporary published account of Sir Rogerio is found in Abbe Cottineau's Journal. Cottineau had been to his house, which he describes as "commanding a most lovely view of the sea, the ramparts, the suburbs, the city, the Colaba island, and the West coast as far as the so-called Malabar Point". He also recounts that Sir Roger's old father was fairer than the son, who was then a widower with one son and eight daughters. Cottineau had dined with the family, and he tells us that after dinner Sir Roger smoked a pipe in the Indian fashion whose reed passed through a cooler.[17] This small concluding detail tends to suggest that Rogerio de Faria was smoking opium. It was in opium-peddling that he had made his fortune. He was one of those in Country Trade which changed the face of Bombay in the first half of the 19th century. It is unfortunate that Gillian Tindall's very recent study of the growth of Bombay has only the Parsee community into focus and the Indo-Portuguese have been dismissed with a passing comment amounting to a taunt : "They are known for their sallow countenance, slovenly gait, and mimicry of the European fashions."[18]

It is not sufficiently known that there were several small Indo-Portuguese firms that tried their luck in the commercial world of nineteenth century rising Bombay. Most of them were small-fry and did not survive beyond the first quarter of the century, when the mortality among the small firms proved to be very high. Following the end of Company's monopoly in 1813 the process of survival of the fittest among the participants in the Country Trade had begun.[19] The history of many of those little concerns that were wiped out will never be sufficiently known, and that deprives us from details which alone could complete the picture of the rise of Indian business world.

We are not able to fully corroborate the statement, but we are told by the otherwise critical Indo-Portuguese administrator-historian, J.H. da Cunha-Rivara, that Sir Jamshetjee Jeejeebhoy, the most glamorous Parsee figure of the mid-nineteenth century in the annals of Bombay, started his prosperous career as a simple clerk in the firm of Rogerio de Faria.[20] Reporting the death of Sir Roger's daughter, Miss Margaret de Faria, the *Bombay Gazette* of 7 October 1889 added that Sir Jamsethjee had made his first voyage to China in a ship belonging to Sir Roger de Faria. A short, but informative life account of Sir Roger in Gujarati language was published in Bombay in 1874 by Rathanjee Faramjee Wacha. It refers to a severe setback in business suffered by Sir Roger in 1835 as a result of a loan given to a Governor of Goa, and which led to Sir Roger's bankruptcy in December 1838. The author concludes saying that Sir Roger had no one to look after him during the sunset of his life, and that Sir Jamshetjee assisted him while he was alive and provided a bungalow and regular living allowance to his descendants in perpetuity.[21] This seems to be confirmed by what Sir Jamshetjee was writing on 26 November 1838 to his correspondent Willin Jardine in Canton :

> You will be sorry to hear poor Sir Roger de Faria delivered his affairs to the Court, his assets apparently 50 per cent which will keep out from going to jail—my good friend...I have some regard to his family and cannot help of avoiding this very large number of persons to provide with.[22]

For nearly half a century, till the financial disaster overtook him in 1838, Rogerio de Faria had been riding quite high on the crest of the opium wave. When Macau route was the only legitimate exception to the Canton system, Rogerio de Faria had claimed right on the basis of his Portuguese nationality to enjoy the privileges of Macau residents in China trade in spite of much resentment and resistance of the local interests. With his base in Bengal, Rogerio de Faria had opened a branch house in Macau in 1798.[23] Due to deteriorating health of his father who was assisting him in Bengal during his business trips to Macau and Canton, Rogerio de Faria shifted his base to Bombay around 1803.[24] Rogerio de Faria had kept up his contacts with the State authorities in Goa, and opened trade contacts with Brazil in the wake of the shift of the Portuguese royal seat to that country following the occupation of Portugal by the Napoleonic forces. When Faria's ship entered Rio for the first time, it brought for Faria an award of knighthood from the King. Apparently, Rogerio de Faria had little regard for honours that did not bring financial benefits along. Writing to Mhamais in November 1811, Rogerio de Faria complaints about getting an honour with no exemption in customs duties to maintain such an honour.[25]

The award of knighthood did earn for Rogerio de Faria the title of *Sir* in the Bombay circles. He was also appointed Director of the Portuguese counter in Surat for three years from 1926.[26] Rogerio de Faria exploited his standing with the Portuguese authorities to the full to promote his business interests. From 1820's he had joined the Country Traders who were shipping opium directly to Lintin, by-passing the claims of Macau. He had also the most advantageous position among the Country Traders, because his standing with the authorities in Daman gave him a near monopoly of shipping the Malwa opium that was evading the monopoly controls of East India Company. Two-thirds of the Malwa was carried by the circuitous route of Daman, and only one-third via Bombay until the Company decided to combat this last challenge to its monopoly controls and introduced 'transit passes' in Bombay in 1831. As a result nine-tenths of Malwa began moving out via Bombay.[27]

It is obvious from the above that the noose was tightening, and the end of Rogerio de Faria and Cia was drawing near. His involvement in the Goa affairs and the problems of the Prefect may be explained as sentimental as well as a business calculation. He had raised loans to meet the expenses of the expeditionary force and had issued bills in favour of Sir Jamsethjee of Bombay and Motichund in Ahmedabad. The bills were to be paid by the Prefect on taking charge of Daman administration in cash or through exemptions in customs duties. Apparently, the Prefect failed to keep his word, because the bureaucracy of Daman that had upheld his legitimacy boldly, was equally bold in questioning the legality of his procedures for clearing the debts.[28]

By failing to honour the bills after repeated reminders of the creditors, Rogerio de Faria lost his credibility in the business world, and that was the last thing he could afford. Sir Jamsethjee had sounded a warning to this effect in a letter he addressed to Sir Roger de Faria on 29th July 1835 :

> *You seem to be quite ignorant of what the result will be in the end* (emphasis is mine). Had it been known to the Marwadies that the Bill granted to Motichund and me was dishonoured after its being put off from day to day for so long a time, I am sure that both the Marwadies and Ahmedabad merchants would always willingly follow Motichand's advice. You are perfectly aware of Motichand's influence over them. (...) In conclusion I have only to add that if they do not choose to pass the Bills in payment of the duty or pay the amount in cash the Bills must be protested for non-payment and we must make our agents to send back to Bombay as they are afraid to do anything of this sort. I trust you will write to Daman confidentially and see that the matter is arranged without delay as we must hold you responsible."[29]

CONCLUSION

It is not important for us to conclude with the very end of Rogerio de Faria's misfortunes. After losing his financial world, he also lost his only son a couple of years before he died in 1848. Both the losses were beyond his control. His son died of tetanus after an accidental fall.[30] His financial strangulation may be regarded also as unavoidable, while his bungling in Goa's freedom struggle provided only an occasion that accelerated the pace of the fall.

It is more important and significant for us to end this essay with a hope that fresh efforts in bringing fresh evidence to light and greater determination to interpret Goan history in as wide and stimulating a frame of reference will be undertaken.

NOTES

1. Seal, A., *The Emergence of Indian Nationalism, Competition and Collaboration in the Later Nineteenth Century* (Cambridge, 1968).
2. The works of Bipin Chandra, J.C. Masselos, Amles Tripathi, A.R. Desai, Leonard A. Gordon, Dietmar Rothermund, Gordon Johnson, Christine Dobbin may be usefully consulted for their analyses of Indian nationalism.
3. Abreu, M.V. de, *Relação das Alteracões Politicas de Goa desde 16 de Setembro de 1821 a 18 de Outubro de 1822* (Nova Goa, 1862).
   Costa, A.A. Bruto da, *As Revoluções Politicas da India Portuguesa do Século XIX*, (Margão, 1896).
   Miranda, J.V. Barreto de, *Quadros históricos de Goa* (Margão, 1863-1865).
4. Moniz, A.F., *Noticias e Documentos para a História de Damão*, (Bastorá, 1900-17) (4 vols.). Documentation relevant for the present essay are found in vols. 2 & 4.
5. Fonseca, J.N. da, *An Historical and Archaeological Sketch of the City of Goa*, (Bombay, 1878), pp. 59-61. *Cf.* Livermore, H.V., *A New History of Portugal*, (London, 1967), p. 264.
6. Costa, *op. cit.*, 14.
7. *Ibid.*, 42.
8. Abreu, M.V. de, *Noção de Alguns Filhos Distintos da India Portugueza*, (Nova Goa, 1874), p. 53.
9. Abreu, M.V. de, *Relaçã das Alterações Politicas*, 36.
10. Moniz, *op. cit.*, IV, 121 ff.
11. *The Bombay Courier* editorials were quite critical of the Prefect and his plans. This attitude invited many letters from the part of the Prefect and are published in the bi-weekly. The controversy is enlightening.
12. Boxer, C.R., *Portuguese India in the Mid-Seventeenth Century*, (Delhi, 1980), p. 23 ff.
13. Moniz, *op. cit.*, IV, 125.

14. De Souza, T.R., Mhamai house records: A new indigenous data-cache for Indo-Portuguese historiography (1750-1850), paper submitted to the *2nd International Seminar on Indo-Portuguese History*, (Lisbon, 1980).
15. Ms in author's collection. It is a letter of Rogerio de Faria, dated 30 November 1823.
16. Drewitt, F.D., *Bombay in the Days of George IV: Memoirs of Sir Edward West* (London, 1907), p. 185.
17. *Instituto Vasco da Gama*, (May, 1874) n. 29, p. 105.
18. Tindall, G., *City of Gold* (London, 1982), pp. 182-183.
19. Greenberg, M., *British Trade and the Opening of China 1800-1842*, (New York, 1951), p. 51 ff.
20. Cunha Rivara, J.H. da, Jornadas as praças do norte em 1859, *Instituto Vasco da Gama* (Nova Goa, 1872), 189.
21. Wachha, R.F., *Mumbayno Bahar*, I, (Bombay, 1874), pp. 235-237.
22. Sir J.J. Papers (University of Bombay), Ms. [illegible]58, p. 213.
23. Goa Historical Archives, Ms. 1296 (Correspondencia de Macau), fls. 74, 281.
24. MSS in author's collection. Letters of Rogerio de Faria, dated 5-8-1803, and 22-1-1816.
25. MS in author's collection. Letter of Rogerio de Faria, dated 10-11-1811.
26. Moniz, A.F., "A Feitoria Portuguesa de Surrate", *O Oriente Português*, XXV (1918), nn. 1 & 2, p. 27.
27. Greenberg, *op. cit.*, 124 ff.
28. Moniz, *Noticias e Documentos para a História da Damão*, IV, 178 ff.
29. Sir J.J. Papers (University of Bombay), MS 351, fls. 169v-171v.
30. Cunha, A.M. da, *Sir Roger de Faria*, Nova Goa, 1928 : 12. This little booklet of 30pp. gives more details about the numerous progeny of Sir Roger than about him. The author fits distantly in one of the lines, and the work seems to have been undertaken to trace this link.

10

Portuguese in the Deccan Politics

A Study of New Marathi Documents from Lisbon

A. R. KULKARNI

DR. PANDURANG S. PISSURLENKAR, a renowned historian of Indo-Portuguese relations, had collected and published numerous Marathi as well as Portuguese records. But it seems that a few Marathi documents preserved in the Bibliotheca de Ajuda, Lisbon,[1] remained unnoticed by him or any other research scholars. An attempt has been made in the present paper to discuss these new documents throwing some light on the Portuguese involvement in the Deccan politics. These letters, addressed to the Viceroys of Goa, belong to the years 1700-1701 except one which is of the year 1683. They are in Modi script, and beset with numerous Persian words, particularly in their format. They cover a period which is politically of great significance as the Mughal army led personally by the Emperor Aurangzeb was deployed in the Deccan with the sole object of uprooting the Maratha power, and thereby bringing the Deccan under their complete control. The premature death of Rajaram, the Maratha Chhatrapati, in 1700 had shaken the Maratha power for a while, but the dynamic leadership of Tarabai, the widow of Rajaram heroically resisted the Mughals and saved the Maratha Kingdom.

Konkan was the home of contention during the period under review among the Mughals, the Marathas, the Portuguese and the semi-independent Desais of the region. In fact, the Portuguese power during this period was on its decline, but from the documents under review, it appears that the Marathas, the Mughals and the Desais of Konkan were trying to keep them in good humour to realize their own political ambitions. The Marathas were the immediate neighbours of the Portuguese, and minor skirmishes between them were quite frequent. But it seems that they were now prepared to ignore their disputes to ward off the danger of the Mughals. It would have been difficult for the Marathas to fight the enemy on two fronts. The Mughals desired the sympathies of the Portuguese to check the activities of the Marathas in the Konkan. The Desais of the Konkan never fully supported Shivaji or his successors in their efforts of creating an enduring Maratha power. In fact, they preferred the Portuguese to either the Marathas or the Mughals to promote their self-interests in Konkan. This political situation explains the strategic position of the Portuguese in the Deccan in the last decade of the 17th century and a little later. The Portuguese were yet a major naval power on the West coast, and their cartazes were still required for other powers to ply their ships in the Indian Ocean. This system of issuing cartazes by the Portuguese was officially abolished only in 1774.

Sambhaji, who succeeded Shivaji in 1680, invaded Goa in 1682, but due to the non-coperation of the Desais of Goa, he could not fulfil his mission of annexing Goa to Maratha Kingdom by expelling the Portuguese from that region. Keshav Prabhu, the Desai of Pedne, supplied secret information about the Desais in the Konkan and a detailed account of Sambhaji's forts from Ankola to Rajapur in his letter to the Viceroy in 1683. His only condition was that the Portuguese should not destroy the Hindu temples after their occupation of Konkan.[2] Khem Sawant, the Desai of Kudal, and also the leader of all the Desais in Konkan, had also entered into a secret alliance with the Portuguese against Sambhaji. It is quite clear from the letter of 1683 and other documents that the non-coperation of the Desais thwarted the ambition of Sambhaji and thus helped the survival of the Portuguese in Konkan.

Except the above mentioned document, the rest belong to

1700-1701 period. The letter of Parashram Pandit, the minister of Tarabai, is quite interesting as it at once threatens the Portuguese for their disturbances in the Maratha country and also seeks their friendship during the period of their struggle with the Mughals. This letter reiterates their former alliances of friendship and enjoins them not to exploit the situation in which the Marathas were currently involved due to Mughal invasion, and disturb the Maratha territory. It further points out that they should not think that as the Marathas were deeply engaged against the Mughals, they would ignore their predatory activities. In fact they should note that the Marathas would not only tolerate it, but they would even not hesitate to destroy their territory if they did not behave. The same letter says that if the Portuguese have any complaints against the Maratha Sardars, punitive measures would be adopted against them. It also requests them not to be swayed away by the words of petty people, who would not lose any opportunity to poison their ears against the Marathas.

It is quite clear from the tone and contents of this letter that while preserving their superiority in Konkan, the Marathas were also anxious to maintain friendly relations with the Portuguese to ensure their neutrality in the current Mughal-Maratha conflict, as they could not have continued fighting on two fronts at one and the same time.

A few letters from this collection are written by the Subhedars or district officers of the Desais to the Portuguese Viceroy or other officers. In most of these letters the Subhedars have sought the assistance of the Portuguese in mitigating disturbances in their areas. They also throw some light on the various transactions between them.

Vithal Pundalik, the Subhedar of Dicholi or Bhatgram, a district in the possession of Khem Sawant of Kudal, was earlier pointed out by the Goa government that his Rajput officers in Narve and Pilgaon villages, demand custom duty on each and every article of the Goans ; object to carry fuel and fodder, and that he should issue orders to his officers prohibiting them from such acts. Vithal Pundalik, while agreeing to comply with this request from Goa, reminds them of his earlier letter in which he had requested the Viceroy to grant a general permission to the Marathas to carry money-bags to Karwar and Karnatak through their territory. The officers of the Goa government had allowed the passage once, but the contention of the Subhedar was as the money-bags were sent to those areas as and when the money was collected, they should get a general permission and their bags should not be checked every time. This argument was not acceptable to the Goan officers who maintained that they must verify the contents of the bags every time they pass through their territory. Being dissatisfied with this reply, the Subhedar further argued that as the money-bags were sent not for any commercial purposes, and they were sending them through their territory, as the administration of Phonda, the most convenient route, had fallen into the hands of their enemy. It was further pointed out that as the Marathas were not blockading their movements, they should also reciprocate. How this tangle was settled is not known for want of records.

In another letter Vithal Pundalik lodges a complaint that a merchant going to Goa was kidnapped by Mir Bujnikh, a Mughal officer in charge of Phonda, occupied by the Mughals since 1689, with the connivance of the Portuguese captain. Vithal Pundalik in his letter censures the act of the captain in view of the perpetual friendship between the Sawants and the Portuguese.

A similar letter was addressed to the Viceroy by Chenbasav Lingayya, the army-chief of Sonda in 1701. According to this letter, a Desai of chandravadi under the jurisdiction of Sonda had failed to pay the dues of the government and had eloped to the Goa territory where the captain of Kukali (Sashti) gave asylum to him. After mobilizing some forces, he raided from there a village called Balli, appropriated the properties of many merchants and fled back to Firangan, that is, the Portuguese territory. He also captured seven or eight persons including a Nadkarni and tortured them. The letter further points out that such acts unnecessarily lead to border disputes, and one does not know whether the captain of Kukali was acting with the knowledge of the government or in his personal capacity. The army chief of Sonda, therefore, urges the Goa government to enquire into this matter and punish the captain concerned if found guilty, and return the captives along with their belongings.

Plundering the villages on the border line of Goa, and taking shelter under the Portuguese areas, with or without the knowledge of the government, was a common practice in the 17th and 18th centuries. The Viceroy of Goa was thus flooded with complaints of this type from the neighbouring powers. Vithal Pundalik, the Subhedar of Dicholi, writes in one of his letters that Ramajirau Desai, probably a rebel of the Sawant family of Kudal first wounded a few poor ryots of village Narwe, of whom one died of severe wounds shortly. He then raided a nearby village called Pilgaon, sacked one house, wounded a few people of whom one died on the spot, collected about 200 to 300 'ashrafis' and fled away. After this event five people of Haldone village from Bardez area landed in a village called Shirgaon, set fire to six houses of the ryots, molested one woman, and burnt four oxen. The Subhedar after narrating all these events persuades the Goa government to punish all those culprits involved in such anti-social activities. One can get an idea of the insecurity of human life and property of the people residing in the border line areas in the medieval period.

A Sarparpatyagar, an officer of a prant, Jumbavali in the Sonda principality, also lodges a complaint with the Viceroy regarding the disturbances on the border of his district. The Desais of Chandrawadi 'tapa' had taken shelter under the Portuguese. A team of officers sent to negotiate with these Desais was put to death. These Desais had maintained a naval force consisting of 75 or 100 small boats for roaming on the border of Sonda, and when they were chased by the officers of Sonda, they used to disappear in the Portuguese territory. They entered into the villages usually at night, plucked coconuts from the trees, burnt a few houses and ran away. It is pointed out in this letter that the captain of Kukali was a party to these acts, as he was bribed by them. The letter further suggests that as these small people violate the laws of the boundaries, they need be warned against such illegal activities. The captain of Kukali was also accused of arresting innocent people of Sonda who used to visit Kukali for their own personal work. This letter also reminds the Goa government that whenever people from Sashti or Kukali came to Sonda, their movements were not restricted. A reciprocal treatment for the Sonda people from the government of Goa was, therefore, naturally expected by the Sonda officer.

Aan Shenvi, the Sarparpatyagar of Ashtagar, also complains that some of his Desais assisted by deceitful people had plundered the market of Hebarbad, killed a son of Harsheti, a grocer, burnt one or two houses, robbed a few shops and merchants, collected three to four thousand hons and took away as captives a few merchants to Kukali. The Viceroy was, therefore, requested to look into this matter and take necessary action against those involved in this affair.

The Subhedars sometimes also acted as the secret agents of the Portuguese. Vithal Pundalik informs the Goa government about the activities of the Arab merchants on the west coast. The Arabs had commercial contacts with India since the early medieval period. Hormuz and Muscat were known for trade with India. But their activities on the west coast were checked with the advent of the Portuguese in the 16th century. This resulted into rivalry between these two powers.

Goa used to receive its quota of rice mainly from Karnatak which was regarded as the granary of the Deccan. The naval force of the Arabs posted at port Basrur in Karwar was blocking the movement of rice from Karnatak to Goa, as per the injunctions of the chief of Muscat. The cargoes of Karnatak sent to Muscat were captured by the Arabs, and supply of rice to Goa was cut by them. Rice being the staple food of the people of Goa, this economic blockade must have imposed many privations on the people of Goa.

This letter is important in two respects : firstly, it reveals the bonds of friendship between the Desai of Kudal and the Portuguese, and secondly it shows how the political rivalries between two powers could affect the prospects of the trading community. The Karnatak merchants who had established commercial relations with the Gulf areas had to suffer as a consequence of this rivalry.

Another example of espionage was the information supplied by Vithal Pundalik to the Portuguese about Aurangzeb's siege of the Maratha fort of Panhala. In this letter of 1701, he writes that the Panhala fort will be captured by the Mughals shortly, and that an agent named Bhaskarrao has been sent to collect latest information about the Mughal Maratha conflict. He further assures that as soon as he gets any additional information, he would come personally to Goa to deliver the message.

Vithal Pundalik also broaches another topic in this letter in which he was personally interested. He had arranged to procure one hundred sacks containing ten khandis of rice and other minor commodities from Karnatak which had reached Goa, for a big feast called *Mejwani* at his residence in favour of his son. He, therefore, makes a personal request to the Viceroy that his agent should be given necessary permission to transport rice from Goa to Dicholi. One wonders whether the purpose of this letter was to supply the secret information about the Mughals or to get personal things done.

In another letter Vithal Pundalik had requisitioned 20 khandis of rice from the government of Goa to meet the requirements of the army stationed in the Konkan areas, particularly for making provision for the rainy season. This payment to the army in kind has been referred to as 'adisheri', that is 2½ shers.

The Desais of Kudal and Sonda were the most powerful chiefs of the Konkan, and they were trying to maintain their authority intact in their respective areas, by currying the favour of the Portuguese or the Mughals as circumstances demanded. For instance, the Khem Sawant did not forget to send ten baskets of mangoes of Goa and two boxes of wine to the military camp of Aurangzeb at Panhala. As the head-loads of these articles were to pass through the Portuguese territory, the Viceroy was requested not to arrest the men carrying them. This letter indicates how the friends of the Mughals were supplying provisions, fruits and articles of luxury from various places.

The advice and assistance of the Goa government was sought by the chiefs of Konkan including the Mughal officers. When Phonda was occupied by the Mughals their Faujdar requested the government of Goa to settle the disputes of the Desais of

Phonda. It was believed that the decision of the Goa government will be acceptable both to the Desais and the Mughals. The confidence reposed in the verdict of the Portuguese by a Mughal officer speaks eloquently for the importance of the Portuguese in the Deccan politics. Another Mughal officer, Mirza Muhammad Bakr, the Faujdar of Mirzan (Karwar) conveys his welfare to the Viceroy and expects a similar letter from him, as he did not receive any news from him since a long time. The Mughals were naturally interested in maintaining friendly relations with their neighbours in Konkan.

Like the Desais, their Sardars also sometime sought the favour of the Portuguese. For instance Tan Sawant, a Sardar under Lakham Sawant of Kudal writes to the Viceroy of Goa that he did not receive any news from him since long, and that he should give him the satisfaction of receiving his letters of well-being off and on. He reminds him of his earlier visit and tells him how the Viceroy showered his favours on him which he would never forget. The humble tone of this and other letters reveal the eagerness of the people of Konkan to maintain cordial relations with the Portuguese particularly to avert the threat of the Marathas.

This brief account of the new Marathi documents from Lisbon, addressed to the Viceroy of Goa between 1700-1701 by the Desais, their officers and the Mughal officers posted in Konkan are very useful for understanding the politics of Konkan in the 17th and 18th centuries. After reading these letters, along with other published documents on this topic, one gets the impression that the people of Konkan never whole-heartedly joined the main stream of the Marathas. They never associated themselves with the Maratha movement launched by Shivaji. The history of Marathas thus remains essentially to be dominated by the people of Desh or Western Maharashtra in spite of Shivaji's efforts to create a strong base for the Maratha power in the Konkan and particularly on the west coast. Shivaji did succeed in capturing some parts of Konkan, but the core of Konkan which was under the Desais and the Portuguese never came under the Maratha control. Phonda, Kudal, Sonda, and so on, never became the integral parts of the Maratha Swarajya. Just as the petty rulers of the North India sought the favour of the Muslim powers, the Desais of the Konkan found a friend in the Portuguese who would help them to preserve their independence. It was, therefore, they repeatedly wrote to the Viceroy to continue their assistance friendship and favour in the future, as they did in the past

A comprehensive history of the Konkan including that of Goa is a desideratum. The Marathi and Portuguese documents preserved in Goa and Lisbon archives would be useful for presenting a connected account of the political, social and economic history of Konkan. It is hoped that the new Marathi documents discussed in this article would add a little bit to the information on the history of Konkan.

NOTES

1. Vol. No. 51/V/49-1-182 pages 152(81) - 215. The author is grateful to Mrs. Melba Maria Olivia Ferreira Lopes da Costa, the Director of the Biblioteca Ajuda and Dr. Blanco, Administrator, Gulbenkian Foundation for their help.
2. A copy of this letter is in Ajuda library. Dr. Pissurlenkar included it in his book *Portuguese Marathe Sambhandha*, Pune, 1967, Appendix I, pp. 339-341. See also pages 99-100 of the same.

11

Arrest, Spoliation and Exile of the Goa Jesuits According to Father Caeiro's "De Exilio"*

J.P. BACELAR E OLIVEIRA

INTRODUCTION

THE third and the last set of papers of this Seminar is grouped under the theme: "Indo-Portuguese Cultural Influences and Exchanges". A network of exchanges and influences includes also institutions, and not just persons and their deeds. The institutions have their characteristic social individuality and also a relatively long duration. These traits enable the institutions to serve as links for events, to determine their direction, and to embody at times dramatic developments. Against this background, it is relevant, or even important, to refer to an institution that played a very significant role in the socio-cultural East-West relations during the 17th and 18th centuries. I am referring to the Society of Jesus.

The arrival of St. Francis Xavier in the middle of the 16th century marked a good start. In the course of the two centuries that followed, Jesuit presence left its mark. Personal achievements and institutional successes of the Jesuits abound. This first phase ended tragically and abruptly due to a despotic governmental interference in 1759.

I have chosen a theme which is of crucial importance in view of the death centenary of Marquis de Pombal. It calls for a study of events of the time with the effects they had on Portuguese Church and world history. The documents, hitherto

*The Paper is presented originally in Portuguese. The editor assumes responsibility for the English translation.

unpublished, lie in the archives of the different Jesuit "provincias" of Portugal and in the Jesuit archives at Rome. A study of these would greatly aid a seminar of this sort.

I intend to study Pombal's role in the suppression and the politico-ideological background in which it took place. I refer to the events at the court of King José in 1759 which later spread to those of Spain, France and Naples. Its influence was felt in the election of Clement XV and the promulgation of the Brief "Dominus ac Redemptor" suppressing the Society of Jesus on the 21st of July, 1773.[1]

The paper discusses Pombal's opposition to powers opposed to him, particularly the Jesuits who stood solidly behind the Pope in ecclesial matters. It touches upon the opposition between the two and the expulsion of the Society of Jesus in Portuguese territories. However, I have left untouched the documents crucial to the event.[2]

In Portugal, the official antagonism to the Jesuits began in the 1750's heating up in 1759 and spreading to other Portuguese territories by 1762. It led to the flight of missionaries from Brazil and the East, and to the imprisonment of many till their release in 1777 from S. Juliao de Barra and other prisons. Only a critical and systematic analysis of the documented sources relating to the blockade, exile and persecution of a society of 20,000 working in Europe and mission lands, at the service of the Pope, will expose the human and social implications of this event.

The scope of my paper is necessarily limited. I have chosen a particular society, placing it in a certain period of time, highlighting its features by means of an unpublished text about whose author and work I propose to give some relevent information : *The blockade, spoliation and exile of the Jesuits by Pombal's orders*, according to Father Jose Caeiro's narrative.[3]

This is a theme of much historical importance. In the 15th century, the Protestant writer Christoph Gottlieb von Murr said, "The sad destiny of the Jesuits in Portugal . . . calls for an unbiased scrutiny...the atrocities these innocent and able men suffered...make an indifferent observer revolt."[4] He edited unpublished manuscripts which are true accounts by eye-witnesses.[5] Father Anselm Eckart's diary is important in this respect. He suffered under Pombal's despotic rule and its account makes shocking reading. I found Eckart's manuscript in the Archives of Cologne and many eye-witness accounts of Pombal's hatred for the Jesuits, in the Society's archives in Cologne[6] and Rome.

Unlike Eckart, Fr. Caeiro, though a victim of Pombal, was never imprisoned like many others. His escape to Italy enabled him to gather many eye-witness accounts for his work on the Jesuits. Yet his work remains unpublished, in most part. The 1936 bilingual edition of his work, published in Bahia, covers three out of the eight volumes, and is unsatisfactory. For those who seek bibliographical information on Caeiro, a good catalogue on the Society of Jesus will suffice. For biographical information, Fr. Júlio de Morais'[7] work entitled *Historiador Desconhecido—P. Jose Caeiro Grande escritor da epoca pombalina*[8] is a must.

A study of the siege and the arrest of the Jesuits leads one to conclude that in Portugal and overseas, the operation siege-arrest-exile followed the same pattern. It began with the sentence of the *Junta da Inconfidência* condemning three Jesuit priests on some specific charges, and all others indirectly.

Sebastião José de Carvalho, later to be Marquis de Pombal, sent written orders to the Chancellor of the *Casa da Suplicação* to confiscate the wealth and income of the Society of Jesus. His *mandato* shows how he worked out to the last detail the strategy and plan of arrest. As he was a strong disciplinarian his orders were followed faithfully with clock-work precision.

GOA JESUITS IN FOCUS

In the Introduction to his book *De Exilio,* Caeiro relates a humorous incident to show how people were shocked at Pombal's blatant lies. An Algerian Muslim sarcastically commented that the arms used in the attempted murder of King José of Portugal was the result of the collaboration of Jesuits from Brazil to Asia.[9] The attempt took place in Portugal on the 3rd September, 1758. Three Jesuits were implicated and though the charge was never proved, 1800 had to suffer without fault, a fact that brings out the Machiavellian trait in Pombal. Though Caeiro unnecessarily advocates the case of the Jesuits in the early part of his book, yet he gives valuable information regarding names, dates, numbers and places.

Caeiro presents Manuel Saldanha de Albuquerque, the Count of Ega, the future Viceroy of India. He was suspected of having been sent on a secret anti-Jesuit mission to India. He left Portugal on the 13th April, 1758 and landed in Goa on the 18th September, fifteen days after the unsuccessful attempt on the King. During this time, Goa was looked after by a triumvirate consisting of the Prelate of Goa, the President of the Senate and the Captain of Bardez, after the assassination of the earlier Viceroy, the Count of Alva. The new Viceroy took charge on the day after his arrival.

As was the custom, the Viceroy went the very same day of his arrival to the Professed House of the Society of Jesus to pray to St. Francis Xavier. The provincial and the other fathers received him warmly, and the feelings were reciprocated by the Viceroy.

Yet things were not the same. Friends in Portugal kept the Jesuits informed of adverse political feelings against them. What followed confirmed their worst fears. On his next visit, the Viceroy was not the same. Curtly he informed the Provincial that the friendly relations maintained by the former Viceroys and the priests of the professed House were a thing of the past. The priests in future would have no direct access to the Viceroy's palace, and all important matters were to be discussed through letters.

In very many ways, the Viceroy showed his antagonism to the Jesuits. He even insinuated that the Jesuits were involved in smuggling. A ship *Nau de Meca* was searched thoroughly to involve the Jesuits. Later the Viceroy apologised and picked up the choicest goods for himself.

Meanwhile, in Goa the campaign against the Jesuits was gaining ground. The Viceroy gave wide publicity to a pamphlet published in Portugal, namely, *Da Republica Relacao abreviada*.[10] The Goan clergy reacted to it. Although it was banned by them, the power of the printed word prevailed in that lies and calumny left a deep impression on the minds of the readers. Fr. Caeiro tried his best to prevent the work from being published. While engaged in writing a Portuguese *Prosódia*, later used for the compilation of the well-known

Magnum Lexicon, he got hold of the proofs corrected by Carvalho himself.[11]

At last the ship from Lisbon laid anchor on the 23rd September, 1759. Although rumours were afloat, the Jesuits awaited detailed news. Through a slip in the tight security in the ship, they heard the fait accompli of the arrest of Jesuits in Portugal. This was the follow-up of the sentence passed by Pombal on the 12th of January condemning the members of the Society of Jesus. The only safe exit for them was the neighbouring kingdom of Sunda, for they would be safe among the Pagans than the Christians. They decided as one man to stay behind and face the circumstances.

The Viceroy did not delay in executing the orders of Pombal. At the September 25th meeting with his *conselho* the following resolutions were taken :

—judges would be in charge of specific missions according to the various *Casas*, and they would be helped by the army.
—convents, houses and farms were to be seized.
—a census of persons residing in the same house, including servants and slaves, was to be conducted.
—they were to be arrested and the slaves to be kept in public jails.
—a list of the belongings of the Society to be tabulated.

A catalogue of the Society, re-edited in 1906 [12] enumerates the following institutions of the Society of Jesus at the time :

—Colégio Novo de S. Paulo
—Colégio Velho de S. Paulo
—Hospital Real
—Casa do Japão
—Casa do Malabar
—Casa de Provação de Chorão
—Residència de Assolná
—Colégio de Damão
—Colégio de Diu
—Residència de Moçambique
—Residència de Cabaceire
—Residència de Maraguem

—Residência Rios de Sena
—Residência de Verenim

In all, there were 143 priests residing in these houses, and the Colégio Novo de S. Paulo with 54 held the pride of place among the *Casas*. One must admire the age-old tradition of cataloguing people.

The night of the 26th September set things moving. In heavy rain, the Viceroy and his men marched to the Colégio Novo de S. Paulo where the cream of the Society was concentrated. The Viceroy feared a counterattack from the young Jesuits and their African servants, and thus took extra care. The setting resembled a warfront, with the Viceroy delivering an eloquent speech on courage and its rewards, while the commander of the troops, Leonel Antònio, replied in the same vein. All through the Jesuits were wide awake and watchful, silently waiting for things to happen.

Saldanha Albuquerque next moved towards the *Casa Professa*. The seige of this Professed House was under the charge of judge Botelho and captain Francisco de Gusmão. As elsewhere events took place with clock-work precision. The judge knocked on the door and the Provincial Luis Lopes had to surrender the African servants who were handcuffed and taken to the public jail. All the Jesuits therein were put under house arrest, their belongings confiscated. The aggressors even demanded the keys to the tomb of St. Francis Xavier.

The next evening they were taken to the Colégio Novo de S. Paulo which was to serve as the concentration camp for the Jesuit prisoners. At the Colégio de Rachol the arrested Jesuits were kept in the dark till their internment on the 12th of November at the common abode : the Colégio Novo de S. Paulo.[13]

The Colégio Novo and the Casa Professa followed a similar plan, whereas at different places the respective judges in charge had their own ways. Luis França in charge of the Colégio de S. Paulo earned the dislike of all the Jesuits due to his arrogance, but a sad incident made him later a friend.[14] Always suspectful of Jesuit actions, he demanded from them the *Monita Secreta*,[15] a code of heterodox and unethical principles of anonymous origin, yet slipped in asking them for *Mónica*

Secreta instead, a fact which provoked his prisoners to hearty laughter.[16]

But such incidents were few. Those at the Colegio Novo faced hard times. Passages from *De Exilio* (pp. 679 and 681) give an idea of the humiliations undergone by them.

> Everyday they were counted like sheep . . . On his name being called, the Jesuit had to present himself to the judge and bow to him. He was next searched thoroughly.
> They had to ask the permission of the captain to dine and followed by six guards each on the way to the dining-room. They were not allowed to stroll in the surrounding garden or breathe the fresh air, a must in the tropical regions . . . They fell ill . . . and the patients were kept in the underground corridors.

Their sad plight took a turn for the worse when they were shifted to houses owned by different Orders other than the Jesuits, from the 2nd of November onwards. Someone sarcastically remarked, "Do we need sacred hands to torment the Jesuits ?"[17] Caeiro has carefully recorded the names of houses and persons, as well as all the proceedings therein.[18] They enjoyed sad as well as cheerful moments as guests of other Religious priests. The Augustinian monks gave them a lot of trouble,[19] whilst the Capuchins were generous and kind.

Yet every cloud has a silver lining. Caeiro's witnesses are all praise for the Goan citizens who aware of the tribulations at the Augustinian convent showered donations and gifts of all kinds on them.[20]

Thus far I have described the siege and arrest of the Jesuits. I now intend to narrate their exile from Goa and the other Eastern territories.

The arrival of the ship from Portugal on the 24th September, 1760 marked the commencement of another stage for those arrested. As per the conventional sign, the firing of the cannon from the fort, the judges converged towards the various Houses and took the prisoners back to their former abode—the Colégio Novo de S. Paulo. Here the masters of the house were subjected to harsh treatment. The 137 priests and their 20 slaves were all confined to one floor which lacked all amenities. It is interesting to note that all through the security was tight. The prisoners were bound to each other to prevent their escape.[21]

The Colégio Novo was then placed under the care of the Capuchins who with all the means at their disposal tried to minimize the sufferings of those in their charge. At night the Jesuits would throw a rope from their third floor and the Capuchins would attach letters and other commodities which provided relief to the prisoners.

On the Viceroy's written orders dated the 5th of November, the prisoners were taken on board the ship on the 17th of December. After bidding a sad farewell to Old Goa,[22] 127 men were tightly packed into the hold of the vessel, and set sail the next day. The voyage was painful and lasted five months.

The end of their journey did not mark the end of their troubles. They still suffered imprisonment in different forts, a fact that led sixteen of them to leave the Order. Caeiro gives us the final figures : of the 127 who embarked at Goa, 24 died during the journey. Of those who reached barely alive, 16 sought leave from the Order, 26 were put in the prison of St. Julian of Barra, 16 were imprisoned in Azeitão, and 45 were exiled to Italy. It was there that Fr. Caeiro could interview them.

Fr. Anselm Eckart has the final say on the matter when he describes the day of release. "On the tenth of March, José d'Oliveira himself came to S. Julião . . . and asked us what we had done . . . and where we wished to go . . . ". When the news spread that the gates of S. Julião were opened . . . crowds rushed in expressing their joy . . . because happier days awaited us . . . and they expressed their heartfelt sorrow on the extinction of the Society."[23]

CONCLUSION

The last to suffer exile were the 29 Jesuits from Macao. Although arrested on the 5th of July, 1762, they left Macao only on the 8th of November, and after a long halt at Goa, proceeded onwards to Portugal. They suffered such pains and humiliations on the way, that ten of them died as a result.

According to one who underwent the ordeal, the worst part was when all along the Asian and African coasts, they were brought ashore to be exhibited. At last, in Portugal, the 19 survivors were in the dark rooms of the fort of S. Julian, which were really burial places.

The banishment of the Society of Jesus was of sad consequence to the economy, culture and religion of Goa. Only a careful study of the life, occupation and social relations of the people can reveal the extent of the damage.

NOTES

1. Von Pastor, L., *Storia dei Papi*, XVI, p. 1, ch. 4 & p. 2, chs. 4 & 5. As the German edition was not available, I referred to the Italian edition. In the above-mentioned chapters, information is given on the persecutions of the Jesuits.
2. A history of the extinction of the Society of Jesus in Portugal, is the need of the hour. Father Domingos Maurício Gomes dos Santos left a valuable contribution in this field, but died without seeing his work published. The MSS in the Archives of the Society of Jesus at Cologne are also a good source of reference. The book *Licht in der Nacht* by Father Karl-Jos. Klinkhammer, (Frankfurt, 1759), throws light on the history of the German Jesuits imprisoned by Pombal in the fort of St. Julian.
3. Caeiro, Jose, The MS. of "De exilio Provinciarum Transmarinarum Societatis Jesu Libri Tres", (Baia Academia Brasileira de Letras, 1936), is published in bilingual edition under the title *Circa Jesuitas Brasilienses et Goanos in Persecutione Marchionis Pombalii.*
4. Von Murr, Christoph Gottlieb., Geschichte der Staatsverwaltung des Marquis von Pombal, Nurnber, 1787. in *Vorrede* (M. III).
5. Ibid., *Vorrede* I, IV.
6. Father Vaz Serra compiled valuable catalogues after referring to the Archives of the Society of Jesus at Cologne. ("Hoc exemplar descriptum fuit a P. Vaz, Lusitano, in Collegio Exatensi, mense Augusto 1899", by Father Brewer, S.J.).
7. Father Júlio Morais was born at Izeda (Bragança) on 12th December 1879, joined the Society on the 18th September 1896 and died at Braga on 27th January 1946. He wrote a monograph on Caeiro and his work, that was offered to the Portuguese Government in 1940. Fr. Morais suffered persecution in 1910. (Gongaga de Azevedo, *Proscritos*, 1911) ; p. 220-237.
8. Morais, Júlio, *Historiador Desconhecido*, Braga (Livraria Cruz, 1939).
9. Caeiro, José, *De Exilio Provinciae Goanae*, Liber Tertius (I, I).

10. Morais, J., op. cit., pp. 12 & 13 ; and also Rodrigues, Pereira Gomes, J, & Sommervogel, in the *Bibliothèque de la C. de J.*, say that Caeiro is the true author of *Magnum Lexikon.*
11. Morais, J., op. cit., Other authors like Júlio Dantas refer to this incident. However, Caeiro was not caught.
12. *Catalogus Provinciae Lusitanae S.J., 1906, cf.* Appendix "Status antiquae Provinciae... tempore persecutionis pombalinae" (XIV-XVI). The records are based on Caeiro's work.
13. Ch. 3 lists the names of municipal councillors, judges and superiors ; and it is divided into nine parts.
14. Ch. 4 includes the incident about Judge França's change of attitude. He interceded on behalf of some Jesuits who would be dismissed by Viceroy's orders.
15. *Cf.*, J. Pereira Gomes, *S.V.* "Monita secreta" in *Encyclopaedia Verbo*, XIII, Col. 1208. "Monita Secreta" is an anonymous work (1614). It was banned on 16.5.1616. Jeronimo Zahorowski, expelled from the Society, is the supposed author.
16. "At socii, qui scilicet, quo imperia tenderent,
a principio agnoverant, supina hominis, Monica pro Monita usurpantis, ignorantiam multum diuque risere" (III, 6 f.).
17. "Si ad eos torquendos manibus opus esset
magis planum ac simples fore,
religiosos in aedes jesuitarum immitere..." (VI, 5)
18. The description is based on records that were handed over to Caeiro in Italy (VI, 6) after being carefully preserved.
19. Whatever is said in note 17 took place here. Three superiors of that community were to be blamed for the death of three Jesuit prisoners (VIII, 5-9 & IX, 3-8, X, 3-4).
20. The text on praise to the Goan citizens contains some sarcastic passages. "Jesuitae, muneribus acceptis eorum partem ipsis donabant, prudenter rati, carnifices donis mulcendos, ut mitius saeviant" (X, 5).
21. "Meanwhile Judge Vale got busy checking the bags of the Jesuits. He caught hold of their cords... lest they would run away". The house was surrounded by troops. (XII, 3).
22. The Jesuits had such confidence in the Capuchins that they entrusted to them their obligation of masses during their voyage. Ch. 13 has references to the sorrow of Goans on the farewell day.
23. Ch. 18 contains the list that can be confirmed from Fr. Lourençc Keulen's letter from prison, dated 12th December, 1766.

12

Indian Textiles in Portuguese Collections A Problem of Provenance

LOTIKA VARADARAJAN

TEXTILES of oriental provenance found in museums and private holdings in Portugal[1] may be divided into four broad categories : monochrome embroidery and related items, polychrome embroideries, couched embroidery in metallic thread, and painted/printed textiles. The background fabric is either cotton, silk or linen. These have been categorised as Indo-Portuguese cultural artefacts. Joaquim de Vasconcelos[2] opined in 1883 that the term Indo-Portuguese included products fashioned by eastern artisans in Lisbon, those made by Portuguese workers established in Goa and other cities under Portuguese control as far eastward as Malacca[3] of eastern manufacture exported to Portugal. Since extant European traditions also shaped Portuguese taste in command items from the East, this factor has to be taken into consideration. Eastern textile traditions, in so far as these are reflected in Portuguese holdings, can be divided into three broad divisions—those of China, Persia and India. It is to be noted that unlike traditions of dyeing which were relatively localised thus making identification of provenance less difficult, the range of stitches used in embroidery[4] were near universal in the areas mentioned above. It was only variation in colour, the kind of raw materials which may have been used, and treatment of individual motifs which could provide clues to specific provenance.

Tradition of European Embroidery

The two traditions of European embroidery which probably shaped Portuguese predelictions in India were those of monochrome embroidery and the more opulent usage of couched embroidery.[5] Both these coalesced in the magnificent monochrome embroidered church vestments which were further embellished with pearls and precious stones, in evidence in holdings in Portugal, Spain and Italy.

In the Middle Ages the term *Opus teutonicum* was given to embroidery worked in white executed in Germany. White linen thread, sometimes with the addition of a little light coloured silk or dyed wool to emphasise details, was worked on white linen in a great variety of stitches, with openwork effects of cross-stitch type, and patterns such as letters, stars and rosettes, done in darning stitch on drawn thread backgrounds. Such work was also executed in Italy. The Italian pieces had a strong narrative content. These were made against a white linen background, the embroidery being in white linen thread. The stitches used were satin, stem, chain and herring bone.[6] There was also the *Swiss Linen Embroidery* popular in Switzerland among the German speaking burghers. This embroidery was worked on white linen with white linen thread. Sometimes details were highlighted in blue and brown. This development runs through the period *circa* A.D. 1250 to *circa* 1640. It was at its peak in the fifteenth century. *Swiss Linen Embroidery* was a continuation of *Opus teutonicum*, which after reaching its zenith in the late Romanesque and early Gothic periods, was generally abandoned in fifteenth century Germany in favour of embroidery in coloured silk. Habsburg dominance[7] introduced this school to the Iberian Peninsula.[8] However, work executed in Spain combined linen monochrome embroidery with couched work in gold thread,[9] often done selectively in relief to offer further surface variation.[10] The sixteenth century saw the most productive period in couched work.[11] These European traditions need to be kept in mind in any attempted analysis of Indo-Portuguese embroidery.

Chinese Embroidery

The seventeenth century Congratulatory Hanging at the

Gettröra Church, Sweden is a fine example of Chinese embroidery. It shows dragons, kilins, symbolical of happiness, playing ball, various good luck symbols and children carrying flowers expressing good wished for a birthday. The work is done in velvet with couched gold embroidery and polychrome satin stitch.[12] If samplers were provided it is evident that Chinese artisans would have been able to cater to specific demand as successfully as any other group of skilled eastern artisans. Since Malaysia has no major textile tradition it is conceivable that the local artisans may have had a Chinese orientation.[13] Portuguese records refer to "... all ... sorts of embroidered silks" received from China.[14] Charles Lockyer noted *circa* 1704 that *palampores* (drapery for bedsteads), and embroidered items could be commandeered in China, such items being particularly valued for their largeness and the fineness in the execution of figures.[15] Among items which could perhaps be given a Chinese provenance are some of the quilts shown in the catalogue of the Museu de Arte Antiga, Lisbon,[16] and the magnificant altar piece in the Treasury of the Sé Cathedral, Braga.[17] The motif of scalloped sea shells so prominently depicted in the latter, contrary to Portuguese belief, is not of origin. It appears to be associated with Coptic decorative motifs.[18]

Byzantine art may have led to a diffusion of this motif in the Mediterranean belt. From here the Portuguese may have introduced it as a favoured embellishment in the field of Indo-Portuguese art. This motif does not play a part in items fashioned for the other Europeans operating through their companies in the East.

Persian Embroidery

Persian embroidery had a tradition going back to Sassanian times. In the seventeenth century Shah Abbas II is said to have brought Chinese artisans to Persia.[19] Whereas India has had a very weak tradition in linen, this material has been used in Persia since Neolithic times. Items of uncertain provenance worked in *Bombyx mori* (mulberry silk), on linen could perhaps be associated with Persia.[20] Chain stitch embroidery is done at Isfahan, Kazan, Yazd and Shiraz. Embroidery executed exclusively in chain stitch is called *golabduzi.* At Resht chain stitch is done with a crochet as in Saurashtra and Kutch in Gujarat.[21] The hanging in the collection of the Museu de Arte Antiga, Lisbon, inv. no. 1750, described as a linen piece embroidered with *Bombyx mori* could perhaps be assigned either a Persian provenance or be imputed to Persian craftsmanship.[22] The *vaq-vaq* motif (tree bearing humanoid blossoms), is said to be depicted in this hanging. Although mentioned in Indian medieval travelogues and present in Indian miniature paintings, this motif does not form a part of Indian textile tradition.[23]

The Indian heritage in embroidery

Although there is no indication as to the techniques which may have been employed, Indian sacred literature contain references to embroidered garments from an early date. The Maruts (wind gods) are said to have worn gold embroidered mantles. In the Ṛgveda and later literature, the term *peśas* denotes embroidered garments worn by dancers.[24] Buddhist texts such as the *Dīga-nikāya* mention the following kinds of embroidered items : patch work counterpanes of many colours (*chittaka*), woollen coverlets embroidered with flowers (*paṭalika*), coverlets embroidered with figures of lions, tigers (*vikaṭika*) and coverlets embroidered with gems (*katthissam*). The *Jātakas* refer to kings wearing gold worked turbans (*kāñchanapaṭṭam*), while state elephants are decked with decorated golden cloths (*hemakappanavāsa*).[25] Among the sixty-four *kalās* (arts) mentioned by Vātsyāyana in the *Kāmasūtra*, is that of *vāstuvidyā*, anything made with skill, within which is included the term *viracana*. *Viracana*, the making of items such as covers and quilts also embraces the practice of embroidery.[26]

The art of embroidery has thus been widely practiced in India but judging by craft tradition it appears to have been a domestic occupation rather than a commercial one. Three sets of provenance are suggested for the commercial embroideries which fed Portuguese demand : those of Bengal, Gujarat and items which may have been procured from *kārkhānā*, workshops set up under the aegis of royalty or nobility.[27]

Bengal provenance

Embroidery traditions of Bengal can be divided into four

categories : *kānthā*, *kashida*, *chikan* and *zardozi*. *Kānthā* is a quilted embroidery done on cotton by women as a domestic occupation. Its origin is not dated. Stitches used comprise, in the main, darning, satin and stem.[28] Although totally non-commercial, some *kānthā* motifs such as the typical fish form may be found in Portuguese quilts.[29]

Unlike *kānthā*, *kashida* embroidery falls into the category of commercial production. It was embroidery done in muga silk on cotton. Usage of chain stitch in nineteenth century samples is rare. The common link between *kashida* and certain narrative and figurative hangings in Indo-Portuguese ware, is that both categories are worked in monochrome colour. However, *kashida* is embroidered in muga while samples in Portuguese collections are stated to be done in tasar.[30] The development of *kashida* in Bengal is not dated, but could be placed circa 9th century A.D.[31] The workers in the nineteenth and early twentieth centuries were females, either Jaina or Muslim.[3] In the nineteenth century *kashida* was exported mainly to Jedda and Basra. Pilgrims would also take them to the fair held at Mina during the Haj pilgrimage. Arabs used them chiefly as turban cloth or in costume.[33] Although linked with *kashida* tradition, the development of *chikan* embroidery in Bengal is not dated. Apart from differences in stitches used, the main distinction between *chikan* and *kashida* was that whereas in the latter muga floss silk was used in embroidery, in the former, which was also monochrome, white cotton thread was used.[34]

The provenance of Bengal suggested by John Irwin for the category of basically monochrome Indo-Portuguese embroideries, many with a strong narrative content, is quite acceptable.[35] However, the conclusion of the present author is based on analogies with *kānthā*, *kashida* and *chikan* embroidery and usage of tasar, rather than because of the presence of imputed Vaishnavite influence.[36] There is a reference to "quilts of Sutgonge (Satgaon) prepared with yellow silk" in a letter written by Robert Hughes to Surat dated 12 July, 1620, in which an offer is made to procure these from Patna.[37] Haghli, Balasore and Sherpur in Bogra district, were important centres of tasar production.[38] With regard to provenance, there is a discrepancy as to the origin of the quilt, inv. no. 2266, in the collection of the Mus n de Arte Antiga, Lisbon. This is described as a seventeenth century white linen piece embroidered in tasar and is ascribed to India.[39] John Irwin[40] states that *Bombyx mori* (mulberry silk) is used in the embroidery and he prefers to assign its origins to Portugal after a Bengal proto-type. The distortion in depiction of European figures, however, is suggestive of a non-Lusitanian origin. The question may be raised as to whether it could have been fashioned in Goa by the slaves so skilled in needlework mentioned by Linschoten [41]

Zardozi or couched embroidery in metallic thread, is said to have been introduced into Bengal from Basra in the 9th century A.D.[42] The Portuguese are said to have imported satin into Bengal and had these worked by native artisans.[43] Such work was done on a frame called *karchob*. Couched work on velvet or satin has been called *zardozi*, while lighter work done on muslin was called *kamdani*.[44] Whereas monochrome embroidery in muga and tasar was done uniquely in Bengal, *karchobi* work enjoyed a much wider distribution. It is difficult to identify specific regional provenance for this category of work as no local benchmarks of workmanship have evolved. However, Indian *karchobi* and the raised silk embroidery of Gujarat appears to have influenced the development of the Portuguese school of embroidery of Castelo Branco.[45]

Gujarat Provenance

Chain stitch embroidery done with a hook is much in evidence in the vernacular embroidery of Kutch and Saurashtra. Apart from chain, interlacing and darn stitches are also in evidence. Generally, the background colour is white, dark blue, maroon or saffron. The embroidery is in multi-colour. The silk used in embroidery is *Bombyx mori*. The background material may be cotton or *gajji/atlas*, the locally manufactured silk in satin weave. Chain stitch is particularly associated with *Kathi* and *Mochi* embroidery.[46] Whereas *Kathi* embroidery may have been in evidence in Saurashtra in the seventeenth century [47] *Mochi* embroidery is dated at the earliest to the late eighteenth century. *Kathi* embroidery pertained to a domestic tradition and it is unlikely that the Portuguese could have enjoyed access to this repositary of skill.

Linschoten refers to the fine coverlets made at Cambay called *godoriins colchas* which were,"very fine to the eye and are stitched, with silk and also cotton of all colours and stitchings".[48] Duarte Barbosa noted of Cambay that, "There are many washerwomen who do fine and cunning work", in reference to embroidery.[49] Since by tradition the job of washermen included functions like dyeing and mending, this statement of Barbosa appears quite credible. Taking into account extant craft tradition and range of motifs in practice, the provenance of Gujarat is suggested for inv. nos. 2282, 3418, 2126 in the holdings of the Museu de Arte Antiga, Lisbon.[50] Inv. No. 2282 may be compared with an 18th century canopy in the Calico Museum Ahmedabad.[51] The execution of the latter is, however, much more graceful than the former. Inv. No. 3418 is described as a linen piece. The material could well have been provided to the artisan by the Portuguese. The form of the tree is evocative of Gujarat vernacular tradition while the *Kalash* (vase of plenty) motif in the outer border panel could be connected with Jaina symbolism.[52] The vase in the ground appears of Persian inspiration. Inv. No. 2126 may be readily identified as springing from the *Pacchitpati* (embroidered wall panel) usage in Gujarat.[53] Instead of mica insets, which, indeed, are absent in Indo-Portuguese embroideries, the border panel has repeats of a circular motif which is fully embroidered.

Karkhana tradition

Items marked by extraordinary fastidiousness in execution as well as some of the Indo-Portuguese couched items could perhaps be accommodated within the Indian *Karkhana* tradition. These would include inv. nos. 2136, 2232, 3704 in the collection of the Museu de Arte Antiga, Lisbon.[54] Prominently, on display in inv. no. 2136 is the pineapple motif, the fruit having been brought to India by the Europeans. The central medallion shows a cock crowing. In Gujarat, the cock was associated with the Mother Goddess, Bahuchara.[55] Inv. no. 2232 has a medallion pattern strongly suggestive both of painted/printed export cottons as well as Persian carpet design. The outer border is of European inspiration. Inv. No. 3704 may also be compared with painted/printed palampores. The central motif shows the Christian motif of the divine heart.[56]

Painted/printed textiles

The provenance of items in this category poses no difficulties. Such items in Portugal were used more for their utility value, rather than being prized for their aesthetic appeal. Except for one sample in a museum collection, the majority are in private hands having been subjected to much rough usage. Hangings with the Tree of Life motif are easily recognizable as of south Indian provenance.[57] The printed item at the Museu Nacional de Machado de Castro, Coimbra, can be identified as of Diu/Ahmedabad provenance. Despite the paucity of samples in Portuguese collection,[58] Diu was a flourishing centre of dyeing and printing at least until the turn of the present century.[59]

Since Indo-Portuguese items are among the earliest samples of Indian textiles in European collections, they merit more detailed study by Indian scholars. Definitive assignment of provenance would mark an important stage in an understanding of the development of Indian craft tradition.

NOTES

1. Thanks to the support extended to the author by the Calouste Gulbenkian Foundation, Lisbon in 1980, she was able to visit Museu de Arte Antiga, Museu Calouste Gulbenkian and the Museum of Decorative Art, Lisbon, Museu Biblioteca Paco Ducal, Vila Viçosa, Museu Nacional Soares dos Reis, Porto, Museu Machadó de Castro, Coimbra, and examine the treasures of the Sé Cathedral at Braga. Among private collections mention may be made of those belonging to Eng. Bernardo Ferrao at Porto and Maria Isabel Mexia. Unfortunately, it was not possible to examine the latter collection which is said to be very rich in the painted/printed textile category.
2. Catalogue of exhibition of *Embroidered Quilts from the Museu Nacional de Arte Antiga, Lisbon*, India, Portugal, China, 16th/18th Century, held at Kensington Palace, London, November 1978 (henceforth *Embroidered Quilts*), p.13.

3. Macao must also have played a part in this trade. Macao was handed over to the Portuguese in 1557 and enjoyed its peak in the China trade from 1582-1598. See *Burlington Magazine*, 77, G. F. Wingfield Digby, "Some silk woven under Portuguese influence in the Far East", p. 59.
4. For graphic depictions of the range of embroidery stitches used and their nomenclature see M. Schuette, S. Muller-Christensen, *The Art of Embroidery*, London, 1964, pp. VII-XII ; J. Irwin, M. Hall, *Indian Embroideries* (Ahmedabad, 1973), pp. 203-208.
5. For a description of this term see publications cited above in note 4.
6. M. Schuette, S. Muller-Christensen, *op. cit.*, pp. XVIII-XIX, figs. 131, 133, 134, plate 95. See particularly fig. 330. The theme of this embroidered piece is Orpheus seated amidst foliage scrolls, playing fiddle to assorted animals.
7. Emperor Maximilian (1493-1519) of Austria had married Mary of Burgundy, heiress to the Netherlands, in 1477. Their son, Philip, contracted a matrimonial alliance in 1496 with Joan, heiress to the kingdom of Ferdinand and Isabella of Spain.
8. A mid-fifteenth century altar frontal of Henry IV of Castile bears a strong imprint of Flemish painting. See M. Schuette, S. Muller-Christensen, *op.cit.*, fig. 279 This shows the degree of cultural diffusion which was taking place.
9. *Ibid.*, figs. 288-291.
10. In India such work was called *Zardozi*. The desired areas were padded with same material over which the gold thread was couched. See below pp. 12-13.
11. For a fine example of work of this *genre* see the illustration of a chalice veil executed in France before 1668 and gifted by Henrietta Maria, widow of Charles I of England (1625-1649), to the Carmelites of Amiens. M. Schuette, S. Muller-Christensen, *op.cit.*. fig. 372.
12. *Ibid.*, fig. 433. For Chinese symbolism see *Revue des Arts Asiatiques*, II, 1925, L.C. Waterlin, "Contribution à l'étude du tissu en Perse au point de vue decoratif" p. 25.
13. This is particularly relevant for the identity of the embroiderers, killed in shipwreck, whom Afonso de Albuquerque was said to have been bringing back with him to Portugal from Malacca. See *Embroidered Quilts*, pp. 13-14.
14. *Documentação Ultramarina Portuguesa*, II, Lisboa, 1962, 17 (98), Riquesas que Produz o Estado da India, p. 113.
15. Charles Lockyer, *An Account of the Trade in India*, (London, 1711), pp. 122-123.
16. *Embroidered Quilts*, plates 13,27. Plate 28 could also be Chinese, John Irwin (*Arts and Letters*, N.S. XXVI, 1952 (henceforth *A.L.*), "Indo-Portuguese Embroideries of Bengal," p.72), assigns plate 13

to Malacca. The piece discussed by C.G.E. Bunt (*Burlington Magazine*, 1942, C.G.E. Bunt, "An Indo-Portuguese Embroidery in the Bargello", pp.277-278), bears a close resemblance to plate 13 cited above. There is a difference in the ornamentation of the outermost panel but the workmanship of the Bargello piece is much finer. It can be assigned an Indian provenance. It is possible that the same muster may have been sent to another centre for plate 13. Provenance of Indian 26 remains problematic until a more intensive study of Indian embroidery has been made.

17. Some 19th century samples of Indian embroidery executed at Tonk, Jaipur, (both in Rajasthan), and Chamba (Himachal Pradesh), bear some resemblance in technical detail to this item. Despite the discrepancy in chronology an Indian provenance for the Sé Cathedral alter piece cannot be ruled out.
18. A Coptic grave stele from Karnak, Byzantine period, 5th-6th century A.D., portrays a scalloped shell on top of a standing figure, See *Bulletin of the Cleveland Museum of Art*, December, 1974, "Saints and a 'sinner' on two Coptic textiles", fig. 6, p. 335.
19. A.U. Pope, *A Survey of Persian Art*, III, Text, (London, New York, 1939), p. 2159.
20. In China *Linum usitatissimum* was grown for extraction of linseed oil rather than for the preparation of flax fibre. Cloth tended to be woven from hemp. B. Laufer, *Sino-Iranica*, Chicago, 1919, pp. 293-294. In India, although linen, *ksauma*, finds reference in the Maitrayanisaṁhitā (3.6.7), as in China, *Linum usitatissimum* was cultivated for extraction of oil rather than for fibre content. Some fibre may have been available in North India, but the remaining supply must have been procured from other sources. See Lotika Varadarajan, "Indian Textile Technology in the Pre-Industrial Period", MS, p. 2, to be published in *Proceedings of Seminar on Technology in India (Ancient and Medieval periods)*, Ananthacharya Indological Institute, Bombay. The Maitrāyanisaṁhitā is dated by P.V. Kane (*History of Dharmaśāstra*, V. Part II, Poona, 1962), to *circa* B.C. 4000. For Linen in Persia see H.E. Wulff, *The Traditional Crafts of Persia*, (Cambridge, London, 1966), p. 178.
21. *Ibid*, p. 218. According to G. Watt (*Indian Art at Delhi 1903*, Calcutta no date, p. 392), Armenian merchants may either have brought the technique from Gujarat to Resht or the movement may have occurred in the reverse order. There is no indication as to how the chain stitch may have been worked in Bengal in the seventeenth century. In present times a needle is used. For 17th-19th century Persian embroidery see A.U. Pope, *op. cit.*, pp.2159, 2161.
22. See *Embroidered Quilts*, plate 11. There has always been migration of craftsmen along the Northwest regions of India. In view of the links between the Shia Deccani Sultanates and Persia, it is possible that Persian craftsmen received patronage in Bijapur and Golconda.

It is of interest that the embroidered *masnad* cover used at the time of the coronation of Shivaji at Raigad in 1674 is said to be Persian fabrication. The workmanship bears a strong resemblance to some Indo-Portuguese embroideries. This cover is now on display at the Shri Chhatrapati Shivaji Mahararaj Museum, Satara, Maharashtra.

23. *Vaq-Vaq* is clearly depicted in an anonymous illuminated manuscript written in Braj *circa* 18th century in the possession of Dr. T. Donaldson, Cleveland State University, U.S.A. The motif is found in Persian carpets. It is depicted in a hanging of Bengal provenance in the collection of A.L. Davison. See *Gazette des Beaux Arts* (henceforth *G.B.A.*), 1948, M.E. Moeller, "An Indo-Portuguese Embroidery from Goa", Fig. 7, upper left corner. The form however, is different from that found in miniature paintings and Persian carpets. The piece was probably executed on the basis of a sampler. Since the *vaq-vaq* existed in Spanish art, the Portuguese were probably familiar with the theme. See *ibid.*, p. 126.
24. A.A. Macdonnell, A.B. Keith, *Vedic Index of Names and Subjects*, II, Delhi, Varanasi, Patna, 1958, pp. 22, 291, *Peśas* are said to have been made by female embroiderers called *peśas-kāri*. *Ibid.* p. 22.
25. M.M. Singh, *Life in North-eastern India in Pre-Mauryan Times*, Delhi, Varanasi, Patna, 1967, pp. 210-211. The *Dīga-nikāya* forms a part of the *Suttapitaka* and is dated *circa* B.C. 600-A.D. 100. The *Jātakas* art dated between *circa* 3rd century B.C. to the 6th century A.D.
26. A.B. Ganguly, *Sixty four Arts in Ancient India* (New Delhi), pp. 124-125.
27. For insight into the working of these *karkhanas* see G.N. Bahura, *Literary Heritage of the Rulers of Amber and Jaipur*, Jaipur, 1976, pp. 14-15, 103, n. 46. According to Dr. Chandramani Singh (Registrar Maharaja Sawai Man Singh II Museum, Jaipur), in the Jaipur *kārkhānā* tradition, artisans were free to cater to outside demand provided they had fulfilled the needs of their own patron. This would explain how the Portuguese, if at all, could draw upon the reserves of *kārkhānā* skill.
28. *Chhavi*, Golden Jubilee Volume, Bharat Kala Bhavan, 1920-1970, (Varanasi, 1971), Kamladevi Chattopadhaya, "Kantha Embroidery of Bengal" p. 78.
29. Inv. No. 548, Museu de Arte Antiga, Lisbon.
30. Muga is derived from the worm *Anthera assama*, Helfer and *Saturnia assama*, Westwood. The tasar silkworm is called *Anthera paphia*. T. Wardle, *Handbook of the Collection Illustrative of the Wild Silks of India*, (London 1881), pp. 5-6, 55.
31. See G. Watt, *op. cit.*, pp. 384-385.
32. *The Journal of Indian Art* (henceforth *J.I.A.*), No. 18, April 1887, B.A. Gupte, "Bombay Embroidery", p. 11 ; *Marg*, 1965, J. Dhamija, *Textiles and Embroideries of India*, p. 36. The Jaina connotation is of interest. Jainism existed in Bengal before A.D. 479, and in the 10th century, north Bengal was an important centre for Jainism. (R.C. Majumdar, *History of Ancient Bengal*, (Calcutta, 1984), reprint 1971,

p. 522). In the same century Jainism gained a firm footing in Rajasthan from where it spread to Gujarat. The earliest Jaina temples in Gujarat are those dated to the 11th century at Satrunjaya Hill, Palitana, and the Parasnath Temple at Girnar built in 1114. It is possible that Jainas from Gujarat/Rajasthan may have had contact with their conferers in Bengal. Chain stitch is peripheral to Bengal embroidery tradition, but is much in evidence in Indo-Portuguese embroidery of Bengal provenance. It is possible that it was through the Jainas from western India that chain stitch was introduced into Bengal.

33. E. Balfour, *Encyclopaedia Asiatica*, II (New Delhi, 1976), reprint, 1884, p. 832.
34. *J.I.A.*, VIII, Nos. 61-69, 1898-1900, N.N. Banerjei, "The Cotton Fabrics of Bengal", p. 71. It was only in Lucknow that tasar was used for *chikan* embroidery T.N. Mukharji, *Art Manufacturers of India* (New Delhi, 1974) reprint (Calcutta, 1888) p. 371.
35. Inv. No. 3413 (*Embroidered Quilts*, plate 6) shows a curious artistic convention whereby faces in profile are endowed with both eyes set in frontal perspective. This may be compared with usages in Madhubani paintings of Mithila, north Bihar, See U. Thakur, *Madhubani Paintings*, New Delhi, no date, fig. 16.
36. *A.L.*, 1952, J. Irwin article cited, pp. 65-72, plates 1-16. Even if it be granted that Vaishnavite symbolism may have played a part, it is very difficult to associate Vaishnavite iconography with the forms depicted. The half-human half-fish figures appear closer to the forms of European mermen and mermaids rather than the *nāgas* and *nāginīs* of Hindu tradition. The analogy drawn by John Irwin between these embroideries and motifs found in some of the Bengal terracotta temples, however, is quite feasible. See *A.L.*, 1952, J. Irwin, article cited, p. 70 and fig. 6). Of particular interest are depictions of the Portuguese portrayed at the Ananta Vasudeva Temple, 1754 A.D., and the Siva Temple, dated 1753 A.D. in Kalna, Burdwan district, and the Radha Govind Temple, 1784 A.D. at Atpur, Hughli district. See P. Das Gupta, *Temple Terracottas of Bengal*, (New Delhi, 1971), plates 50, 52, 96. Even after the eviction of the Portuguese from Bengal by Shah Jahan in 1632, individual Portuguese soldiers found ready employment as mercenaries in Bengal. *Ibid.*, p. 21. This would explain their delineation in 18th century terracotta art. A striking feature of these artefacts is the ribbed effect depicted in clothing. This may be compared with the visual impact created by the chain stitch filling-in device of 17th century embroideries. Discrepancy in chronology may be overlooked as the salient feature is similarity in treatment of surface areas which may thus be invested with the specific attribute of regional style.
37. *The Indian Historical Quarterly*, XV, 1939 (henceforth *I.H.Q.*), J.N. Sarkar, "The Silk Trade of Patna in the early 17th century", p. 215. Among embroidered patterns in textiles mentioned in a 14th century

Bengali text are *jātrā-sid*, auspicious journey representing people singing and dancing, *manja-phal* sari in which borders show depictions of hills and forests while the *pallu* (cross border), had scences of Vrindavan with flute playing cowherds and Krishna receiving gifts of betel-nuts. Refer to University of Calcutta, *Journal of the Department of Letters*, XVIII, 1929, T. Das Gupta, *Aspects of Bengali Society*, pp. 230-231.

38. *I.H.Q.*, 1939, J.N. Sarkar, article cited, p. 222 and n. 30.
39. *Embroidered Quilts*, p. 41 and plate 1.
40. *A.L.*, 1952, John Irwin, article cited, p. 71.
41. Linschoten had noted that in Goa many Portuguese lived off the earnings of their slaves. Among the latter, "The women slaves make...... much fine needlework, both cut and wrought works". A.C. Burnell, trans., *The Voyages of John Huyghen Van Linschoten to the East Indies*, I (London, 1885) p. 186.
42. *J.I.A.*, No. 18, 1887, B.A. Gupta, article cited, p. 11.
43. *Imperial Gazeteer of India*, III (Oxford, 1907) p. 222.
44. G. Watt, *op. cit.*, p. 370.
45. See *Embroidered Quilts*, plates 19, 21. As has been pointed out above, p. 3, couched work reached its peak in Europe in the 16th century. The inference that Gujarat embroidery influenced that of Castelo Branco is based upon examination of samples available at the Calico Museum, Ahmedabad. Moreover, the Portuguese had direct access to Gujarat tradition resulting from their presence at Diu and Daman.
46. J.M. Nanavati, M.P. Vora, M.A. Dhakky, *The Embroidery and Bead-work of Kutch and Saurashtra* (Baroda, 1966), pp. 18-20.
47. According to Gazeteer of Bombay Presidency, VIII, *Kathiawar* (Bombay, 1884, p. 136), the first band of Kathis moved into Kutch from Sind in A.D. 1400. They should then have penetrated into Saurashtra. The Gujarat State Gazeteer, *Kutch District* (Ahmedabad, 1911, p. 74), assigns the date A.D. 714 for Kathi presence in Kutch. Khodidas Parmer (Bhavnagar), the well known folklorist of Kathiawar, dates Kathi presence in Saurashtra to *circa* A.D. 1316 on the basis of regional poetry. Oral communication to the author by Khodidas Parmar.
48. A.C. Burnell, *op. cit.*, I, p. 61. Even in contemporary times in Gujarat quilts are called *godri.*
49. M.L. Dames, *The Book of Duarte Barbosa*, I (London, 1918), p. 142.
50. See *Embroidered Quilts*, plates 10, 12 and 5.
51. J. Irwin, M. Hall, *op. cit.*, plate 21.
52. Cf. *ibid.*, plate 37A.
53. Cf. *ibid.*, plate 54.
54. *Embroidered Quilts*, plates 14, 16, 17.
55. For the Bahuchara cult in Gujarat see *Gazeteer of the Bombay Presidency*, IX, Part I, Bombay, 1901, pp. XI, XXVI, 227, 366, 386 ; *ibid.*, VII, *Baroda*, Bombay, 1883, pp. 610-611 ; Census of India, 1961, V.

Gujarat, Part VII-B, *Fairs and Festivals* (Ahmedabad, 1965) pp. 111, 268-69, 274 ; M.R. Majumdar, *Cultural History of Gujarat* (Bombay, 1965) p. 225.

56. With regard to motifs some note needs to be taken of the bicephalous or double headed eagle. This image in Indian art can be traced back to Hittite origins. In course of time it became transmuted into the *Gandabherunda*, shown clutching elephants in its claws. S. Gorakshkar, *Animal an Indian Art*, (Bombay, 1979) p. XVIII. Europe received the double-headed eagle by way of Byzantium. It was adopted as the crown emblem by the Hapsburgs. *G.B.A.*, 1948, M.E. Moellar, article cited, p. 124. By and large, the bicephalous eagle in Indo-Portuguese hangings appears to be of European inspiration. However, there is mention of the Gandabherunda in one Bengal quilt. See *Embroidered Quilts*, plate 6 and p. 24.

57. Cf. Lotika Varadarajan, *Sputh Indian Tradition of Kalamkari* (Bombay, 1982), p. 29.

58. Apart from the factor of divergence in taste in Portugal mentioned above in the text, another aspect may exp'ain the absence of printed items in sizable numbers in Portuguese collections despite ease in availability at Diu. This was the demand for such items in Mozambique which was met through imports from Diu. See *The International Journal of African Historical Studies*, IX, 1, 1976, E.A. Alpers, "Gujarat and the Trade of East Africa, c. 1500-1800", pp. 34-44.

59. Techniques of dyeing and printing in vegetable and mineral colours at Diu are described in detail by Narayan Daji (*Art of Dyeing in Western India*, place and date of publication not known). The author did not enjoy access to the original publication but K.V. Chandramauli (All India Handicrafts Board, Bangalore), who had a typescript copy of the printed work was kind enough to allow her to read the material.

13

A Portuguese Creole in Sri Lanka

A Brief Socio-linguistic Survey

M.H. GOONATILLEKA

THE Portuguese sojourn in the island of Sri Lanka, known to them as *ilha de Ceilão*, was of shorter duration than in India. Nevertheless, the impact of the Portuguese on Sri Lankan society was as strong here as in parts of India. They arrived in the island in A.D. 1505 and sometime after involved themselves with the local administration. They dominated the maritime provinces of the island for nearly a century and half from about the mid sixteenth century till A.D. 1658, when they were forced to handover the territories they controlled to the Dutch.

During their presence here they had to be content with the maritime bases, perhaps on account of their basic reliance on naval power. Their intervention in the affairs of Sri Lanka was motivated by self-interest. Nevertheless their task was made easier when they were openly wooed by the Sri Lankan chieftains because of schisms among themselves.[1]

They were pushed into the circumstances of operating in a multi-lingual and multi-racial community of Colombo's commercial enclaves comprising Sinḥalese, Tamils and Moors and in consequence thereof the Portuguese were pre-occupied with the task of learning the language of the trade.[2] The task was an urgent one, because they opened up a trade centre (factory) to compete with the local traders. In other parts of the island where the Portuguese ventured later, they were compelled to work within a large concentration of Malayali-speaking fisher-folk[3], who had migrated from the coastal regions of Western India. The Malabar language was in fact characterised by writers as a language which was in common usage in the littoral belts of the island. ("Língua malavar hé ordinária em todos os lugares marítimos da ilha").[4]

Thus the circumstances led the Portuguese to adapt themselves to a multi-lingual speech community and its behavioural norms. The lead was given by the Portuguese and Indian missionaries. While learning this language they in turn taught their language as well. As much as economic necessities prompted the Portuguese to study the trade language of the people, the political necessities prompted the Sinhalese chieftains to study the Portuguese language. The Sinhalese ambassador Salappu Aracci (also known as Pandita or Panditer) who led the first Sinhalese overseas mission to Portugal is described as a person "who spoke Portuguese extremely well".[5]

S.G. Perera relates how children of rich families were educated in the two languages, Portuguese and Latin at the Collégio dos Jesuitas in Colombo in the latter half of the 16th century.[6] According to Robert Knox king Rajasinghe II "understood Portuguese and spoke it well".[7]

This is the result of missionary activity started by Frei João de Vila de Conde of the Província da Piedade de Portugal[8] and continued by Portuguese and Goanese priests. Their activity resulted in a process of acculturation and language borrowing which culminated in a large number of Portuguese vocables entering the indigenous languages.[9]

This process was made easy because of the presence of a fairly large number of Portuguese settlers at the time. They were of different descent. Some of them were soldiers who came thither from Portugal. Others were mercenaries enlisted in the service of the Portuguese battalions and came from the Portuguese colonies in East Africa.[10] There were in addition, a large number of *casados* or "married Portuguese settlers" and *mestiços* or "those of mixed stock".[11] Women too have been brought down for the specific purpose of 'peopling the colony'.[12] Moreover some Sinhalese princes who went to Goa for higher education and military training during the 16th and the 17th centuries had married either Portuguese or Goanese women and returned to the island with or without them. There is also the unique case of two Sinhalese princes who settled down in Portugal and lived the life of another 'Don Juan' in the city of Lisbon.[13] Mention is made of a daughter born to one of them, and named Dona Maria da Candia.

The Portuguese appear to have mixed with the local population more freely than the Dutch or even the British. The question may be raised whether this was the result of the social status of the average Portuguese who came here ? Whatever be the answer to this question the fact remains that this type of adaptation both here and abroad not only led to a process of acculturation but also to the establishment of small pockets of converts[14] with either Portuguese settlers or descendants or of *mesticos* occupying leading community positions such as the Headmen of villages.[15] It is no doubt the existence of small communities that leads Smith to observe that "By the time the Dutch arrived on the scene, there was a reservoir of mother-creole speakers established in Lanka, and their language was in wide-spread use as a lingua franca".[16] If we modify this statement from "a reservoir of mother-creole speakers" to "small pockets of mixed communities" and from "a lingua franca" to" a lingua franca of the colonial and colonized elite" perhaps Smith's statement may be more acceptable.

It is certainly true that the Dutch were compelled to use the Portuguese language in their official dealings with the Sinhalese long after the Portuguese left our shores. This alone is an indication of the tremendous influence the latter exerted on the official correspondence between the Sinhalese royalty and the foreign powers. The impact was so great that even the British Governor Frederick North as late as the early 19th century had to employ a Portuguese-Sinhala interpreter to accompany his ambassador to the court of the Kandyan king[17]. Nevertheless the Dutch colonial Governors issues numerous regulations prohibiting the inhabitants from mixing with the Portuguese, and even the Portuguese settlers from practising their way of life.[18] But this was ineffective. Despite the fact that the Dutch Governor, Maetsuyker was strongly opposed to the indiscriminate use of Portuguese by the official printers of the Dutch East India Company, an Amsterdam-based publisher, Allewin and Collé, published a Portuguese-Dutch dictionary as late as A.D. 1718, Coelho quotes from a letter sent by a Portuguese missionary from the island of Ceylon on November 13, 1825 which refers to the language used by the Dutch missionaries as being the language of the Portuguese and Dutch descendants of the island.[19]

But this type of activity was not prompted by a desire to uplift the Portuguese language which was in vogue in the island at the time. The purpose was politically motivated, Nevertheless Portuguese words gained currency in the indigenous languages to such a degree that these still form a part of the living languages of the country.[20]

In effect what we observe is a two-way process of acculturation at work : the Portuguese settlers and the Sri Lankans studying each other's languages resulting in (a) a large number of vocables entering the Sinhala and Tamil languages and (b) the emergence of pockets of Portuguese-creole-speaking settlers in the coastal areas close to the main ports and in parts of the hinterland. They were found in Kotahena and Mutwal near the port of Colombo ; Galle, Matara and Weligama in the Southern province ; Negombo and Chilaw in the Western and Northern periphery where the population was largely Sinhala. There were other pockets in Batticaloa in the Eastern Province ; Jaffna Kalpitiya and Puttalam in the North and the North West of the island which were predominantly Tamil at the time the Portuguese were administering these areas. Of these settlements creolized language persisted only in Batticaloa, Puttalam, Parangi-teru in Jaffna, Akkaraipattu and Trincomalee in the Eastern province and in a very few places to which they migrated later.

Not all these settlers could have come directly from Portugal. Instances are often recorded of Indian, East African and Malay (Javanese) soldiers making Sri Lanka their home once their military contracts were over. They came here as members of naval forces commanded by Portuguese captains. Most of them appear to have sailed in relatively small crafts called 'patachos' or two-masted vessels and galliots thus indicating that they came here from areas in the Indian Ocean region. It would normally have taken several months to reach Sri Lanka from Lisbon.[21] During emergencies naval task forces from East African ports and Malaccan service stations were despatched to Sri Lanka to supplement the garrisons. Trindade says that among these in-coming soldiers were both black and white men.[22] Moreover many a Portuguese captain-general who came here had previous African military experience.[23]

Portuguese intervention in Sri Lanka was part of a process of historical interaction where the activities of the colonial establishments and Lusitanian settlers in the Asian and African region project themselves on the internal conditions and structures of Sri Lankan society. C.R. De Silva examining the land tenure system of Sri Lanka during the early Portuguese period comments : " . . . by 1615, there had emerged a solid phalanx of Portuguese landed gentry consisting of army officers, casados and a few soldiers".[24]

Of these Portuguese settlements I am here concerned with the larger creole-speaking community—the Batticaloa Portuguese-speaking community. I have worked among 250 nuclear families in Batticaloa during the last 13 years. Through time they have assimilated features of Sinhala and Tamil social structures. But in their intimate situations they still preserve their older traits. These people are generally known as Portuguese-Burghers and not as Mechanics as some writers would prefer to call them. In fact their formal association is known as the Portuguese Burgher Union of Batticaloa and is housed in a building rented out for the purpose by Mr. Ronald Rosairo its President at the Old Rest House Road in the heart of the Batticaloa town.

This brings us to the question : Who is a Burgher ?

Burgher in Sri Lankan context

One cannot locate their origin by examining their status in modern Sri Lankan society. The Sinhalese people in their usual patois call them *'Lansi'* of *Lansi Minissu* which is an ethnic classification, very often used with racist overtones, the most derogatory from being *Karapotu Lansi* (Kärapotu= Carocha (P)=Cockcroach (E) applied to darker skinned types of those of mixed stock. The term '*Lansi*' is however a localized form of the Portuguese term *Olandês* used to identify the Dutch. This type of expression confuses issues and makes one wonder whether the Sinhalese people were not confused in their own minds owing to the colour of the skin of the Portuguese and the Dutch—which to them meant the same. The same is however not true of the descendants of the Portuguese. Whatever be the colour of their skin, they were offsprings of mixed marriage. Don Peter identifies them as "mestizos also called Luso-Indians or Eurasians, who later came to be known as Burghers".[25]

An ironical situation arises when we notice that the Dutch for their own purpose, employed these terms of identification almost in a derogatory sense in connection with the Portuguese descendants ! *Mestizo* (also written as *mestiço*) that Don Peter mentions and other terms as *Tuppahi* (also written as *Toepas/ Tupassi/Tuppassi*) have been used in this sense although their original meaning was not the same.

Mestiço refers to a half-caste or the cross-bred. We have in Sri Lanka still the Sinhalese family name *Mestiyagè*. This is common in the Kalutara-Panadura area in the Western littoral belt about 25 miles away from the city of Colombo, in an area where the Dutch stockade was garrisoned by them. For instance Tennent records how the Anguruwatota stockade was garrisoned by "a Mesties sergeant and two toepas soldiers".[26] The term *Tuppahi* was originally used in the sense of a person skilled in two languages thus tracing its etymology to the Sanskrit term Dvibhāṣā and the Konkani Dubash. It was also used to identify the Interpreter Mudaliyar who played a significant role during the Dutch period of rule in Sri Lanka. He was called the *Tuppahi Mudiyanse*. Tennent apparently does not deal with the deeper etymological meaning and is satisfied by merely stating that the word was applied to a somewhat degenerated class of mixed Portuguese of native descent thus making it easy for the inexperienced Western writers of a later date to use Tennent almost as an authority on the subject to avoid going through a difficult process of linguistic exercise. The Tuppahi class in later times absorbed the libertines or emancipated slaves of the Dutch and many of them, while wearing European dress and using Portuguese as their colloquial, were of darker complexion than any of the indigenous natives of the island.

Sophia Anthonisz the Dutch translator remarks that the term is of uncertain origin but being "of mixed Portuguese and native descent were employed by the Dutch in various inferior handicrafts".[27] The term *Tuppahi/Toepas* as far as we can see, is employed in relation to local descent and domicile and is at times cognate with the term *Mestiço.*

The term Burgher was later used to denote the local counterpart of the European, and those closer to the "European Masters". The difference in the "colour of the skin" of many of the Portuguese descendants would have perhaps made them recede to the background. They were probably kept out of the normal Dutch-Burgher community in the cities, while a majority of the Dutch-Burghers do not recognise the existence of such a community.

Dutch-Burghers and Portuguese-Burghers

Census reports of Sri Lanka do not categorise them as a separate entity. In fact the earliest Census reports classify the island's population into caste groups and not racial units. Europeans and Burghers were then included as distinct "castes". Race was made a basis for Census purposes only as late as 1911. Sir Ivor Jennings once remarked that races are "enlarged editions of castes".[28]

The distinctive feature of community segregation in Sri Lanka especially amongst Sinhalese and Tamils is the existence of a relatively strict endogamy within communities or subcaste groups. This same phenomenon applied at some point of time to the Portuguese-Burghers too.

This classification into the category of Eurasians and Burghers does not appear to be based on any scientific system but merely on the admission of the individual concerned whereas in similar ethnic classifications the criterion adopted was father's race. The Burghers were however not differentiated into Dutch or Portuguese-Burgher. This is the case in the most recent Census too. In 1963 there were 46050 Burghers and Eurasians in the whole island and this figure includes the Batticaloa

Portuguese-Burghers too (although not differently categorised). Neveretheless the figure of 1500 (1250 in the urban block and 250 in the rural sector) in the Batticaloa area does not reveal the true position.

Table of Census Figures since 1871

				1000
1871 :	Burghers and Eurasians	15.3	All races	2400.4
1881 :	-do-	17.9	-do-	2759.7
1891 :	-do-	21.2	-do-	3007.8
1901 :	-do-	23.5	-do-	3566.0
1911 :	-do-	26.7	-do-	4106.4
1921 :	-do-	29.4	-do-	4498.6
1931 :	-do-	32.3	-do-	5306.4
1946 :	-do-	41.9	-do-	6657.3
1953 :	-do-	46.0	-do-	8097.9

It may be possible that the Burghers were not divided into the categories of Portuguese and Dutch as a result of the pressure exerted by the Dutch-Burghers who were close to the Government administrators forming an "elite group" so to say. Translator Peters put it very clearly when he says :

> The Portuguese had left behind some of their race, more or less mixed, to whom the Dutch in the early years of their occupation gave the privilege of Burghership. As the number of Dutch-Burghers increased, these dwindled away until the few remaining were merged with the Toepasses and went to form rank and file of the Burghery or trainband.[29]

The Portuguese-Burghers were thus left to neglect and disrepute : the remnants in the main cities were categorised as of menial stock. C.M. Fernando refers to them as "mechanics" and "shoe-makers"[30] which is a local patois only. This position may have been the result of the neglect of this group by the administrators, but it has to be clearly stated that the more affluent of the group conveniently entered the fold of the Dutch-Burgher. At times, as Dr. Colvin R. de Silva remarks :

> The Burghers of Ceylon, condemned to permanent exile, succumbed to greed and degenerated in the adulatory atmosphere of a slave-ridden home.[31]

Nevertheless physiognomically some of them are as fair as the urban Dutch-Burghers while others are darker than the darkest Sri Lankan. Some display African characteristics such as dark curly hair, flat broad lips and other negrito features. As with many Sri Lankan communities instances are not rare of families displaying all these features within the same circle. The port of Batticaloa was used by the king of Kandy as his Eastern maritime outlet so that in order to isolate the king from foreign contacts a fortress was constructed by the Portuguese.[32] The Portuguese garrisons arrived there with Malay, Canarese, Bengalese, Kaffir, Paravar and other troops in addition to Topasses and casados.[33]

But the historical origin of the Batticaloa-Portuguese community cannot be fixed to any such wave of troop movements alone. Although no authentic records of their earliest migrations exist the balance of probability is that they belong to a mixed stock of Portuguese and Portuguese-speaking people who arrived in the island either as soldiers or as casados or even as servants or slaves employed by Portuguese soldiers and officials. Nevertheless many of these people still take pride in tracing their ancestry to Portugal itself though none has been to that country.

Batticaloa-Burgher Community—its location

The Portuguese-Burgher community in Batticaloa live in and around the town and its environs such as the Koolavaddy (Sinna Koolavaddy and Periya Koolavaddy) colony, the Mamangam colony, Uppodai (Sinna Uppodai and Periya Uppodai), the Dutch Bar (sand bar built by the Dutch), the Old Rest House Road and in the heart of the town.

A complex ethnic distribution is noticed among the population in the area. The Tamils constitute the majority. Muslims outnumber the Sinhalese. In fact the Muslims are mostly the descendants of the Moors settled in this region by king Senerat and form an ancient settlement. It is also a significant fact that this is the one area of Sri Lanka where there is a Muslim peasantry.

Both Tamils and Moors play a historical role in the affairs of the Batticaloa region. The early Portuguese settlers were not normally friendly towards the Moors perhaps due to traditional religious rivalry and the commercial competition on the Fishery and Coromandel coasts. Nevertheless as C.R. De Silva points out : "The opinion among the Portuguese in Ceylon as to the question of the Muslims appears to have been less rigid than that in Lisbon".[34] Thus in Batticaloa although the Portuguese-Burgher community as a whole maintained rather distant and sometimes hostile relations with them many perhaps "acting on specific motives"[35] as Joseph Grenier says developed closer relations with the other ethnic groups. This process has continued. For instance the brother of Ronald Rosairo (since deceased) was married to a Sinhalese lady while his father's parentage is traced to Jaffna. Names such as Innacia Manonmani Piregasamuthu and Sebamalai Granvill Roy are the result of Portuguese-Tamil intermarriages. Maureen Jonathan was married to Jehan, a Malay from Colombo.

Although these people could have maintained their social boundaries in intimate situations such as club functions, church weddings, funeral services and the weekly (now monthly) *baila* parties they were however forced by economic circumstances to learn the language of the people.

There are approximately 250 families in the Batticaloa region alone. Some of them migrated to cities such as Colombo and Trincomalee in search of lucrative white-collar jobs whereas several skilled workers among them have taken up temporary residence in places like Valachchenai, Tirukkovil, Akkaraipattu, Ampara, Pottuvil, Chenkaladi and Paluta in Trincomalee. In the circumstances the researcher who selects the central urban area in preference to the outlying settlements where the less affluent sections of the community lives will fail to find the more relevant data in studying the Portuguese-Burghers of Sri Lanka. A comparative study with the other major pockets of Portuguese-creole-speakers of the island[36] will throw much more light on this historical phenomenon which is now fast disappearing.

Immediately after my return from Portugal in 1970 I was drawn to the Batticaloa region as I was at the time working on a thesis on the indigenous theatre for which purpose I had to interview several Tamil folk drama artists in the area. It was during these trips that I came across the Batticaloa Portuguese Union officials led by the late Mr. Rosairo. If the inquiries of the folk theatre brought me to Batticaloa it was the lure of the Portuguese-Burgher community which prolonged my stay there. I was therefore able to gather a great deal of information about these people in a somewhat natural and organic way rather than as an anthropologist or historian working on a specific assignment.

Residential segregation

A list of family names recorded in a *Book of Census* found in the house of Mr. F.W. Ragel of 22, St. Anthony's Street, Batticaloa, provides some useful information to reconstruct a fair picture of the geneology of the Batticaloa Portuguese-Burgher community. It is interesting however to note that there are more names of Dutch or even English origins rather than those of Lusitanian origin. This is probably an interesting aspect of 18th and 19th century social history buried in the fact that the Portuguese creole-speaking people of Batticaloa do not all have Portuguese family names.

Residents in the town area are the more affluent members of this community. Some with substantial means (when taken in a comparative sense) are employed as white-collar workers and school teachers. We notice among them a couple of bank managers, staff officers in Government departments, telephone operators and typists. One or two of them *were* employed in the Police Department as Police Inspectors and Police constables while one *was* an Excise Inspector (since retired from service). There is a medical practitioner and a tide waiter and some insurance agents attached to the Insurance Corporation. My main informant Mr. Rosairo owned a series of small commercial establishments and a tyre rebuilding shop in the heart of the town. This business is now in the hands of his sons who are English educated and hold prominent positions in the welfare organisations of the area. Another son of his is a Catholic priest who had his education in India. Ferdinands is their professional photographer.

Those in the suburbs and in the rehabilitated colony nevertheless eke out an existence and are engaged in sundry jobs such as masonry, carpentry, tinker work, smithy welding and minor house repairs. It is true that these people are skilled mechanics but that is no reason to dub the entire community as 'Mechanics'. Fishing appears to be a communal exercise of those living in and around the Bar road and the colonies.

The late Mr. Rosairo was a Justice of Peace and a distinguished citizen of the area. Mr. Ragel stood for the Municipal Council elections this year.

Unlike their counterparts, the Dutch-Burghers, who successfully migrated in large numbers to Australia, the Portuguese-Burghers have been denied opportunities for international migrations. Because of the extended family system and the interdependency of kinship structures, any inclination towards international migration on the part of a Portuguese-Burgher may often be frustrated by his social and moral obligations to the rest of his family. It was very lately that some of them could find jobs in the Middle Eastern countries but that is a very wide phenomenon in Sri Lanka today, not confined to any race or nationality.

Education

It has however to be noted that none of them now receives an education through the Portuguese language. Since the middle of the last century they received their education in one of the following three schools in Batticaloa : St. Mary's (predominantly Tamil medium), St. Cecilia's (English and Tamil media for boys) and St. Michael's (English medium). In earlier times there had been a Roman Catholic School imparting knowledge through the medium of Portuguese but the maintenance of private institutions could not have been possible without sufficient funds. This school seems to have closed down nearly a century ago.

Since the advent of the British in the latter part of the 18th century their general preference had been to study English, which was a *sine-qua-non* for application to clerical and other white-collar jobs. The Portuguese-Burghers had a better opportunity to study this language especially as they were more closer to the Catholic priesthood which enjoyed privileges under the British administrators. The position however changed when Sinhalese language became the official language with reasonable use of Tamil. A Sinhala Maha Vidyalaya was established in Batticaloa and the Portuguese-Burghers started sending their children to this institution. The other Catholic schools in the area were therefore forced to become bi-lingual. This new development resulted in further cultural interaction.

This however did not dampen the enthusiasm of the Portuguese-Burghers to maintain Portuguese as their mother tongue. In their social gatherings and marriage ceremonies, funeral services and all church services the Portuguese language still predominates. All prayers are sung in Portuguese or Tamil, but not in Sinhala.

Similarly at wedding ceremonies the entire ritual is conducted in Portuguese creole dialect. I have noted how the Tamil partners of these families normally stay away from these ceremonies or if they attend them, keep at a cool distance because they find it hard to accomodate themselves to this type of intimate situation in a meaningful way.

Use of a Script

A majority of Batticaloa Portuguese-Burghers do not know to write in their creole language. I was earlier under the impression that this was due to the lack of a previous script. But new material has come my way which throws new light on this subject. Owing to years of neglect, the very little importance attached to the creolized language outside their orbit appears to have been lost and the dialect was confined to the most intimate situations. The elders would have lost touch with it and the younger members would have through disinterestedness neglected further study. I am aware of attempts made by the Portuguese Burgher Union spearheaded by Mr. Rosairo to rekindle enthusiams of the younger generation in studying the creolized language and the folk literature associated with it. But these attempts appear to have fallen on deaf ears due mainly to pecuniary considerations and lack of economic result.

Nevertheless the present situation is no criterion to dismiss the possibility of the use of a script and literature in Portuguese. The data now available shows that there was a script, not necessarily in a developed form as in Portugal or in Goa but a kind of 'sound language' reduced to a script. This is precisely what Adolpho Coelho described as "Ceylão-Português" and Sebastião Rodolpho Dalgado as "Indo-Português".[37] Referring to a 19th century verse book written in Ceylão-Português reprinted in Portugal Coelho states that the work was first published in a magazine entitled *O Bruffador* published in Colombo. The publication could not be found. But Dalgado gives details about this magazine and some specimens in its content.[38] According to him the magazine was published by the Wesleyan Missionaries of Colombo and its first publication is dated July 1883.[39] I have with me a handwritten manuscript containing some of these stories belonging to the family of Felthmens of Jaffna which was thrown to the dusty attic of one of the town dwellers and came to me through Mr. Rosairo. The manuscript is written in ink and some of the pages are missing while a part of it is defaced. The work contains thousands of verses and I find two stories, "Istori de Urson e Valentyn" and "Istory de Lazarus". The text compares well with the type of writing that we notice in the stories reproduced by Dalgado in the *Dialecto Indo-Português*".

The script displays an archaic type of Portuguese characterised by Dalgado as "A orthographia do crioulo não é exclusivamente etymológica nem sónica ; é um mixto ; um tanto incoherente, de ambos".[40] I would however prefer to characterise the dialect as "sonica" and "coherente" viewed in the context of the times. This type of script is noticed in other Eastern creoles as well. Silva Rego provides us with sufficient examples which we could use in support of this contention. Some specimens are as follows :

"Ta fala Joana sa fila ja fuzibos ja oubi ?
Sim ca ? Bos ta reca.
Eh, nunca, dreito, Antonio nobe esti ja fala com eu.
Paulo, bos nunca sabe, qui ta fica na campo diante di

butica.
Ah ! sabe, eli qui ramedi ta faze ?"[41]

A close look at the Batticaloa Portuguese dialect reveals a kind of 'sound spelling' with a penchant for economy of terms. Following examples will no doubt throw some light on the nature of this dialect :

Alternate use of vowels a/əe/e/a/ə ;e/u ; u,e
Sema ; na/suma : nə (week); MP-*semana* ; resi : bə (receive) MP-*recibe* ; inchi : du/ inche : du (full) MP-enchido ; cursan/ curəsan/cursã (heart) MP-*coracao* ; otro : s/ otru:s (they)- *otros* ; eu/yo : (I) MP-Eu ; esci : sə/ iski : sə (excuse, forget) MP-*esquise* ; me : nus/ me : nis (less) MP-menos

Free phonetic variations of b/v/ ; v/y ; y/j ; g/v/w ; nh/n/n
sa : bə/sa : be/savə/sawe (known) MP-*sabe* ; ba : rbə/ba : rvə/ ba : rbe (beard, moustache) MP-*barba* ; subi :/suvi :/ (climb) MP-*sube* ; bacə/ ba :cə/ va : cə (cow) MP-*vaca* ; acəba :/cava ; / caba : (complete) MP-*acabar* ; bonta : di/ vonta : de (intention, advantage) MP-vontade ; oibi/o : vi/ ouve (hear)MP-*ouve* ; fi : vu/fi : yu (ash-plantain, fruit) MP-*figo* ; ago : re/ avur (now) MP-*agora* ; nu : n/nu : v/nu : k (never) MP-*nunca* i : gre : y/ igre : j (church, temple) MP-*igreja*

Solidifying of phonemes
oya : / olja : (see, look) MP-*olha* ; conse : ju / conse : yu (counsel) MP-*conselho* espi : ju / ispi : ju (mirror) MP-*espelho* ; fi : y / fi : jə (daughter) MP-*filha*

Glossing over and reduction or permutation through elision
a : mana : / amiyan / amiyə (tomorrow) MP-*amanha* ; a :rbore/ a : rvor/avri/ alri (tree, vegetation) MP-*arvore* ; manisa : / ma : nise (day-break) MP-*amanciar* ; ningə/ninge : m (none) MP-*ninguem* ; siri : su/servi : s (service, work) MP-*serviço* ;

Simplification of dipthongs including nasal dipthongs
ba : su/ ba : isu (low, below) MP-*baixo* ; ma : s / mai : s (more) MP-*mais* ; re : (king) MP-*rei*; capitan, kapitã / kapitan (captain) MP-*capitão* ; na : na : (no, no) MP-não não ; cunsa/kumsa

(commence) MP-*começo*

Compounding of clusters

osiya/sinho/siño (You, sir) MP - *o senhor* ; namas (no more) MP - *não o mais :* acalo : re/acalo :rə (then) MP - aquela hora; prə lis (to them) MP - *para eles ;*

Syntax influenced by contact situation

SVO (Subject + Verb + Object) syntax of the MP., (Modern Portuguese) as also of other European language such as E., (English) has not been adhered to. Instead we notice the SOV Subject + Object + Verb) syntax in common with Sinhala (S.,) and Tamil (T.,) being freely employed. In the examples given below MP., is given first followed by Bcr., (Batticaloa creole), S.,T., and for comparison Sk , (Sanskrit), P., (Pali) and H., (Hindi) have been included.

MP - Eu vou a casa (SVO) ; E - I go home (SVO) ; Bcr-Eu ca : sa pə tanda (SOV) ; S - Mamə gedə r əyan əva (SOV) ; T - Na : n viTTə po : ran (SOV) ; Sk - Aham gṛham gaccha : mi (SOV) ; P - Ahaṁ gehaṁ gaccha : mi (SOV) ; H - Mai ghar ja : ta : hu : m (SOV)

Mp - Eu como arroz (SVO); - I eat rice (SVO) ; Ber - Eu aro : s tə cume (SOV) ; S - Mamə bath kanə va (SOV) ; T - Na : n so : ru sa : ppiTuran (SOV) ; Sk - Ahaṁ o : dənam bhunajmi (SOV) ; P - Ahaṁ bhattam bhunja : mi (SOV)

MP—O rapaz leia o livro (SVO) ; E—The boy reads the book (SVO) ; Bcr—Podi : bukku le : s (SOV) ; S—Laməya potə kiyəvai (SOV) ; T—Pillai puttəkan paTikkira : n (SOV) ; Sk—Kuma : ro pustakam paṭhati (SOV) ; P—Kuma : ro potthakaṁ paṭhati (SOV) ; H – Ladka : kita : b padhta : hae i (SOV)

Morpho-syntactic qualities relating to the Dative and Genitive cases

SVOTN (Subject+Verb+Object+Termination+Nominal) syntax as in MP and E has been abandoned in preference to the SONTV (Subject+Object+Nominal+Termination+Verb) syntax of S and T

MP—Eu dou o livro a ele (SVOTN) ; I give the book to him (-do-) ; Bcr—Eu akə bukku eli pə da : (SONTV) ; S—Mamə e : potə ohuTə denəva (-do-) ; T- Na : n ində pustəkattei avənuku kodukere : n (-do-) ;

It is thus seen that the creole is more closer to the syntactical formation of S and T. Following select examples will be more clear :

MP	*Bcr*	*S*	*T*
jantar	Ano:tisu kume:rə	Rəɐ:kəɐ:mə	ira:sa:ppa:Tu
(dinner)	(night, of, food)	(night, of, food)	(night, of, food)
almoço	middiyəsu kume;rə	daval kae:mə	maTTia:nə sa:ppa Ta
(lunch)	(noon, of, food)	(noon, of, food)	(noon, of, food)
frango	gali:nhasə ka:rni	kukulu mas	ko:li iracci
(chicken)	(hen, of, flesh)	(hen, of, flesh)	(hen, of, fiesh)
buscar	encu:lcə oya:	hoyəla balənnə	teTi pa:r
(search)	(inquire, see)	(inquire, see)	(inquire, see)
prepara	ləɐ:sti faya:	ləɐ:sti kərənnə	adukkupannu
(prepare)	(prepare make)	(prepare make)	(prepare make)
agua quente	ke:nti a:vu	aṇn vaturə	suTu tanni
(hot water, water hot)	(hot water)	(hot water)	(hot water)
jovem, nove	pikini ida:i	kuda: viyə	
(young)	(small age)	(small age)	
Quando está pronto	Kvando: ləɐ:sti faya: ?	Kavədadə/lae:sti venne ?	Enne;ram adukku ?
(when it is ready ?)	(when, prepare make ?)	(when, prepare, make ?)	(when, hour, prepare ?)

These examples taken at random (many more left out due to want of space) make it difficult to agree with Smith's contention that "There are several phonological developments in Batticaloa Portuguese which can be attributed to Tamil influence, and *none* which are solely the result of Sinhala influence,[42] although it is true that a large number of vocables of Tamil origin entered the Batticaloa Portuguese. For instance, Smith quotes the following two examples as illustrations to show the influence exerted by the Batticaloa Tamil language on the Portuguese dialect there :

1. "kə podiya:s-pe mule:re nikədə sirwi (BP)—the Bcr.
   ante Pillay-kal-ukku-mu:lə ve:lə cey-r-a-illə (T)"—the Tamil lang.
   ("Those children's brains do not work").

2. "Isti nuw justu isti me: ju:stu fai:" (BP)"
   Itu cari illa itu ta:in cari eNTu "(T)"
   ("They say This isn't right. This is (the) right (thing)")

These two forms are found even among the Sinhalese of the area in almost exactly the same sense and context :

1. "E:kollange mole: hariyətə vəeda kərənne nəe:"
   (Those children's brains do not work well")
2. "Me:kə hori nəe:, me:kəyi hari"
   ("This isn't correct, this (the) correct (thing)")

In view of these circumstances it becomes difficult to suggest only onesided influence. One has to consider both languages and the behaviour of the creole language in normal conversational situations. For instance one notices a strong Sinhala influence on the umlaut pronunciation generally used by the creole-speakers. For instance "ve:l" (honey) is pronounced as "vəe:l", "ve:yə" (old age) as "vəe:yə" and "me:ste" (must) as "məe:stə" thus retaining the Sinhala umlaut pronunciation as opposed to the Tamil. Moreover in the use of the Future Tense the creole usage is cognate with S. rather then T.

Examples : *Will come* *Bcr.*—Lo: vi: *S*—HeTə enəva In both these forms a qualifying adjective is used to indicate the Future while the verb has not been inflected for the Tense. In Tamil it is different. So is it in the verb *Will go*. *Bcr*—Lo: andə *S*—HeTə yanəva. The form *Lo*: is equivalent to the Portuguese word *Logo*.

Similarly the verb is not inflected for Person as well.

Examples : *1st Person*

Bcr—Eu, No:s ANDA (I, We—ANDA)	*S*—Mamə, Api YANəVA (I, We—YANəVA)	*T*—Na:n PO:RAN (I - PO:RAN) Na:nkal POVAN (WE—PO:VAN)

2nd Person

Bcr—Vo:s, Vo:ssu ANDA (You, You all ANDA)	*S*—Obə, Obəla: YANəVA (You, You all YANəVA)	*T*—Ni:r PO:RI:R (You—PO:RI:R) Ni:nkəl PO:RINKAL (You all PO:RINKAL)

3rd Person

Ele, Fles ANDA (He, they—ANDA)	*S*—Ohu, Ovuhu YANəVA (He, They—YANəVA)	*T*—Avar PO:RAL (He—PO:RAL) Avarkal PO:RA:RKAL (They—PO:RA:RKAL)

But normally Case Terminations show the influence of both S and T.

Examples :	*Locative*	*Dative*	*Genitive*	*Ablative*
Bcr—	Ca:santu (Ca:sa+ntu)	Ko:vilpə Ko:vil+pə)	Murukənsu (Murukən+su)	Aki-impə (Aki+impə)
	house, in	Kovil to	Murukan, of	Here, from
S--	Gehi/Geyi (Ge:+hi)	Ko:viləTə (Kovilə+Tə)	Murukənge Murukən+ge	Metəe nin Metəeh+in
	house, in	Kovil, to	Murukan, of	Here, from
T—	Vi:TTilay (Vi:TTi:+lay)	Ku:yilukku (Ku:yil+ukka)	Murukən inray (Murukən+inray)	IngəirunTu (Ingə+irunTu)
	house, in	Kovil, to	Murukan, of	Here, from

The use of the copula indicating any aspectral mood or state or thing compares well with S. and T.

Examples : *Bcr*—Ja: vi: te: m (came and is) meaning 'had come'
S—Ae villa tiyenəva (—do—) —do—
T—Vanirikkəra:n (Came and is) —do—
Bcr—Eli to:rnə ma:l o:mi (He, is come, bad man) meaning "He is a bad man"
S—Ohuəevilla narəkə minihek (—do—) (—do—)
T—Andə Ku:TTə manisan vanda:n (That bad man, came to be) (—do—)

Other usages peculiar to the creole where we notice the influence of S :—

Verbal usages : Vi:

Vi : come *Bcr*—Vi: aki (come here)
S—Enəva meha:Tə (—do—) ;

Bcr—Vo:s minhə juntu vi: (You me with come)
S—Tamuse ma: ekkə enəva (—do—)

Tira : take *Bcr*—Tira: isti (take this)
S—Gannəva me:kə (—do—)
Bcr—Ki bo:s tira ? (You me with come)
S—Monəvadə tamuse ganne ? (—do—) ;
Bcr—Eu lo: da: isti bukku (I will give this book)
S—Mamə dennan me: potə (—do—)

Oya : See, look *Bcr*—Andə oya: (Go, se)
S—Gihillə balənəva (—do—)
Bcr—No:s ung taxi para me:stə oya: (We, a taxi must see)
S—Api taxiyak o:nae balandə (—do—)

Degree of comparison is very different from that of MP and is cognate with Sinhala usage. For example :

	Positive	*Comparative*	*Superlative*
Bcr—	pikini (small)	sinnə pikini (little) small	tudu pə pikini (of all, small)
S—	kuda: (do)	tikak kuda: (—do)	okkoTəmə kuda: (—do—)

(In this, the Superlative appears to be a word-to-word translation of S. into Bcr.)

	Positive	*Comparative*	*Superlative*
Bcr—	gra:ndi	ma:s gra:ndi	tu:do pəgra:ndi
S—	loku	hungak loku	okkoTəmə loku

(Even here, the Superlative displays the same influence as in 'pikini')

There are some forms of expression which cannot be explained other than by referring to the Sinhalese idiom. One such term is "mara:" which is used in the contexts of 'tying something' and 'building or constructing something'. If one were to trace this term back to Portuguese word 'amarrar' both these meanings will not be clear ; in fact the issue will be complicated. The word has to be explained by connecting it with the Sinhalese term 'bañdinəva' which has been used in the context of 'tying' and 'building'.

Examples :

S—Konde bandinəva—Tie the konde or the tiny knot of hair on one's head.

Bcr—Mara: konde —do—

S—Geyə bandinəva—Build the house

Bcr—Casa pa mara: —do—

S—Harəkə baňdinəva—Tie the cow

Bcr—Ba:cə tə mara: —do—

One must not mistake the term 'mara:' as equivalent to the Sinhalese word 'mara:' which means 'to kill'. In fact this mistake cost the life of one of the Dutch Vice-Admirals: Seebald De Weert. It appears that this Admiral and some myrmidons who were the worst for liquor made coarse remarks regarding the queen of Vimaladharma Suriya (1603) whereupon the king bade his attendants to tie him. The words of command were in Portuguese. He said "Mara isto cão",[43] but the attendants who knew only one meaning of the term 'mara' in Sinhalese, that is 'kill', apparently did the needful.

An examination of the Portuguese—Burgher community of Sri Lanka should not be attempted in the way these attendants executed the Sinhalese king's orders so that a repetition of history may be avoided.

NOTES

1. For detailed information, see, Goonatilleka, M.H., "Um Príncipe Cingalês em Coimbra", *Panorama* (Lisboa, 1971) No. 37 : 19-21.
2. "come um meio de trafico", See, Dalgado, Sebastião Rodolpho, *Dialecto Indo-Português de Ceylão* (Lisboa, 1900), XXII, n. 3.
3. Pieris, P.E., *Ceylon, the Portuguese Era* (Colombo, Ceylon, 1913), Pt. I, pp. 406-407.
4. See, *The Ceylon Antiquary and Literary Registrar* (Colombo, 1951), Vol. VII, Pt. I.
5. Trindade, Paulo da, *Conquista Espiritual do Oriente*, (ed) Félix Lopes (Lisboa, 1961), Pt. III : 24.
6. See, *The Ceylon Antiquary and Literary Register*, 1915, Pt. I : 8.
7. *ibid.*, Vol. VII, Pt. I : 47.
8. See, Goonatilleka, M.H., *An Examination of the Sinhala Nadagama*, Ph. D thesis, University of Peradeniya (Ceylon, 1974), ch. I : 48-53.

9. See, Goonatilleka, M.H., "Relações Culturais entre Ceilão e Portugal", *Studia* (Lisboa, 1970), Nos. 30/31.
10. See, Goonatilleka, M.H., "Report made of an interview with the Portuguese-speaking community in Puttalam", Historical Manuscripts Commission, Dept. of National Archives, Sri Lanka, 10th August, 1974.
11. See, for a discussion on 'casados' and mestiços', Abayasinghe, Tikiri, *Portuguese Rule in Ceylon* (Colombo, 1966), p. 13.
12. "mulheres que traziam para povoarem", See, Trindade, (ed) 1961, II, Cap. 22.
13. See, Goonatilleka, M.H., "Two Sinhala Princes at the Court of Lisbon", *The Ceylon Historical Journal,* Dehiwela (Sri Lanka, Oct. 1978), pp. 186-192.
14. Mention must be made of the following missionaries : Pierre Bergoim (1629-1634), José Vaz (1658-1688), Jácome Gonçalves (1735-1742), António Peixoto (early 17th c.).
15. "Senhor da aldeia", See, Trindade Paulo da, (ed) 1961, III, Cap. 43, fl. 874.
16. Smith, Ian R., *Sri Lanka Creole Phonology*, Cornell University, (USA, 1977).
17. Ferguson, Donald, "The correspondence between Rajasinghe II and the Dutch", *The Journal of the Royal Asiatic Society, Cey. Branch,* No. VIII, 1904.
18. See, "Instructions from the Governor-General of Council of India to the Governor of Ceylon, 1656-1685" (tr) S. Peters, Dutch Translator (Colombo, 1908).
19. Coelho, Adolpho, "Os Dialectos Romanicos ou Neo-Latinos da África, Ásia e America", *Boletim da Sociedade de Geografia de Lisboa* (Lisboa, 1880), 2a. série, No. 3 : 157.
20. The following Vocabularies throw much light on the subject : Callaway, John, *A Vocabulary with Useful Phrases and Familiar Dialogues in the English-Portuguese and Cingalese-Partuguese* (Colombo, 1818) ; Godinho, Caetano e Farino, *Vocabulário Chingalático Et Lusitano,* Colombo, undated ; Freres, Garnier, *English-Portuguese, Portuguese-English Dictionary,* Colombo, ? ; Dalgado, Sebastião, Rodolpho, *Dislecto Indo-Português de Ceylão* ; Gonçalves, Jécome, *Vocabulário Português-Tamul-Chingalá*, (ed) Barbosa Machado (Lisboa, 1838).
21. "A armada de que foi Capitão-mor Diego da Silveira partiu de Lisboa a 25 de Março de 1543 e chegou a Goa de 3 de Setembro". See, Trindade, Paulo da, (ed) 1961, XII, fl. 725.
22. See, Trindade, Paulo da, (ed) 1961, III, Cap. 88.
23. For instance Lopo Soares de Albergaria reached Colombo in 1516 A.D. having earlier engaged in a navel exercise off the shores of Africa.
24. See, Peter, W.L.A. Don, *Education in Sri Lanka under the Portuguese,* (Colombo, 1978) p. 260.

26. See, Tennent, James Emerson, *Ceylon, an Account of the Island, Physical, Historical and Topographical* (London, 1859), p. 70, n. 3.
27. *Memoir left by Hendrich Becker, Governor and Director of Ceylon to his successor Isaac Augustyn Rumpf, 1716* (tr. Sophia Anthonisz, Dutch translator) (Colombo, 1914), p. 49, n. 47.
28. Quoted by Sarkar, N.R., *The Demography of Ceylon* (Colombo, 1957), p. 191.
29. *Instructions from the Governor-General of Council of India to the Governor of Ceylon 1656-1665*, (tr. Peters) (Colombo, 1908), p. 6.
30. Fernando, C.M., *The Music of Ceylon* (Colombo, 1904).
31. de Silva, Colvin R., *Ceylon under the British Occupation* (Colombo, 1953), p. 14.
32. See, Silva, C.R. De, 1972 : 66.
33. *Ibid.*, pp. 88-92.
34. *Ibid.*, p. 85.
35. Joseph, Grenier, "The Portuguese and the Dutch in Ceylon", *Dutch Burgher Union Journal* (Colombo), VII : 87.
36. See, Goonatilleka, M.H., 1974 August.
37. See, Coelho, 1880 ; Dalgado, 1900.
38. Dalgado, 1900 ; 108-116, 120-128.
39. Dalgado, 1900 : 80.
40. This was the type of language used by the settlers at the time Dalgado was making his investigation, namely the end of the 19th c. In the words of Dalgado : "muito pessans quem to use iste lingua". See, (Dalgado, 1900), p. 82.
41. Rego, Silva, "A Communidade de Luso-Malaia de Malaca e Singapura", *Actas do V Colloquio International de Estudos Luso-Brasileiros*, 1965, Vol. I ; See also Barbosa, George Morais "Contacto de Linguas", *Boletim da Sociedade de Geografia de Lisboa*, 1965, série 83.
42. Smith, Ian Russel, 1977 ; Dennis B. McGilvray apparently relies on Smith's contentions. See, McGilvray Dennis B., "Dutch Burghers and Portuguese Mechanics : Eurasian Ethnicity in Sri Lanka", *Comparative Studies in Society and History*, Cambridge University Press, 1982, Vol. 24.
43. *Ceylon Antiquary and Literary Register*, VIII, Pt. I.

ANNEXURE I

From a Book of Census found in the house of F.W. Ragel

(Copied by M.H. Goonatilleka in 1972)

1. *Felthman Family*

John Peter Felthman m. Benedicta Paterson

Francis m. fr. Jaffna | Harriet | Ann (Ragel m. fr. Colombo | Mary | Dorah

Ebley Felthman fr. Jaffna m. Ann Ragel

Pauly Mary | Edda | Pithy | Claude | Dorothy | Mutty (b. 2-9-1895)

Claude Felthman m. 1. Blossom Barthelot
2 Emily Weber

Jessy | Vincent | Cyril | Hugh | Donald | Jane | Theophilus Cloe | Ruth Donald (b. 28-4-1915 m. 29-6-1938 m. 29-6-1938)

2. *Sellar Family*

Marnes Jackovis Mathes Sellar m. 1. Mary Nonnochi Barthelot
2. Anna Vincent

Bernard Benny | George Joy | Minnie | Lissie | Joseph Josey (b. 5-10-1878 m. 16-1-1904) | Cyril | Jerol

Bernard Benny Sellar m. Regina Mariya Andrado

Eddy Adolphus | Sonny Sunny boy | Sellor

3. *Casather Family*

Francis Casather (b. 25-6-1890 m. 8-11-1911 m. Emma Ragel (b. 16-11-1893 m. 8-11-1911)

Justin Adolphus, Girlie Mary, Camilus, Violet Mary, Lourdes, Edward, Gladys Mary, Lilly Trodda, Justin

Arthur John Casather 1982 m. Ancilla Mary Teresa de Cruz 1893

Clara Josephine Agnes Francis Stephen John Berchmans Aloysius Teresa Rita Girlies

4. *Regel Family*

John Ragel (b-1-12-1852) m. Lissie de Zilva (Lissie-Elizabeth)

Stany (Stanislaus) Wickwar Joseph (b-27-5-1882 m. 11-6-1908) Kevalee Benedict (b. 21-3-1884 m. 5-1-1920) Ebert

Joseph Jollyboy Ragel (b. 10-10-1878 m. 27-5-1901) m. Victoria Ragel (b. 26-9-1881 m. 27-5-1901)

Victoria Maria Anna Francis Whitley Canicius Lourde Mary Antony Hubert Mary Bertha

5. *Rosairo Family* (Sec, Felthman)

Alick Joseph Rosairo m. Pauly Mary

Ruth, Delicia, Roland, Concy, Ronald Albert, Margaret, Agnes, Aloysius

Note : b=birth m=married d=death

Ronald Rosairo (b. 5-6-1906 m. 5-8-1933) m. Mary Felicia Milrose Ockersz (b. 30-5-1917 m. 4-8-1933)

Harison Joseph, Esmine Lourdes, Stella Irene, Quintus Consie, Winton, Wilson, Agnes Clare, Wesley, Christine, Marcelline

6. *De Zilva Family*

Peter De Zilva (b. 2-6-1899 m. 18-10-1920) m. Luisa De Lima (b. 4-5-1909 m. 18-10-1920)

Teresa, Mary Valentine, Antony, Clarisa

7. *Zilva Family*

Godfrey Zilva m. Magdaline Balthazar

Francis Celestine, Sebastian, Adolphus Patrick, Maria

8. *Andrado Family*

Niclas Andrado m. 1. Francisca Ragel
2. Victoria Ockersz

1. Francisca

Joseph, Seraphine, Clara, Cyril, Basil

2. Victoria

Mabel Richard | Lourde, | Mary Rutty | Cicily | Alphonsus

9. *Perera Family*

Jsolin Joseph Perera (b. 10-10-1887 m. 24-10-1906) m. Margaret Jonathan (b. (?) d. 13-12-1934) (m. 24-10-1906)

Anton Andrew Perera (b. ? m. 29-12-1941) m. Mary Violet Lourdes Casather (b. 3-3-1922 m. 29-12-1941)

Anton | Reginald | Elmo | Halloy

10. *Tenarena Family*

Pietersz Tenarensz fr. Kalmunai m. Mable Andrado

Hendrick | Denzil | Camila | Berny | Anala | Anton (adopted)

11. *Pietersz Family*

Edmund Edwin Pietersz (b. 16-11-1884 m. 1-25-8-1915) m. 2-11-7-1927) m. 1. Constansa Mary (d. 6-8-1926 m. 25-8-1915) 2. Emily Speck (b. 31-10-1910 m. 11-7-1927)

Gertrude | Edward | Benedict Joseph | Constantina | Mary Irene | Mary Emmy | Joseph Antony | Mary Magdaline | Celinda

12. *Vanderhoven Family*

Walter Vanderhoven (b. 11-1-1899 m, 8-7-1926) m. Bridget Sellar (b. ? m. 8-7-1926)

Maro Magdaline | Agnes | Matilda Lilly | Julien | Edith

13. *Sparks Family*

Thomas Spark m 8-10-1894) m. Joesai Elizabeth Lourdes Mary (m. 8-10-1894)

Margaret | Vincent Francis | Mary Lilly | Isene Ruby | Grace

14. *Specks Family*

Edward Ebo Speck (b. 29-9-1875 m ? m. Caroline Joseph (b. 6-7-1874 m. ?

Catherine | John Collin | Vincent Wilson Francis | Mary Magdaline | Nelson Zavion | Clara

15. *Vyse De Lima Family*

Henry Thomas Vyse m. Anna Rachel De Lima

Mary Teresa 'Leena' | Joseph Antony 'Jacky' | Catherine Cicily 'Tiny' | Rebecca Shirly

16. *Wetterbrown Family*

Bobby Wetterbrown m. Jane Hendrick

Regina | Rosalind | Emily | Helistan

17. *Balthazar Family*

John Joseph Balthazar m. 1. Mary Outschoorn
2. Mary de Rosairo

ANNEXURE II

(From Oracans Per Mortes)

Consoladora de afflictos
Soccorro de Christans
Rainha de Anjos
Rainha de Patriarcas
Rainha de Apostolos
Rainha de Martyres
Rainha de Confessores
Rainha do Virgens
Rainha de todo Santos
Rainha concebida sem peccado original
Rainha de Santissimo Rosairo
— *Roga par nos*

Cordeiro de Deos, quem te tira o peccados de mundo - Perdoa nos, O Senhor.

Cordeiro de Deos, quem te tira o peccados de mundo - Benignamente ouvi nos, O Senhor

Cordeiro de Deos, quem te tira o peccados de mundo - Tende misericordia de nos.

Christo ouvi nos.
Christo beniguamente ouvi nos.

Ant Nos te corre por vossa protecean, santa Mai de Deos; nan descuida nossa rogos ne nossa necessidades, mas livra nos de todos perigos sempre. O gloriosa e bendita Virgem.

V Roga par nos, O Santa Mai de Deos.

R Que nos pode fica digno de promissos de Christo.

Rogamos

Inche, O Deos, nossa almas com Teu favor, que nos quem ja ouvi de boca de Anjo e encarnacan de Jesus Christo, Tue Filho, pode, pela sua paisan e morte, fica juntado ne gloria. Amen.

Oracans per fiels quem ja descanca de iste mundo

Nan Tu lembra, O Senhor, per nossa offensos, ou offensos de nosso parentes, nem toma vinganca de nossos peccados.

V Eterno descanco da par ello-tros, O Senhor.

R E desse eterno lume luze sober ellotros.

V Desse ellotros descanca ne paz.

R. Amen.

O Deos Creador e Redemptor de todo fiels da par as almas de Tue servidors defuntos a perdan de todo sue peccados, desse ellotros acha, por nosso rogos, a perdan que ellotros sempre ja desea. Quem te vive e reina por sempre e sempre. Amen.

V. Eterno descanco da per ellotros O Senhor.

— 18 —

R தெஸ்ச ஓ ஆதேயுஸ் த தேயுஸ் ப்றசெந்தா பர் எல்லி/எல்ல அகோற நியாந்தி த சேய ஸெஞோரா.

V செஞோர் தேந்த மிசறிக்கோர்திய பர் எல்லி/எல்ல

R. ஜெஸ்து தேந்த மிசறிக்கோர்திய பர் எல்லி/எல்ல

R. ஜெஸ்து தேந்த மிசறிக்கோர்திய பர் எல்லி/எல்ல

V. செஞோர் தேந்த மிசறிக்கோர்திய பர் எல்லி/எல்ல

(பல்லா பாத்றி நொஸ்சு . ...)

V எ ஞன் தொஸ தெஸ்ச கயி னெ தெந்தசாம்.

R. மயிஸ் லிவ்று நோஸ் து மால்.

V எத்தார்னு இஸ்காலசு தா பர் எல்லி/எல்ல ஓ செஞோர்.

R. எ தெஸ்ச லூமி எத்தாணா லுசி சோபர் எல்லி/எல்ல.

V. த போர்த்த த இமபார்னு.

R. லிவ்று சுல ஆல்ம ஓ செஞோர.

— 19 —

V. தெஸ்ச எல்லி/எல்ல இஸ்கனசா ன பாஸ்.

R ஆமென்.

V. ஓ செஞோர் ஒவி மிஞு ஒறசாங்.

R எ தெஸ்ச மியூ ப்ரேகு செகா பெர் தி

றுகாமுஸ்

பெர் து ஓ செஞோர், நோஸ் தெ எந்றகா அ ஆல்ம த தேயு செர்விதோர் நோ .. .. முறந்து பா இஸ்தி மூந்து கே எல்லி/எல்ல லோ வீ கும் தீ. எ ஒஸ் பெககாதுஸ் கே எல்லி/எல்ல ஜ பயாஸ் ன இஸ்தி மூந்து த ப்றுகுளன்சு த சுவ நசதுவேஸ், பெர் துவா கும் துவ மிசறிக்கோர்திய. பா நொஸ்சு செஞோர் ஜெசுஸ் கிறிஸ்து — அமென

ஓ தேயுஸ், நோஸ் அகோற அக்ஹி தெ சுரு சோபர் அமோர்த்தி த இஸ்தி தேயு செர்விதோர், தா பர் நோஸ் சாம்பிறு பற லெம்பிறு கே நோஸ் தம்பேம மின்த சிகுய பேர் எல்லி/எல்ல, எ தா பர் நோஸ் துவ வன்சு பெற

(From Dalgado's text)

120

Meu piquins non tem perdido,
Masque de o mundo ja vai,
Tórna lo ser ascertado
Ne ceos juntado lo morai.

ISTORI DE REY DE GRIS E MESTRI DOUBAN

(1889)

1

Ne terra de Persia
Zouman chomado,
De um leproso rey
Está governado.

2

Inteiro sua corpo
Cum léper e gafo,
Elle te travia
Per ficá curado.

3

Bastanto mestris
Moito ja travia,
Per o leproso rey
Nompódi cura.

4

Bem capas um mestri
Ne-terra ja chegá
Elli sua nomi
Douban te chomá.

5

Elli foi um hómi
Um grandi prendido,
Bastanto lingos
Elli tem sabido.

6

Syriano e Hebreos
Persiano e Arabic,
Turco e Latin
Tambem lingo de Grik.

7

Todo isti lingos
Elle tem sabido,
Javi ja chegá
Isti hómi prendido.

8

De dovensè de rey
Elli ja ouvi,
Seu nehum resia
Per palaso javi

9

Per grandis de palaso
Jadá per sabê,
Logo leva per elli
Diante de rey.

10

Fazê curtesia
Ja ficá impido
Té pidi cum rey
Mande dá ouvido.

(*From an old Mss in Batticaloa*)

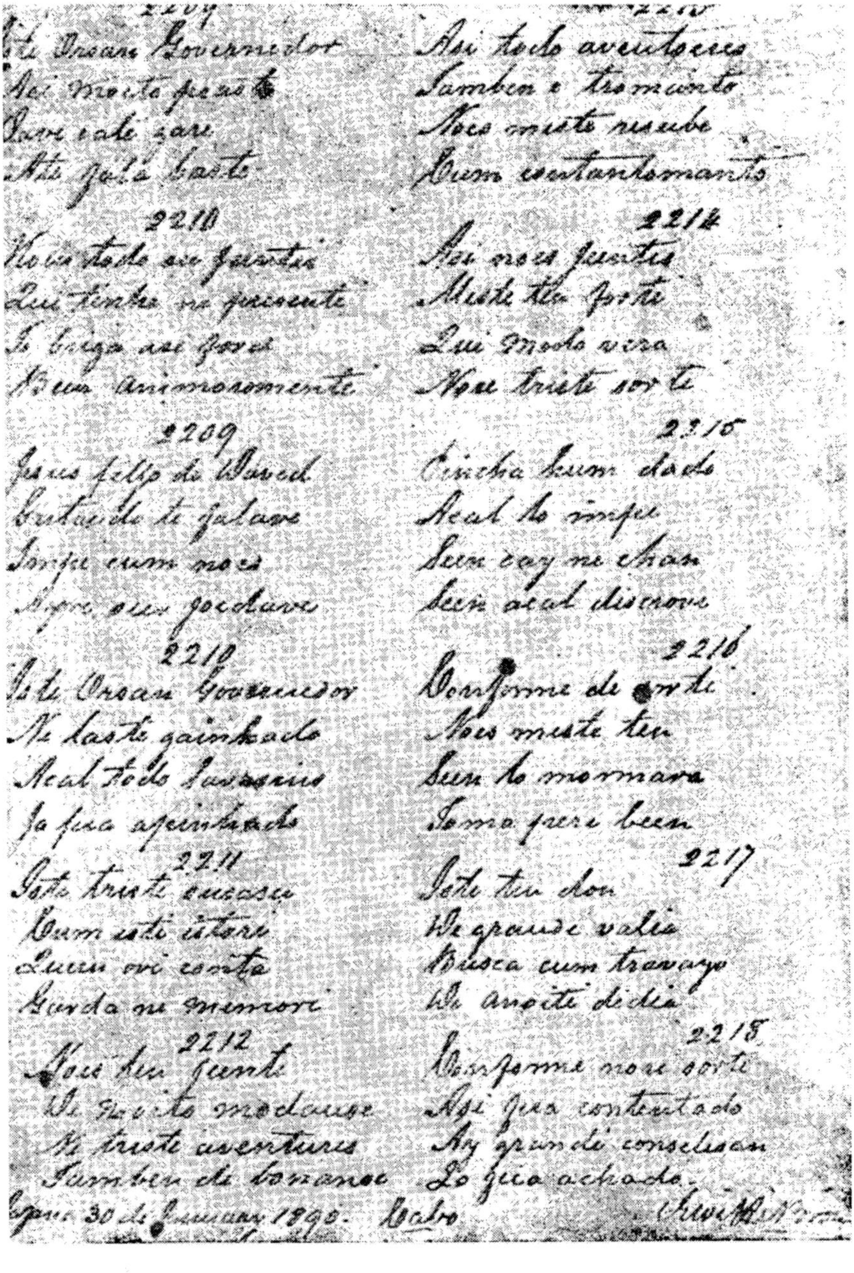

2207
Este Orsan Governedor
Nos muito penso
Ouve este zare
Ate gala baste

2208
Nosso todo ajuntes
Lei tinha na presente
Te broga nos Gozos
Bem animosamente

2209
Jesus filho de David
Entrado te galavra
Sempre cum nos
Pope nos peccadore

2210
Este Orsan Governedor
Ne laste gainhado
Acal todo sucessos
Ja fica apuntado

2211
Este triste ocasan
Cum este istore
Quem ovi conta
Guarda na memori

2212
Nos tem gente
De muito modanse
Ne triste aventures
Tambem de bonanse

2213
Asi todo aventures
Tambem e tromento
Nos muito recebe
Bem contentamento

2214
Nos nosso gentes
Muito tem forte
Lei modo vira
Nos triste sorte

2215
Cricha bem dado
Acal to impe
Bem cay ne chan
Bem acal discanse

2216
Conforme de sorte
Nos muito tem
Bem to mormara
Tomo pera bem

2217
Este tem don
De grande valia
Busca cum travayo
De noite de dia

2218
Conforme nos sorte
Asi fica contentado
Ay grande conclusan
Lo fica achado.

Iapur 30 de Januar 1890. Catro [illegible]

Annexure-IV (Cont

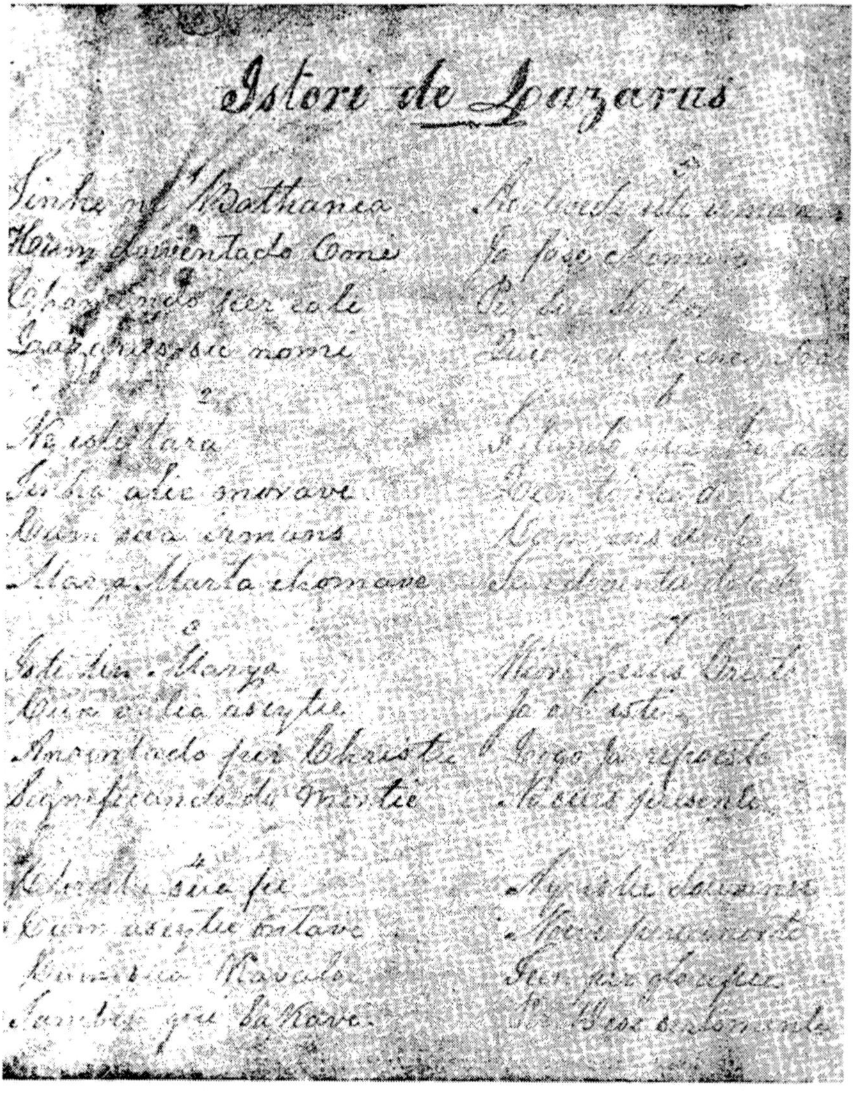

Istori de Lazarus

Tinha na Bathania
Huma aventado Ome
Chamando ser ele
Lazarus esse nome

2

Na istu tara
Tinha ale morave
Quen sua irmans
Maria Marta chamave

3

Isto hun Maria
Qum ali aseytie
Anuntado per Christu
Significando da mortie

4

Christu sua fe
Cum aseytie tratave

14

The Image of Goa[1]

CAROLINE IFEKA

EUROPEANS visualise Goa as a verdant paradise lapped by sparkling seas, swept by cooling winds and showers; Goa the Golden, clinging like a limpet to the edge of a hot, tropical hinterland. The Golden Goa vision is unequivocal in its radiant clarity.

Goa Dourada is a remarkably resilient ideology transplanted onto Indian soil by a southern European civilisation struggling for long against the Moors and an interventionist Castille and perhaps in consequence becoming deeply imbued with an idealistic, sometimes bucolic romanticism, tempered by a certain quiet stoicism.[2] Those great poets of the Age of Expansion, Camoes and Gil Vicente, convey in many a lyric and verse the intelligentsia's yearning - fanned by the great discoveries of Vasco da Gama and his successors—for life lived in a distant land (and therefore remote from close, critical inspection) whose people dwelt in pastoral simplicity, at peace and in prosperity.

> And now land was close at hand, the land so many others had longed to reach, that lay between the Ganges, sprung from the earthly paradise, and the Indus. Take courage, my brave men, who have set your hearts on the Victor's palm. You have arrived : the land of wealth abounding lies before you.[3]

Goa is 'golden' in another sense too. The epithet is popularly believed to refer to the gold which adorns the altars, pulpits and images of cathedrals in Old Goa and churches in Ilhas and Bardez that the conquerors built in rapid succession,[4] wonder-struck worshippers gazing at them in awe.[5] Others[6] though imply that such term as 'Goa Negra' may be more appropriate on account of the colour of the labour force which dug up the gold and which helped build Old Goa's religious houses and places of worship. Whatever the case, *Goa Dourada* is a most compelling image for many Goans of all walks of life who believe theirs is a special land—not an Indian land but of India, not Hindu but 'really Catholic, a tiny piece of Catholic Portugal transplated onto tropical soil.

This writer does not set out to trace the genesis and development of the Golden Goa vision or to outline its impact upon a people's self image and, equally important, upon the writing of Indo-Portuguese history. Perhaps others more qualified than myself will pursue the line of enquiry suggested below and undertake the necessarily pains-taking research. My purpose is somewhat different. The discussion that follows takes a closer look at aspects of life in the *Estado da India* that at first seem to mirror the *Goa Dourada* image. The results of this brief enquiry do not confirm, rather they challenge the historical accuracy of the Golden Goa vision and suggest another way of looking at the *Estado da India.* Hopefully this perspective, a new idea about how to look at Goa, will help generate fresh interpretations of Portuguese India in times past and present.

Goa : 'Limpet' Port ?

In the age of sea-borne discoveries several European powers resorted to the strategy of establishing and maintaining 'limpet' ports ; some were convict settlements as in eastern Australia or St. Helena, others were intended to be trading posts and military camps. Blainey[7] has stressed the maritime importance of location in the Australian case where, as Allen[8] notes, the British set up several 'limpet' ports in northern Australia 'to solve the problem of distance from the commerce of the Indian Archipelago'. On their part, the Portuguese congratulated themselves greatly on capturing Goa for it was destined to become the capital of their Indian empire. Goa provided the Portuguese with a deep water port, refuelling facilities, steady access to the pepper and horse trade and hopefully a lucrative outlet for European luxury goods. As Barros once wrote,[9]

> A ilha em si é terra graciosa e de boas águas, e não alagadiça, mas empolada com alguns capeços, que gazem a maneira de vales, fértil de todalas cousas que se nela plantam e semeam.

By the mid-sixteenth century the Portuguese had evolved several kinds of settlement, from the fortified to the unfortified, The fortified ports (*fortalezas*), principally Old Goa on the Mandovi river and Vasco da Gama close to the Zuari river, constituted the commercial and political centre of the Estado da India ; then there were trading factories (*feitorias*) all along the western coast which were generally unwalled and only lightly defensible ; lastly there were small forts (*praças*) like Cabo da Rama in southern Goa which were built at the head of a promontory overlooking the mouth of a major inland waterway. These forts, often equipped with only one or two cannons, were intended to secure access to inland waterways for ships sailing in and out to distinations east and west of Goa, as well as the Viceroy's customs officers and the militia. Goods produced locally were transported down river to coastal entrepots while imported goods of European provenance as well as goods manufactured in India were carried upstream. Some writers[10] have called these three kinds of coastal settlement a *talassocracia*, sites held together by Goa's economic role in the region as a sea-based power.

This perspective is nicely attested in two maps of the sixteenth and seventeenth centuries (reproduced in Baião).[11] Linschoten's (c. 1599) depiction of the port, the river Mandovi and the city of Old Goa nestling at the foot of the western Ghats, is true to the seaward image. Note the prominent position given to the Indian ocean, the river Mandovi and the endless convoy of caravels and *naos* entering the deep water channel. True to the *Goa Dourada* image, Linschoten's drawing (reproduced in Baião) [12] of the market-place (*mercado*) abutting the Rua Direita transforms the *mercado* into a place where anyone who was anybody assembled. Here rank-conscious members of an hierarchical colony convey to one another their station in society through their mode of transport, dress and comportment. Portuguese, not Indian, notions of hierarchy constitute the organising framework. However, although outwardly Iberian in content—the Portuguese imposing their hierarchies on indigenous patterns of social interaction—this market-place is Indian in form. For Indian markets, as illustrated in Sinha[13] and Pereira [14] are also places where local dignitaries, merchants and low caste hawkers assemble, dress and occupation distinguishing one and all in terms of their various castes. In respect to form and function, then, there is little to differentiate an Indian market-place from the Portuguese-imposed *mercado*.

Although the *mercado* reflects a seaward conception of Old Goa, Indian princes saw the city and the surrounding districts of Ilhas, Bardez and Salcete (the 'Old Conquests') rather differently. The Nayar potentates, the Sultan of Zamorin, and the dreaded Shah Adil Khan of Bijapur regarded Goa as an extension of their land-based empires which needed access to the maritime trade between western India, Arabia and Malacca.[15] They, and the Maratha kings two centuries later, tried every now and then to wrest Goa from the Portuguese. More often than not, though, they were content to control trade routes that connected their kingdoms to the Indian Ocean through entrepots like Old Goa. Thus did these satraps, Muslim and Hindu, shape in ways known as yet for limited areas only of the Konkan coast[16] (and for particular commodities destined for the European market, that is, pepper, silks, cotton) the economic development of the region and the terms of trade. These, through a chain of transactions, connected producers along the coast and far inland to local merchants, and thence to agents buying for the Portuguese, who in turn oversaw the transhipment of gods to European and Arbian markets.[17] Political upheavals notwithstanding, the *Estado da India* and neighbouring states traded over the years to their mutual advantage. In the fifteenth century Goa received exports from the Bahmani kingdom of Bijapur and the Vijayanagara empire. Two hundred years later Goa imported from them wheat, meat, horse feed, and rowers for 'oared boats'.[18]

Here, then, is some evidence that Indians going about their everyday business on the land and in the market-place saw Goa in landward terms. The historical flaws in the 'limpet port' conception are patent. Some years ago Disney[19] and Ashin das Gupta[20] argued for radical rethinking about the landward contribution to the maritime economy of the Konkan. The latter writers note especially the dismal dearth of published material on commercial networks and exchange systems that linked different kinds of producers to one another and to merchants buying goods intended for sale in overseas, coastal and inland markets. They might also have added that Goa extended inland through trade and not the church. But commentators from 1510 onwards have been faithful for the most part to the *Goa Dourada* image.

Hierarchies and houses

By the eighteenth century or so travellers and administrators were glossing over divisions amongst the rural population, forsaking the realities of factionalism for an ideological view of the Goan village. It is typically described as follows. The village comprised a *communidade* of ranked co-parcenors[21] living according to their allotted status in happy harmony,[22] *gaonkars* (shareholders in the land and its products) and *mundkars* (non-shareholders) cultivating the rice fields, *gaonkars* distributing annually to families their portion of the village rice harvest and of fruits garnered from coconut and cashew trees. Assuredly is this image richly documented in many a traveller's description of life in these verdant districts of the Konkan, as it is in household sketches and faded photographs depicting the Goan gentry at home.[23] The old century houses of well-to-do families in Ilhas, Bardez and Salcete, the elegant rosewood furniture in recoco style, the verdant gardens aflame in bougainvillea speak more strongly than mere words. Several generations of *colonados* and their descendants enshrined for posterity in a Portuguese family name, country mansion and town house their image of the Goan happily adjusted to life in a plural society where continuity not change, consensus not conflict, became the dominant *weltanschaung*.[24]

As is well known Afonso Albuquerque, Governor of Goa

from 1509-1515, did much to foster this notion, so that the white, brown and black races could live in harmonious interdependence : different but equal in their mutual distinctiveness, each needing the services of the other. This *jajmani* model of race and ethnic relations rationalised political inequalities and perhaps facilitated widespread acceptance among elite Christians especially of Albuquerque's policies, which would result in the majority of the population assimilating to the culture of a dominant minority committed to Portugal. The policy of assimilation, though, remained an ideal ; as Boxer[25] has argued, it was doomed to failure. For did not Lisbon retain control over the metropolitan and viceregal levers of power ? Did not the missionary orders remain very much under the control of headquarters in Lisbon and Rome ? Little wonder, then, that paler-skinned Goans were apt to justify their priviliges by invoking their Portuguese and not their Indian ancestry.

The harsh underbelly of *realpolitik* aside, cleavages within the Indian population also ensured that assimilation would remain a chimera—perhaps the chimera of the Indo-Portuguese world. On the whole Goans holding senior government positions in any period of Portuguese rule have hailed from Brahmin and Kashatriya castes ; though some, perhaps, may have been recruits from the ranks of the Sudra population who, donning Christian and Kshatriya names, were accepted after a couple of generations or so. High ranking men and women would in all likelihood have claimed that they were of Indo-Aryan descent and by comparison with the Sudra castes and the untouchables were 'white' complexioned.[26] Persons of aboriginal descent or low caste status could be distinguished by their physical appearance, their dark brown to black skins, their family and clan names, their occupational calling within the *jajmani* system.[27]

Portuguese artists of the eighteenth and nineteenth centuries were well acquainted with these beliefs about the Indian population of Goa, and some sketches reprinted in Baiao[28] demonstrate Portuguese sensitivity to Indian hierarchies. A sketch of an Indian trial by fire,[29] reminiscent perhaps of the Inquisition's relentless pursuit of heretics during the seventeenth century, is of interest on account of the artist's assiduous attention to dress and physique as symbols of racial difference. The unfortunate (low status) miscreant is distinguished from his amply proportioned (high status) judges on account of his headgear and skinny body, while his judges confidently bare their curly locks to the world's gaze.

Outsiders reporting on their travels along the Konkan, and industrious priests (Jesuits and Franciscans), played an important part in supplying information to the Viceroy and his officials about the aboriginal peoples, lower caste Christians and Hindus of all castes. Those intrepid travellers of the fifteenth and sixteenth centuries Linschoten, Abdur Razzaq, Nuniz and Conti—recorded for posterity many south Indian customs which later generations of scholars subsequently 'assimilated' into their own commentaries. And in the process they frequently switched the original writer's interpretative focus into one that accorded well with the *Goa Dourada* image. Compare for example Linschoten[30] who writes detachedly of the 'Kurumbars', Goa's 'aboriginal' farmers or Gaudes, with the account by D'Almeida Azevedo,[31] a ninteenth century writer who romanticises the 'Chorumbins'; while some contemporary renderings of the 'Aboriginal Kunbis' reflect an even more idealised perception.[32] Note the slide from careful description to accounts that reinforce the central assumption of the Golden Goa vision, that all the races and ethnic groups live in happy harmony. The peaceful and gentle 'Chorumbins', for examples, exemplify the European and high caste Hindu stereotype of the 'happy savage'; thus this stereotypical image reproduces the *Goa Dourada* vision.

Compared to the highly idealised generalities about Goa's different peoples that more recent reporters promulgate, these early writers are careful to present the inhabitants in their daily social context – living in houses, cultivating rice fields, and marrying off their children. We also learn something of the variation in customs between districts. Consider now Linschoten's account written in 1583 of the tribal people he calls 'Kurumbar' or alternatively 'Canarin', who lived in Karnataka and the sonthern Konkan. He reports:[33]

> The Canariins and Corumbiins are the Countrimen, and such as deals with Tilling the Land, Fishing and such like

> labours . . . They are in a manner blacke, or of a darke browne colour, many of them Christians, because their chief habitation and dwelling places are on the Seaside, in the Countries bordering upon Goa, for that the palm-trees does grow upon the Sea coasts, or upon the bankes by River sides.

Kurumbar houses were described by Linschoten as being little straw huts with low doors and a pit or hole in which to bear rice.[34] People of modest means and the wealthy residents of communities along the Konkan coast lived in houses built of bricks and burnt tiles.

A Karnataka inscription[35] dated A.D. 1372 emphasises that houses were built according to standards and rules laid down in sacred texts. The inscription runs thus :

> Five foundations, . . . domes, pinnacles, crests and the sixteen signs of the original house, the signs of the sacrificial hall, the sign of the pit for consecrated fire, the sign of slopes, according to standard rules, for these and all other signs.

According to Hocart[36] Indian cities were often planned so that one main street ran from north to south while the other street ran from east to west. The streets formed a cross, a gate marking each cardinal point. The king's palace usually faced east, as should the residence of a god, while the four major varnas were assigned as follows : the Kshatriyas to the east, the Vaishyas to the south, the Sudras and artisan to the west, and the Brahmans to the north. Prior to the nineteenth century caste communities and the varnas in south India were often openly identified with the right or left hand, but today this division is more covertly expressed. Throughout 'right and left country,[37] people used to associate right with high rank and left with lower rank *jati*, but as Beck[38] recounts for south India a *jati* of the Kshatriya varna, for example, ranked as being of the left hand in relation to the Brahmans but of the right in relation to the Vaishyas.

It is, however, unclear whether Goan Hindus built their houses according to the ritualised precepts recounted above, since the written record is equivocal regarding the extent to which various castes might have practised the sacred precepts when constructing houses. Nonetheless Bragança Pereira[39] found evidence that in more recent times the two and four fold division had been important among Maratha *jati* in Goa. Bragança Pereira describes in some detail habitations common among caste Hindus in the 1930s, and supplies illustrative materials. Consider, for instance, Bragança Pereira's[40] photographs of some prosperous Maratha families and their commodious houses. Though casual inspection suggests that the houses might conform to the design noted by Hocart for south India, we are not told in which direction the houses are located, so until further research is carried out nothing definite can be said. We can note, meanwhile, Bragança Pereira's account of house building. When folk are about to commence building in earnest they chant the 'north-east song' while digging the first hole, and bury in the prescribed ritual manner coagulated milk and seven different kinds of vegetables. 'Este canto Nordeste passa a ser o lugar sagrado da casa', writes Bragança Pereira,[41] implying that in the 1930s at least building was still conducted according to ancient precepts which stress the sacred meaning of right and left and the fusion of epiphenomenal divisions in the ultimate unity of 'The One That Is'.[42]

These reports on Hindu house styles and rituals highlight the importance of the four cardinal points : it would be easy to conclude that Hindu houses are very different to those of the Catholic gentry. But were we to look no further we would be falling into the same trap as awaits those whose critical faculties the *Goa Dourada* image stifles. Information from southern Salcete villages today suggests we should pursue the matter for a while yet.

Here,[43] abutting high caste quarters, we find low caste Hindu families living in dwellings whose starkly simple interiors follow a similar design to those inhabited by low caste Christians, whose houses in general are located in a separate quarter. In Hindu and Christian homes the kitchen is situated at the back of the house beyond the sleeping area. It abuts the well and toilet shelter and frequently faces east while the balcony and verandah look west to the setting sun. Though anthropologists[44] do not tell us if particular zones in Goan houses are identified with the four cardinal points, we can be confident that the eastwards orientation of the kitchen area amongst and Christians of low and high castes is a well established preference which accords with beliefs about the four cardinal points important in both religions. Consider, for instance, Hindu precepts concerning the sacred status of fire and of those activities associated with it, in this case food preparation and consumption. As Veena Das[45] notes for Hindu domestic rites in general. 'The sacred fire is placed to the east of house for the rituals of marriage, pregnancy, rituals of childhood and initiation'. But Christian families too regard the east as symbolically powerful, the especial source of creative energy or Spirit, the Godhead. Do not the high altars of the churches and great Cathedrals in Salcete, Ilhas and Bardez face towards the east while the massive doors front westwards ?

Heertz[46] demonstrated very tellingly in his study of lateralism that right and left in Indo-European cultures are always associated with superior and inferior ranked groupings or individuals, man and woman included. The four cardinal points are also identified symbolically with ranked statuses. Very likely this parallel orientation towards east and west among Hindus and Christians indicates some striking similarities in self images and culture orientations. It seems the similarities have always been present, independently of the policy of assimilation, but helping to fashion a Goan identity that is hardly in accord with the *Goa Dourada* vision of the races living in harmonious interdependence and striving to become 'Portuguese' Goans. The evidence on house-styles supports our findings above, namely that there are major flaws in the historical adequacy of the *Goa Dourada* image. As said earlier, according to this image the races are interdependent but different : the inhabitants of the Old Conquests were *either* Hindu or Catholic. (There is nothing Hindu about the converted Goan.) But history tells otherwise. For information about house-styles and market-places suggests there is another kind of Goan, a person whose heritage is a culture that is both Christian *and* Hindu ;[47] a man or woman who personifies *Goa Indica.*

This can be demonstrated in respect to sacred images to

be seen today in the churches of Old Goa, Ilhas and Bardez. Consider the image of St. Joseph in the church of Espirito Santo Ilhas.[48] The carver has emphasised the physical concomitants of assimilation, for the visage combines features from both races. A familiar member of the Catholic hierarchy of saints is imaged as 'Goan' man, one who is *both* Indian and European. Then there are images of angels—so exuberant and unmistakeably Indian – adorning pulpits in the great cathedral of Bom Jesus and elsewhere. On the other hand some images are very European in appearance, specially those fashioned during the baroque and neo-classical periods ; for example, the figure of St. Ignatius Loyola (founder of the Society of Jesus) encrusted in gold and towering over the high altar and basilica of Bom Jesus.[49] The interesting point is not so much the existence of religious objects reflecting now a Hindu, now a Catholic and sometimes a syncretic vision of the holy, but rather what these objects tell us about the artists and their times. We know these men were Christian converts, so they would be expected by priests and the faithful to abide by Iberian-Catholic conceptions of form and style. Consequently a carver would have to suppress his Indian-Hindu sensibilities. The artists presumably believed this to be so as did the missionary orders commissioning these works of art ; had they scented the least taint of anything Hindu the works would have been rejected. The artists, then, did not see themselves as producing Indian or Hindu-derived images. But in point of fact they were producing figures whose visages portray European and Indian features. This is hardly surprising, for the similarities between Hindu and Catholic cultures, which existed prior to contract, favoured the evolution of not just a Portuguese society but a nice working out of the Portuguese and the Indian.

Goa Indica

The purpose of this essay had been to critically examine a dominant image of the *Estado da India* by exploring aspects of life that seem to mirror the *Goa Dourada* image. But rather than confirming, the results of this enquiry challenge the image's historical accuracy whilst also printing the way towards a different conception of Goan culture, one that emphasizes the Indian contribution to Goan identity.

Although historians researching matters of time and place would be disinclined on account of their training to accept house styles, church images, and maps of ancient fortifications as historical evidence, it does seem that the kind of materials used here do enable one to test time-worn verities : because such data are 'new' (compared to the official documents favoured by Indo-Portuguese historians) one achieves a fresh perspective. Ashin das Gupta[50] argued at the first seminar in this series that historians should be more sceptical about the values and world views enshrined in their documents, especially those papers 'at the top of the pile'. These, administrators often tailor to conform with their elite perceptions of events and so they are attractive to historians because they seem more 'complete'. Das Gupta suggests that scholars sifting uncritically through public papers perpetuate interpretations of the past that accord with views of Goan society regarden 'from the top down, (*Pace Goa Dourada*). Perhaps we can avoid some of these value-laden traps if only we realise that conventional research methods are ill-suited to the problems discussed here which confront scholars interested in exploring the interaction between the land and seaward factors in Goa's past, and eager to reconstruct the *weltanschaungs* and social practices of the people.. For Das Gupta archival research will always be important, but maritime historians should also be able to apply techniques that lie 'on the edge' bordering the disciplines of history, anthropology and demography.

Like Das Gupta I am interested in combining the skills of the anthropologist and the historian so we can fashion research techniques that can cut beneath dominant images and expose hitherto 'muted' perceptions and patterns of social organisation. In this regard the advice of Mare Bloch merits the careful attention of anthropologists as much as historians. In the prolegemna to *The Historian's Craft*, Bloch[51] writes.

> The variety of historical evidence is nearly infinite. Everything that man says or writes, everything that he makes, everything that he touches can and ought to teach us about him.

And so the new historian will surely be someone who looks.

beyond the dusty pile of official documents to other texts and even to the field. He or she will be able to read, write, and speak the local languages, not only in order to give access to documents in Marathi and Konkani but to acquire some insight into self images and cultural orientations that language enshrines. Speech idioms, house styles and religious art are all instances of vernacular sources that can challenge time honoured truisms. These all comprise Bloch's 'nearly infinite' variety of historical evidence.

These 'vernacular' sources also point to important differences between on the one hand the kind of man depicted as being 'Goan' in the *Goa Dourada* image, and whom the carvers believed they were representing in figures made for Old Goa's great cathedrals, and on the other hand 'Goan man' as imaged in the carvers' minds. *He* was certainly not cast in the Portuguese Goan mould. Evidence considered above suggests many people in the past and today think they are Portuguese Christians when in reality they often behave and think in ways that indicate they are Indian Christians. Christian Goans see no contradiction in this, nor did they in the past, for being blind to one's enacted (as distinct from one's self elected) identity is part of being human and is an essential aspect of the real Goa, *Goa Indica.*

NOTES

1. I wish to thank Barbara Fisher for very helpful and detailed comments on earlier draft of this paper, participants at the third ISIPH, Panjim, for their suggestions, and James Urry for persuading me to think further about images of Goa.
2. Bell, A., *Portuguese Literature*, (Oxford, 1970), pp. 67-8, 132-55; Oliveira Marques, A.H., de., *Daily Life in Portugal in the Late Middle Ages*, (Madison, 1971), pp. 154-81.
3. Camoes, L., *The Lusiads*, (Harmondsworth, 1952) Canto VII, Stanza 1, p. 161.
4. Azevedo, C. de., *Arte Cristã na India Portuguese*, (Lisboa, 1959).
5. Azevedo, C., Goa Dourada e Outras Imagens de Goa, in *O Heraido*, (Panjim, 18-5-1983), p. 2.
6. de Souza, T.R., *Medieval Goa*, (New Delhi : Concept, 1979), pp-93, 157-8, 184-6.

7. Blainey, G., *The Tyranny of Distance*, (Melbourne, 1966), pp. 82-96.
8. Allen, J., Port Essington—A Successful 'Limpet Port' ?, *Historical Studies*, (Melbourne, 1971-3), Vol. 15, p. 342.
9. Barros, J., *Asia. Segunda Decada*, (Lisbon, 1945), p. 189.
10. See Azevedo, C., Porto-Patela, in *O Heraldo*, (Panjim, 24-5-1983), p-2, quoting C.R. Boxer.
11. Baião, A., Cidade, H. and Murias, M., *História da Expansão Portuguesa no Mundo*, (Lisboa, 1939), Vol. 2, p-90.
12. Baiao, A. *et al.*, *op. cit.*, Vol. 3, p-73.
13. Sinha, D., *Culture Change in an Inter-Tribal Market*, (Bombay, 1978), fac. p. 64.
14. Bragança Pereira A., *Etnografia da India Portuguesa* (Bastora, 1940), Vol. 2, p. 188.
15. Logan, W., *Malabar*, (Government Press, Madras, 1951), Vol. I, pp. 294-318 ; Panikkar, K.M., *Malabar and the Portuguese*, (Bombay, 1929), pp. 23-5.
16. Disney, A., "The Portuguese Empire in India, c. 1550-1650", ed. Correia-Afonso, J., *Indo-Portuguese History*, (Bombay, 1981), pp. 148-150.
17. Cf. Kulkarni, A.R., *Portuguese in the Deccan Politics*, (Panjim, 1983), 3 ISIPH, mimeo ; Shastry, B.S., *Socio-Religious Impact of the Portuguese on Karnataka : Some Observations*, (Punjim, 1983), 3 ISIPH, mimeo.
18. Pearson, M., *Coastal Western India*, (New Delhi : Concept, 1981), pp. 77-8.
19. Disney, A., *op. cit.*
20. das Gupta, A., "Some Problems of Reconstructing the History of India's West Coast from European Sources", ed. Correia-Afonso, J., *op. cit.*, pp. 174-*et. seq.*
21. Cf. D'almeida Azevedo, A.E., *As Communidades de Goa*, (Lisboo, 1890), pp. 81-13 ; Xavier, F.N., *Bosquejo Historico das Communidades*, (Bastora, 1903), Vol. 1, pp. 26 *et. seq.*, pp. 146-150.
22. Da Fonseca, J.N., *An Historical and Archaeological Sketch of the City of Goa*, (Bombay, 1878), p. 20 ; Bragança, Pereira, A.B., *op. cit.*, pp. 261 *et. seq.*
23. Cf. Bragançe Pereira, A.B., *op. cit.*, Vol. 2, p. 82 ; also this writer's field notes.
24. Rodrigues, L., *Cancoes Populares*, (Bastora, 1899).
25. Boxer, C.R., *Race Relations in the Portuguese Empire, 1415-1825*, (Oxford, 1963).
26. Cf. Boxer, C.R., *Mary and Misogyny*, (London, 1975), pp. 68-84, on preferences for marrying 'white' in sixteenth and seventeenth century Goa ; *vide* photographs of forebears in Salcete houses in which the honourable lawyer, doctor, priest or entrepreneur is notably pale-skinned.
27. Cf. Xavier, F.N., *op. cit.*, pp. 78-81.
28. Baiao, A., *et. al.*, *op. cit.*, Vol. 3, p. 200.

29. Baiao, A., *et. al.*, *op. cit.*
30. Cited in Saletore, B.A., *Social and Political Life in the Vijayanagara Empire*, (Madras, 1934), Vol. 2, p. 47.
31. D'Almeida Azevedo, *op. cit.*, pp. 19-19.
32. Cf. Mascarenhas, A., A Tourist's History of Goa, in *Boletim do Instituto Menezes Bragança*, (Panjim, 1981), No. 129, pp. 73-95.
33. Saletore, B.A., *op. cit.*, p. 47.
34. Saletore, B.A., *op. cit.*, p. 266.
35. Saletore, B.A., *op. cit.*, p. 293.
36. Hocart, A., *Kings and Councillors*, (Cairo, 1936), p. 247.
37. Hocart, A., *op. cit.*, p. 267 ; also Das, V., *Structure and Cognition*, (Delhi, 1982), pp. 142-146.
38. Beck, B., *Peasant Society in Konku*, (Vancouver, 1972), pp. 7-16.
39. Bragança Pereira, A.B., *Etnografia da India Portuguesa*, (Bastora, 1904) Vol. 2, pp-40, *et. seq.*
40. Bragança Pereira, A.B., *op. cit.*, pp. 82.
41. Bragança Pereira, A.B., *op. cit.*, pp. 83.
42. Rawson, P., *The Art of Tantra*, (London, 1973), p. 38 ; Reymond, L., *My Lile in a Brahmin Family*, (London, 1958), p. 124.
43. Noted by this writer during fieldwork in southern Salcete during 1983.
44. Cf. Bragança Pereira, A.B., *op, cit.*
45. Das, V., *op. cit.*, p. 104. 'Brahman is food' records Zaehner, R.C., *Hinduism*, (Oxford, 1966), p. 51. Also on food see Dubois, Abbe, J.A., *Hindu Manners, Customs and Ceremonies*, (Delhi, 1906), pp. 245 *et. seq.* On fire see Dubois, *op. cit.*, po. 549-552.
46. Heertz, R., *Death and the Right Hand*, (London, 1961).
47. Cf. Newman, R., *Goa : The Transformation of an Indian Region 1961-1981*, (Mimeo. Monash, Melbourne).
48. Marg, *Golden Goa*, (Bombay, 1980), pp. 24-4.
49. Marg, *op. cit.*
50. das Gupta, A., *op. cit.*
51. Bloch, M., *The Historian's Craft*, (Manchester, 1976), p-66.

15

Diogo Ribeiro's Vocabulario da Lingoa Canarim and its Historical Significance

ROCKY V. MIRANDA

Vocabulario da Lingoa Canarim is a Konkani - Portuguese and Portuguese-Konkani dictionary compiled by Diogo Ribeiro in Salcete, Goa, in 1626. Konkani is referred to as Canarim in early Portuguese writings. The full title of the work describes it as a dictionary of the Konkani language compiled by the fathers of the Society of Jesus who reside in the Christian settlement of Salcete and newly augmented with various modes of expression by Fr. Diogo Ribeiro of the same Society.[1] Neither the original version nor the enlarged version prepared by Diogo Ribeiro was ever published.

Diogo Ribeiro was a Portuguese Jesuit, who came to Goa in 1580. He is also known for his revision of Thomas Stephens' *Arte da Lingoa Canarim* (printed in Goa in 1640) and for a work on Christian doctrine called *Declaraçam da Doutrina Christam* (printed in Goa in 1632). He died in Goa in 1633.

The manuscript of Ribeiro's *Vocabulario* found in Central Library (formerly, Biblioteca Publica de Nova Goa), Panaji, was for a long time the only known manuscript. However, in 1973, Junta de Investigações do Ultramar published in Lisbon a seventeenth-century Konkani dictionary called *Vocabulario da Lingoa Canarina Com Versam Portugueza*.[2] In his preface to this *Vocabulario*, Faustino Noronha de Almeida stated that it might be the work of Diogo Ribeiro. A close examination of the two works shows that the work published by Junta de Investigações do Ultramar is a revised and enlarged version of Ribeiro's *Vocabulario.* Noronha de Almeida also reported in the same preface that the Ajuda Library in Lisbon had a manuscript entitled *Vocabulario* (Canarim) *da Lingoa da Terra, Composto pelo Padre Diogo Ribeiro da Companhia de Jesu do uzo do Padre Amaro de Azevedo tresladado a sua custa.* A photocopy of several pages of this manuscript was supplied to me by Lee Webster of the Department of Spanish and Portuguese, University of Minnesota. A comparison of the photocopied material with the corresponding material in the Central Library manuscript shows that the Ajuda manuscript is not a mere copy either. The person charged with the task of transcribing Ribeiro's *Vocabulario* for Fr. Amaro Azevedo has apparently made several alterations and revisions. However, it is evident that both the 'Junta' manuscript and the Ajuda Manuscript are based on Ribeiro's *Vocabulario.* In 1982, professor L.A. Rodrigues of Santa Cruz learned about the existence of some dictionary manuscripts at the Government Higher Secondary School, Panaji, which belonged to the library of the old Liceu Nacional Afonso de Albuquerque de Nova Goa. When he went to examine them, he found among them one entitled *Vocabulario da Lingoa Canarim, feito pellos Padres da Companhia de Jesus que residião na Christandade de Salcete e novamente acressentado com varios modos de falar pello Padre Diogo Ribeiro da Companhia.* Anno 1626. According to his report, the text of this manuscript does not differ from that of the Central Library manuscript of the *Vocabulario* in any significant way.[3] So, according to our current knowledge, two manuscript copies of Ribeiro's *Vocabulario* have survived. Both of them are in Panaji, Goa.

Only the Konkani Portuguese part of Ribeiro's *Vocabulario* will be discussed here. It consists of about 14,000 principal lexical entries. The Latin tradition has been faithfully followed in this work in citing the various parts of speech. The nouns are cited in the nominative singular followed by the oblique singular suffix. In Latin, the nominative singular is followed by the genitive singular. It should be noted, however, that the Konkani oblique, having evolved from an earlier genitive, often indicates the genitive case without further marking. Konkani nouns preserve the arbitrary three-gender system of Indo-European, but their gender is not specified in the *Vocabulario.* However, the gender of nouns in Konkani can be determined in almost all cases from the nominative singular and the oblique singular suffix variants that are given. The adjectives are cited in the nominative singular masculine, followed by the nominative singular feminine, and the nominative singular neuter suffixes. The verbs are cited in the first person singular present. Their Portuguese glosses, however, are in the infinitive form. The orthographic representation used in the *Vocabulario* is adequate for the Konkani phonemic contrasts except for the indication of contrast between the single and the geminate consonants.

The *Vocabulario* was compiled prior to the earliest European grammatical studies on other languages of India. Among the earliest studies on other Indian languages. *Naauwkeurige Beschrijvinge van Malabar* (Exact Description of Tamil) of Philippus Baldaeus appeared in 1672, the Tamil-Portuguese dictionary of Antão de Proença was compiled in 1679, *De Lingua Hindustanica* of Johannes Keteaer was written originally in Dutch but was published in a Latin translation in 1743, and *Vocubulario em Idioma Bengalla e Portuguez* of Manuel da Assumpção also appeared in 1743. Ribeiro's *Vocabulario* is, therefore, a valuable document for scholars interested in the earliest phase of European Indology. It takes us back about 150 years before Sir William Jones made his pronouncement on the relationship between Sanskrit and the classical languages of Europe. It is of value as primary source material not only to scholars interested in the history of Konkani and other Indo-Aryan languages, but also to those who are interested in the cultural history of the region since Ribeiro provides a great deal of information on the customs and beliefs of the people.

In illustrating the usage of the lexical items, Ribeiro has—copiously cited Konkani idiomatic expressions and sayings.[1]

Âmbăttu. y. ă. Sour. *Âmbăttă khăe tăcheă gălleădde ddhăe.* One who eats something sour burns his throat.

Angă â Body. *Angă mărnu.* Exerting oneself. *Angă kădditâ.* To shudder. *Angâmellu.* Sexual union.

Anta or *Antăgollâ.* Entrail. *Zăche ăntă zălla, tăcho ddollo găllă.* One whose insides are hurting, has tears flowing from his eyes.

Baỳ. ī Well. *Băĩtu păddălălo zhăddă rămpătâ.* One who has fallen into a well looks for a branch to grasp. Metaphorically, it is said of someone who has gotten into some difficulty and is looking for some means to free himself.

Bhâiră Outside. Also, *Bhâiri. Bhâiri sărătă.* To go outside. *Bhâiră băissătă* To defecate. [lit. 'sit outside']

Bhâkăry. ie. Rice cake. *Châkăry korũchy, bhâkăry ghăũchy.* Whoever wants to eat bread must work for it. The idle do not get to eat bread. Trout are not caught with dry breeches.

Kânkănnă. â. Bracelet. *Hâticheâ kânkănnâkă ârsso nălâgă.* A mirror is not necessary to see the braclet on the hand, or what is obvious need not be demonstrated.

The following three entries show how the early Christian missionaries borrowed terms connected with Hindu religious beliefs and adopted them for Christian religious concepts :

Deuăchâru. â. Devil. [originally, 'a wandering spirit', 'a malevolent spirit']

Yemăkonddă. â. or *Yemăpury. ie.* Yama's pit, taken for hell in popular usage. (Yama is the Hindu God of the dead. The standard term for hell among the Konkani Christians today is *Yɛmkī:d*)

Vâincuttă. â. Celestial paradise (originally, abode of the Hindu god Viṣṇu) *Bhumv - văincuttă.* Paradise on earth (Christians use the tern to refer to the Garden of Eden].

The following items are samples of lexical entries connected with Hindu religious beliefs alone.

Archănă. â. Homage paid to the deity in four ways : *Archănă, Văndănă, Puzănă, Stăuănă.* In *Archănă* one cleanses his own body by bathing. *Văndănă* consists of external homage done with the hands and body. *Puzănă*, bathing, anointing, and incensing the idol. *Stâuănă* laudation.

Auătăru. â. Appearance or form taken in incarnation which is attributed by the Hindus to their gods. They appear in the world taking one form or another in order to fight a battle or slay a demon. On this, many stories have been invented, especially concerning the god Visttnnu [sic], to whom ten incarnations are attributed or which nine have already taken place and one is yet to come about.

Bălli y. Sacrifices the Hindus perform by beheading an animal. As a threat to an adversary, one says : *Tuzy bălli dină.* 'I will sacrifice you' or 'I will decapitate you.'

Yugă. â. An age of the world. The infidels posited four ages, the first called Cretâ, the second Tretă, the third Duâpără. the fourth Kăli. They attribute to each age an infinite number of years—as many as they wish—and invent stories which they would have liked to have happened in those ages.

Entries like the following shed light on the customs and social organization of the Konkani people at the time.

Bâmănnu. â. Brahmin. Also, the husband of a Brahmin woman.

Dântăuăddo. eâ. Cake made when a child is teething.

Tillu. a. Sesame. *Tillă ânchăle.* The sesame stuck. It is a custom among the Hindus to put sesame on the forehead of the newlyweds. If it sticks it is said that they will live in harmony. When there is discord between husband and wife, it is said : *Hâncă tillă băre ânchăle nânti.* [=The sesame did not stick to them well].

Vărnu. â. Color. Also, differences of caste of which there are four : Brămhâ, who are Brahmins and priests. Khetry, who are fighting men like Chararos and others. Văissè, who are Baniyas ; Sudra, who are Choudiris, Curumbis, Mahars and Shoemakers. [The subcastes listed under *Sudră* are problematic. The curumbis consider themselves superior to the Sudras. The other three groups are generally considered inferior to the Sudras].

The *Vocabulario* contains extensive information on the state of Konkani vocabulary and grammatical structure around 1600. The Konkani vocabulary of the time included numerous loanwords from various languages : Sanskrit, Kannada, Persian and Arabic. Some of these are no longer found in the modern Konkani dialects. The extent of Kannada influence on the Konkani of this period is noteworthy. The modern Konkani dialects of Goa have very few Kannada loans. On the other hand, the Konkani dialects spoken by the people who left Goa after the Portuguese conquest and migrated into the Kannada region have a large number of Kannada (and Tulu) loans. One might conclude from this that the Konkani speakers in the Kannada region picked up the Kannada loans found only in their dialects after the migration. However, this hypothesis turns out to be incorrect. The numerous Kannada loans in *Vocabulario* make it clear that Konkani had already borrowed extensively from Kannada prior to the migration of Konkani speakers to the south. Before the Portuguese conquest, Goa was for a long time under Kannada rulers. After the advent of the Portuguese, however, there was not much contact between Goa and the Kannada region. The Konkani dialects of Goa must have lost most of the Kannada loans during this later period.

The items given below are representative of non-Sanskritic loans found in the *Vocabulario.* Like most other India languages, Konkani borrows from Sanskrit in an open-ended fashion. No samples of straighforward Sanskrit loans are included here.

Bărăită. To write. *Bărăpă.* Writing. *Bărăpy.* Scribe. One who can read and write. (<Kannada *Bare* 'write').

Bidi. y. Street. *Bidītuleână.* Through the street. *Bidinăbidi.* From street to street. (<Kannada *bidi* <Sanskrit *vithi*)

Chilă. â. Bag. (<Kannada cīla).

Mâtu. u. Discourse, matter. Mâturi âdd*ă* *Yetă* or *vetă.* To interrupt a discourse. *Hy thoddy matu.* An insignificant matter (<Kannada *mātu*)

Bărkătă. â. Prosperity. Peace. (<Arabic barakat)

Dâru. ue. Gunpowder. (<Persian *daru*)

Dărzy. iâ. Tailor. (<Persian *darzi*)

NOTES

1. *Vocabulario da lingoa canarim feito pellos Padres da Companhia de Jesus que residem na Christandade de Salcete, e novamente acressentado com varios modos de fallar pello Padre Diogo Ribeiro da Mesma Companhia*-Anno 1626.

2. This is an anonymous work and has no date.
3. Professor Rodrigues notes that this title is identical to that of the Central Library Manuscript of Ribeiro's *Vocabulario* except for the substitution of *residão* for *residem* and for the omission of *mesma* before the final occurrence of *Companhia*. See note 1 for the full title given in the Central Library Manuscript.
4. In the *Vocabulario* samples quoted here and later on in this paper, Ribeiro's Portuguese glosses are given in English translation. All notes and comments added by the author of this paper are within square brackets. It should be noted that, in the case of the principal lexical entries, Ribeiro cites the nouns in 'direct' singular form followed by the oblique singular suffix. The adjectives are cited in the masculine direct singular form followed by the feminine direct singular and the neuter direct singular suffixes. Equivalents in modern phonetic transcription for special symbols in Ribeiro's transcription may be given as following :
   ă : [ə]
   â : [ă], *-i-* : [-i-/-y-], *-i* : [-ĩ], *-y* ; [-i]
   -u- : [-u-/-v-], *-u* : (-ũ], -û : [u]
   c, k, q : [k], *ch* : [tš] before front vowels and [ts] elsewhere, z : [dž]/[dz] (with distribution of [dz] and [dz] parallel to that of [tš] and [ts] and *s* : [š]/[s] (with distribution of [š] and [s] parallel to that of [tš] and [ts].

16

The Writings of Francisco Luis Gomes

HENRY SCHOLBERG

INTRODUCTION

FRANCISCO Luis Gomes was at once a child of the French Revolution and of the Church. He was a romanticist who loved liberty and a moralist who judged the world around him against the ethical standards of his Roman Catholic faith.

His life story

He was born on 31 May 1829 in Navelim, Goa. His father, Francisco Salvador Gomes, was a physician and civic leader.

In 1850 at the age of 21, or in 1846 at the age of 17 (depending on which biography one reads), Francisco Luis, a precocious child by any standards, was graduated from the Medical College in Nova Goa and started practicing medicine and involving himself in civic affairs as his father had done.

Finally, in 1860 he stood for election to the Portuguese *Cortes* from the constituency of Margão. He served in the *Cortes* until his death 25 September 1869 at the age of 40 years, three months and 25 days.

His major works

It was during the period of his incumbency in the *Cortes* that his principal works were published. More complete bibliographic citations will appear at the end of this paper, but listed here in chronological order are the first editions.

His first major works were in Portuguese : *A liberdade da terra e a economia rural da India Portugueza* (1862) and his only novel, *Os Brahamanes* (1866.)

The next two were in French : *Essai sur les thoéries de l' économie politique et de ses rapports avec la morale et le droit* 1867 and *Le Marquis de Pombal : esquisse de sa vie publique* (1869).

One sees by these titles a versatile man : economist, novelist, agriculturalist, political scientist, lawyer, biographer and historian.

These are his major works. In addition, we have some of his speeches in the *Cortes*, some letters to his friend Lamartine and articles he wrote for various journals. His first published work was a 34-page pamphlet entitled *De la question du coton en Angleterre et dans les possessions portugaises de l' Afrique occidentale* (1861). His unpublished works include an account of a voyage from Goa to Bombay and a Konkani grammar dedicated to Joaquim Heliodoro da Cunha Rivara 1800-1879).

The Marquis de Pombal

Sebastião José de Carvalho e Melo, Marquis de Pombal (1699-1782) was Portugal's eighteenth century strong man. He was controversial in his liftime, and he is still controversial.

It is axiomatic that most biographers fall in love with the subjects of their biographies. Not so Francisco Luis Gomes. He managed to remain reasonably objective in his treatment of Pombal, admiring the totality of his influence and effect on the history of Portugal, but making severe moral judgements about specific measures the Marquis took.

Whether his judgements were right or wrong and whether his total assessment of his subject was correct are moot points. The point is that the biography remains a standard work on Pombal.

Pombal was born 13 May 1699. Little is known of his early life and education. In 1738 his public career began with his appointment as ambassador to London. He distinguished himself enough in this position to be appointed in 1745 to mediate a dispute between the Pope and the queen of Hungary and Bohemia.

Ween Dom José I ascended the throne of Portugal five years later, Carvalho was appointed Minister of war and Foreign Affairs. He came into a premier position in the government following the Lisbon earthquake of 1 November 1755.

During this period of supremacy he encouraged monopolies as a means of improving the economy, expelled the Jesuits from Portugal, reformed the educational system, decreed that natives of Portuguese Asia were equal before the law to Portuguese born in Portugal, instituted reforms in public finance, waged war against Spain and France and reformed the administration of the Estado da India.

He became Marquis de Pombal in 1770.

At the death of Dom José I in 1777 Dona Maria I ascended the throne, deprived Pombal of his several portfolios, banished him from Lisbon and instituted a legal investigation into his deeds during his time of power.

His enemies descended on him and his last years were spent in fighting them off. He died 8 May 1782, five days before his 83rd birthday.

Gomes is quick to proclaim Pombal to have been a great man, but not a good one. That he undertook to write a biography of him within 100 years of his death was in itself an act of courage ; for Pombal was still controversial – more so than he is now, 200 years later, and somewhat less so than in his lifetime. After all, descendants of the nobility he had persecuted were very much alive, and the Society of Jesus which he had expelled in 1759 had returned in 1814.

The first sentence of Gomes' introduction tells all : "La biographie d'un ministre est toujours une oeuvre morale et politique."[1] Note the word "morale."

Equally revealing of Gomes' approach is the last sentence of the last chapter : "Sa gloire et sa grandeur souffrent des torts qu'il causa á ses prochains et des moyens qu'il employa "[2]

It would be unfair to say of Gomes that he was playing a double game with his biography : extolling Pombal's greatness for his admirers while exposing his faults for his detractors. Gomes was too honest and up front for this kind of intellectual acrobatics. It would be fairer and more accurate to say that

Gomes was primarily interested in the truth. To prove this he went to the archives of both Portugal and France to base his writing on primary documents.

There are several incidents in the career of Pombal that excited Gomes and which he described in some detail : the Lisbon earthquake, the Porto riots, the attempted assassination of Dom José, and the expulsion of the Jesuits.

Pombal was propelled into power by the Lisbon earthquake of 1755 or, rather by the masterful way in which he restored order following it. His ascendancy enabled him to institute measures which he considered necessary for the prosperity of the country. One of these measures was that of farming monopolies, and one of these monopolies was in the wine industry where Pombal established the Wine Company of the Alto Douro.

The provisions under which the Company operated made it illegal for the citizens of Porto to purchase wine other than that of the Company, even that which was locally produced. This created a hardship for local producers and a severe inconvenience for local consumers.

A riot broke out early in 1757 which prompted Pombal to institute a judicial inquiry. These proceedings resulted in the incarceration of 478 persons, 32 of whom were acquitted and 21 of whom were condemned to death on charges of treason.

Gomes regards this whole sordid business as a blot on the career of Pombal. To add to his infamy in this case, he sought to prove that Jesuits were the instigators of the Porto riot. No such evidence was found, outside of Pombal's correspondence, and no Jesuit was brought to trial or convicted.

The attempted assassination of the king 3 September 1758 gave Pombal an excuse to rid himself of some of his enemies, decrease the power of the nobility and bring the Jesuits into disfavour. The accused were the ex-Duke Aveiro, the Marchioness of Tavora who involved her husband and two sons in the plot, and the Jesuit fathers. All conspirators were executed—some in a particularly gruesome way—except the Jesuit fathers. A different fate awaited them.

In 1761 all Jesuit property in Portugal was confiscated to the crown, and 53 Jesuits accused in the assassination attempt on the king were executed. Their alleged leader, a 73-year-

Italian priest, Fr. Malagrida, was hanged and the others burned at the stake in the Rocio. In 1759 the Jesuits were expelled from Portugal.

Gomes shows us in Pombal a man of good intentions, but one who did not always use goods means to realize his good intentions. He allows him the virtues of patriotism, honesty and genius, but is not blind to his faults : "Bon administrateur, mauvais politique, Pombal ne fut pas un heureux legislateur."[3]

We would be remiss in our duty at this the third Seminar on Indo-Portuguese History if we did not touch on Pombal *vis-á-vis* Goa and on what Gomes has to say about this facet of his career.

The Estado da India received from Pombal "une protection presque paternelle."[4] Pombal was offended by the grandeur with which the viceroys surrounded themselves. This may have been tolerable at an earlier time, but not in the late eighteenth century. He instituted a number of reforms, but unfortunately Gomes does not tells us what these reforms were. He sums them up in one sentence : "Ses diverses lois sur les finances, sur l' administration civile, sur l' organization de la justice, et sur les rapports des indigènes avec les Européens peuvent constituer un véritable code indien."[5]

It has already been mentioned that Pombal decreed that natives of Portuguese Asia were equal before the law to Portuguese born in Portugal.

We have discussed Gomes the biographer. Let us now turn to Gomes the novelist.

Os Brahamanes

Gomes was quite modest about his ability as a novelist. "V. exa. sabe que não sou romancista,"[6] he says in his dedicatory letter. Why, then, did he write it ?

He wanted to tell about Anglo-Indian society as he saw it and apply the principles of liberty and equality to it in order to say what was wrong about it and to say what was right about it. If one does so on the pages of a newspaper, his writing is thrown out with the garbage within 24 hours. Ah ! But if one writes a novel, there is a chance it might last.

There are two Brahmans in this story : a British Brahman and an Indian Brahman. The British one, an Irish tobacco planter of Fyzabad, Oudh, named Robert Davis in the fourth chapter manages to insult the Indian one, Magnod, by flinging a plate of roast beef in his face. Magnod is so overcome by this offense to his person and his religious beliefs that he leaves his wife (who hangs herself) and children and joins the Thugs in order some day to seek vengeance.

In a spirit of remorse Davis, with the help of a Portuguese missionary, undertakes the upbringing in England of Magnod's children, a boy and a girl. They return to India as young adults, and the girl has an affair with Davis' young and villainous cousin Richard. To these characters are added : Davis' niece who grows up with the Magnod children in England and a mysterious Jew whose behaviour is a source of bewilderment to the community in Fyzabad—as well as to the reader of the novel.

The ending is a surprise, not in the O. Henry mould, but in a manner that is less of a surprise if one appreciates that the novelist is an incurable romantic.

How does one review *Os Brahamanes* if one is reviewing it, say, for the *Navhind Times* or *Statesman* ? Is it highly readable ? Yes. Absorbing ? Yes. Does it hold the reader's interest throughout ? Yes. Is it believable ? Well, yes. But the ending is a little difficult to swallow. Does the author have something to say ? Oh, yes !

It is not just the principles of the French Revolution which he proclaims here when he attacks Brahmanism of both the Hindu and British variety. He has no time for gambling : "O jogo é a contração de todos os vicios em um só."[7] He would transform the theory of equality into the reality of custom : "De que serve a igualdade teórica e legal quando ela não penetra até aos costumes ?"[8] He saw through the hypocrisy of those nations of Europe who call themselves Christian nations : Dizem que a lei de Cristo rege a cililisação europeia. Mentira. Ilumina-lhe a superficie e não lhe penetra as entranhas."[9] If he were living today, he would not number among those of his compatriots who see the Indian Mutiny of 1857 as "India's First War of National Independence." He called it "A Revolta dos Sipais." Here is how he distinguished between a revolt and a revolution : "A revolta foi o sipai ; a revolução seria o povo ; a revolta foi a vingança ; a revolução seria a ideia ; a revolta foi o fero Oisnu ; a revolução seria o brando Siva."[10]

A Liberdade Da Tarra

Francisco Luis Gomes was always close to Goa, spiritually and mentally. His novel took place in Bihar ; but he mentions Goa several times, and one of the principal characters was a Portuguese missionary. His biography took place in Portugal, but he found space to discuss his subject's concern for Estado da India. It has been mentioned here that among his unpublished work is a Konkani grammar.

But *A liberdade da terra* was the only book he wrote on Goa itself. It is a short book, 102 pages, written in Portuguese and published in 1862 in Lisbon.

The theme of the book is that a citizen should have the right to own land and dispose of it at will. He opposed the concept of village, convent or state ownership of land. One must conclude that if he had been born a century later, he would have walked with Vinoba.

The book begins with a description of Goan agriculture as he new it. This is one of the earliest such accounts recorded. He finds Goa to have been blessed by its rivers with an excellent system of natural irrigation, but cursed with a system of farming that is both ancient and incompetent.

He then proceeds to estimate the value of annual production of the land, but his figures are not notably reliable because he arrived at them partly through guess work.

He next goes into the issue of land tenure. He finds that village communities claimed large tracts of land because in the early days land could be cleared only by cooperative effort. He notes that much land is owned by religious associations (both Christian and Hindu), agricultural groups, the state and a sort of landed gentry.

Gomes proposed a system a laissez-faire and of depriving the state of land ownership.

The chief value of this book is its description of the agricultural situation in Goa in the mid-nineenth century, not in the idealistic, romantic and impractical measures he proposed for its reform.

ESSAI SUR LA THEORIE D'ECONOMIC POLITIQUE ET DE SES RAPPORTS AVEC LA MORALE ET LE DROIT

This book is in two parts : one on political economy and the other on the relation of economics to ethics and law.

Gomes sees work as the basis of wealth, and he defines work as action which results in utility. He defines value as an economic quality that has to do with how much a piece of merchandise can cost, not with how much it does cost. Capital is the accumulation of wealth used for production. He distinguishes between money and currency and says that money should be considered as merchandise. He considers credit to be the lever of production ; and production, he believed, should have freedom of labour, capital and right. In short, he believed that economic freedom was the quickest way to Utopia.

As to the part on political economy as it relates to ethics and law, Gomes has three chapters : the first on the principles of ethics, the second on the principles of law, and the third on the links which connect the economic science with the moral science and with the science of law. That Gomes would treat each of these elements—economics, morality, and law—as sciences is in itself noteworthy.

Morality he describes as the truth. In so doing he admits that not all men are capable of arriving at the truth. And how does one arrive at the truth ? One arrives at it, apparently, through the intellect. How it is that one moralist's moral principles might differ sharply from another moralist's moral principles Gomes does not say.

However, he does arrive at the conclusion that duty is the principle of morality. "Ethics," he says, "is the science of duties, and its principles, perceived by reason, and revealed to us by conscience."[11]

"Law," Gomes finds, "is justice outside its moral source," and he adds: "Law can be . . . defined as the science of the relations among men touching the exercise of their liberty."[12] He recognizes his right to prevent another man from infringing on his liberty. It is the law which must protect both his rights and his neighbour's rights.

This is how he sums up the difference between morality and law :

"La difference qui existe entre la morale et le droit peut se résumer dans les points suivants ; (1) La morale considére le motif pour lequel une action est accomplie, le droit regarde l'action en elle même : l'une envisage plutôt l'acte dans sa source, l'autre dans ses effets. (2) La conscience est le suel juge de le moralité ; mais, comme le droit se laisse reconnaitre extérieurement, on peut établir des lois sociales applicables à chacun par une autorité constituée ; c'est à dire, le droit de chacun peut etre distingué. (3) La morale est une science formelle et subjective ; le droit, au contraire, est une science matérialle et subjective ; il s'attache à l'acte et ne soucie pas de l'intention."[13]

In his chapter on "The Concordances," those "links conneting the economic with the moral science and with the science of law".[14] Gomes finds that "the economic principle is based exclusively on the following principle . . . : buy the maximum pleasure with the minimum of pain ; be happy".[15] And he finds that "as a man is subject to the necessity of physical laws, so he cannot stray at his will from the moral and social laws".[16]

If there is faultiness in Gomes' reasoning, it may be in his belief in the scientific definition of ethics, economics and law and in his belief in the universality of moral and legal behaviour. For example, he is quoted above as saying that law regards the act but does not care about the intent (see footnote 13). This may be true of Portuguese law, but it does not hold for Anglo-American law where intent can be an important issue in determining one's guilt or innocence.

Miscellaneous works

There are two writings outside of Gomes' major works which deserve mention at this point : his celebrated letter of self-introduction to Lamartine who died, by coincidence, in the same year as Gomes and his equally celebrated maiden speech in the *Cortes*.

The Lamartine Letter. Alphonse de Lamartine (1790-1869) won recognition as a leading romantic poet as early as 1820; but he became involved in government during the revolution of 1848, and his popularity went into decline. It was in this period that Gomes addressed his letter to him. It is said that upon reading it Lamartine "broke out into exclamations of delight and admiration".[17] In his declining years Lamartine published a number of books in order to pay off his debts and ultimately died in poverty.

In the first paragraph of his letter, written in Lisbon 5 January 1861, Gomes says he was born in India, "once the cradle of poetry, philosophy and history, and now their tomb".[18] He then boasts of belonging to "that race which composed the *Mahabharata* and invented chess".[19]

He admits to having read everything Lamartine wrote and expressed the desire to go Paris some day. That day came six years later, and Gomes and Lamartine finally met.

The letter is fascinating as a show piece of Gomes' romantic style and as a statement of his belief in the ideals of the French Revolution and in his love of his country. "I ask for India, " he said, "liberty and light".[20]

The Maiden Speech was delivered 18 January 1861, just three days after Gomes had taken his seat in the Chamber of Deputies. It seems the member from Madeira had made a speech in which he argued that since Great Britain did not permit colonial representation in the *Cortes.*

In his address Gomes paid tribute to England as a great nation which "was the first to unfurl the constitutional flag,"[21] but went on to urge that Portugal not imitate England's motives for refusing native representation in her Parliament. He then points out that the great Pombal had insisted there be no legal distinction between the natives of Goa and those of Portugal.

He then called the members' attention to the fact that he himself represented a civilized and educated constituency, and he believed that it had a right to be fairly represented in the law-making assembly of Portugal.

CONCLUSION

Was Francisco Luis Gomes a forerunner of the Indian Independence Movement? Perhaps. We have already quoted from his letter to Lamartine: "I ask for India liberty and light." What did he mean by "light"? Understanding? The ability of rulers to rule with enlightenment?

Was he a forerunner of the Goan Independence Movement? In his lifetime he worked for political and social reform in Goa, but he never actually pleaded for independence from Portugal. But if he had lived a hundred years later, he very well might have.

BIBLIOGRAPHY

Books—by Gomes

Os Brahamanes : romance.—Lisboa : Gazeta de Portugal, 1866.
xi, 314, iv. p. ; 17 cm.

Os Brahamanes.—2. ed.—Nova Goa : Livraria Académica, 1928. 288 p. ; 19 cm. —(Obras completas ; I).

Os Brahamances : romance.—3. ed.—Panaji : Comissão de Centenàrio de Falecimento do Dr. F.L. Gomes, 1969. vi, 177 p., 2 leaves of plates : ill. ; 20 cm.

The Brahmans.—Bombay : Sindhu Publications, 1971. vi, 184 p. ; 22 cm. Appendix : Letter to Lamartine. p. 183-185.

Os brigadeiros Henrique Carlos Henriques e Joaquim José Xavier Henriques. Lisboa : Typ. Universal, 1863, 39 p. ; 19 cm.

De Ia question de coton on Angleterre et dans les possessions portugaises de l'Afrique occidentale.—Lisbonne : Imp. de la Societé Typ. (Franco-Portugaise, 1861), 34 p. ; 82 cm.

Essai sur la théorie de l'économie politique et de ses rapports avec la morale et le droit.—Paris, (Guillaume, 1867), ii, 232 p. ; 22 cm.

Essai sur la théorie de l'économie politique et de ses rapports avee la morale et le droit.—(New York : B. Franklin, 1970).

A libertade da terra e a economia rural de India Portugueza.—Lisboa : Typ. Universal, 1862. 102 p. ; 19 cm.

Le Marquis de Pombal : esquisse de sa vie publique.—Lisbonne : Imp. Franco-Portugaise, 1869, 377 p., I leaf : 22 cm.

Marquis de Pombal.—2. ed.—Nova Goa : Livraria Académica, 1929. viii, 392 p. : front. ; 19 cm.— (Obras completas ; II).

Selected works. Memorial volume.—Bombay zxxiv, 412 p. : port. ; 24 cm.

Books on Gomes

Amzalak, Moses Bensabat, (b. 1892). Francisco Luiz Gomes e os seus estudos sobre economia politica : discurso pronunciado no dia 31 de maio de 1929 na Sociedade de Geografia de Lisboa.—Lisboa : Imp. na Soc. Nacional de Tip., 1929 17 p. · port. ; 20 cm.

Costa, Carlos Trajano. Francisco Luis Gomes : noticio biographica e retrato d'esse eminente publicista indio.—(Bombaim : Nicol's Printing Works, 1887).

Dr. Francisco Luis Gomes.—Lisboa : Agência Geral do Ultramar, 1971, 17 p. : port. ; 20 cm.

George, Evagrio, 1925-1978. Eminent Goans—Panjim : Goa Cultural and Social Centre, 1970. 17 p. : ill., 23 cm. (Gomes' biography appears on pp. 5-13).

Gomes, Olivinho, Dr. Francisco Luis Gomes : jivit ani vavr.—Ponnje : Konknni Sorospot Prokaxon, 1968. 38 p. ; 20 cm. In Konkani ; Roman script.

Newman Fernandes, Inacio P., *Dr. Francisco Luis Gomes, 1829-1869*—Avedem, Goa : Coinia Publications, 1969. 116 p. ; 24 cm. In English, French, Portuguese, or Konkani (Roman script).

Pereira, Felizardo Gonsalves. *Apontamentos para a biographia de Francisco Luis Gomes.*—Bombay : Typ. do Anglo-Lusitano, 1809. 344 p. : port. ; 24 cm.

NOTES

In preparing this paper the author read everything by and about Francisco Luis Gomes that he could find. In some instances he had to content himself with translations or summaries. He is deeply grateful to the University of Michigan for the extended loan of Gomes' *Collected Works*, the only known copy of this book in the U.S.

1. Comes, *Le Marquis de Pombal*, Lisbonne, Imp. (Franco-Portugaise, 1869), p. 5. "The biography of a minister is bound to be a work of moral and political importance".
2. *ibid.*, p. 377. "His glory and his greatness suffer from the wrongs he did his fellow men and from the methods he employed".
3. *ibid.*, p. 374. "Being a good administrator and a bad politician, Pombal was not always a happy legislator".
4. *ibid.*, p. 303. "An almost paternal protection".
5. *ibid.*, p. 303 et seq. "His various laws on finance, on the civil administration, on the regulation of justice and on the relations between the native and the Europeans, might constitute a veritable code".

6. Gomes, F.L. *Os Brahamanes*, 3. ed. Panaji, 1869. "Your Excellency knows I am no novelist".
7. *ibid.*, p. 53. "Gambling is the contraction of all vices into one".
8. *ibid.*, p. 33. "What use is equality in theory and in law, if it does not penetrate to our customs ?"
9. *ibid.*, p. 107. "It is said that the law of Christ governs European civilisation. That is a lie. It shines on its surface, but does not penetrate to the entrails".
10. *ibid.*, p. 147 et seq. "The revolt was the sepoy ; the revolution would have been the people ; the revolt was revenge ; the revolution would have been the Idea ; the revolt was the cruel Vishnu ; the revolution would have been mild Siva".
11. Gomes, P.L. *Collected Works* (Bombay, Centenary Committee, 1931), p. 375.
12. *ibid.*, p. 380.
13. Newman Fernandes, I.P. *Dr. Francisco Luis Gomes.* Avedem, Goa, Coinia, 1969, p. 28. "The difference which exists between morality and law can be summed up in the following points : 1. Morality considers the motive of an action ; law regards the action itself ; the one envisages rather the act at its source, the other in its effects. 2. Conscience is the only judge of morality ; but, as law can be recognized outwardly it is possible to lay down social laws applicable to each one by a constituted authority ; that is to say, individual right can be distinguished. 3. Morality is a formal and subjective science ; law on the other hand, is a material and objective science ; it regards the act and does not care for the intent".
14. *Collected Works*, p. 380.
15. *ibid.*, p. 381.
16. *ibid.*, p. 384.
17. *ibid.*, p. 369.
18. *ibid.*
19. *ibid.*
20. *ibid.*
21. *ibid.*, p. 352.

17

The Presence of Indian Culture in the Work of Some Portuguese Writers*

MARIA DOS REMEDIOS CASTELO-BRANCO
&
FERNANDO CASTELO-BRANCO

EÇA DE Queiroz is one of the greatest personalities of all times in literature in Portugal and the rest of Europe. In his novels, articles for reviews and papers, and even in other writings of his, he transmitted an expression of thought, the interest and depth of which is evidenced by the large series of works devoted to its study.

It is one of his characters, namely Frandique Mendes, whose fictitious biography and correspondence convey Queiroz's ideas. One of such letters was addressed to the poet Guerra Junqueiro, a member of the *Vencidos da Vida*, to which Queiroz himself belonged. Fradique Mendes expatiates on religion and contradicts Junqueiro's belief in a pure and abstract religion. He emphasizes that religion is essentially rituals, and cites illustrations from Catholicism as well as from Indian religious life :

> My dear friend :
> Your letter exudes poetic illusion. You believe very naively that poetry can penetrate the Church, the Priest, the Liturgy, the Sacristies, the Friday Fasts, and the Bones of

*The Paper was presented originally in Portuguese language. The editor assumes responsibility for the English Translation.

the Martyrs, and clear God from the clerical debris (*desentulhar Deus da aluvião sacerdotal*), and raise the faithful (among whom you surely include the State Councillors) to a fully pure and abstract understanding of Religion—a Religion consisting solely in Morality based on Faith. Not even your verses, which are more brilliant than the darts of Apollo, can succeed in this venture. It is just a misconception of the essence and function of Religion. To persist in it will be tantamount to being a stubborn dreamer.

My dear friend :
A Religion deprived of ritual vanishes. All men (excepting rare metaphysicians, moralists and mystics) look upon religion as a complex of rites that permit the faithful to establish an intimate contact with their God and obtain favours. This is the only function and goal of all cult, that is, from the primitive cult of Indra to the more recent cult of the Heart of Mary, which bothers you so much in your parish. You are a naive idealist.

"If you are keen to have historic proofs, leave Viana de Castelo, take a staff and climb with me to a distant antiquity and to a well cultivated and watered site, which lies between the Indus river, the slopes of Himalayas, and the sands of a vast desert. We reach Septa-Sindhou, the region of Seven-Waters, the Happy Valley, the land of the Aryans. In the first inhabited area where we stop you see on a hillock a stone-altar covered with fresh moss. You see the glitter of a lazily burning fire on it. Men dressed in linen and with their long hair held together with clips of fine gold move about the altar. They are the priests, the first chaplains of mankind, busy celebrating on a warm dawn of May the rites of an Aryan mass. One cleans and breaks firewood for the sacrificial flame. Another grinds with pestle in a mortar the aromatic substance that provide *Soma*. The blows of his pestle echo like a triumphant drum. Still another casts oats around the altar, while another by his side intones austere tunes raising his palms towards heaven. My friend, these men are celebrating a rite that embodies the whole religion of the Aryans, and which aims at

> propitiating Goa Indra : the Sun, the fire, the divine power that can strike the Aryan heart with pain and destruction by drying up water, by burning the pastures, by converting lakes into sources of pestilence, by reducing Septa-Sindhou more sterile than a wicked heart. He can also melt the Himalayan snow or with a fiery blow produce water and release it from the womb of clouds, restore water to the rivers, greenery to pastures, wholesomeness to lakes, happiness and abundance to the Aryan dwelling-place. It is therefore a matter of convincing Indra to be always well-disposed and to bless Septa-Sindhou with all the favours that its rural and pastoral inhabitants most desire".[1]

After some considerations which deal largely with Western religions, Fradique Mendes refers to Buddhism in the following terms and pursuing the same line of thought :

> If we could find time to visit China or Ceylon, you would see the same with Buddhism. It is a religion containing the subtlest metaphysics and the noblest morality. However, wherever it reached, be it among barbarians or civilized people, among the hordes of Nepal or to the Chinese mandarins, Buddhism had been for them all nothing more than rites and practices. The prayer-wheel has been the most known of these practices. Have you never handled this wheel ? It is comparable to a coffee-grinder : You find it in all Buddhist countries placed on the streets, at field crossings. Any devotee passing by can give a couple of turns to the handle and thereby cause some written prayers to chime and establish contact with Buddha, who is expected to be grateful for this show of courtesy and be generous with his gifts.[2]

A very interesting reference by Fradique Mendes to Buddhism occurs in another letter addressed to his "most beloved Clara".

> My studious Clara, I greatly approve of your interest in the history of divine Buddha. You sound very disconsolate when you complain that Buddha appears to you as a

very complicated Jesus. My beloved, it is important to exhume it from thick layers of legends and wonder-stories that have piled up in the course of centuries. Once cleared from mythology and seen in his historic clarity, he appears as the best visitor of this Earth, and there is nothing virtuous and heroic to be compared with his Night of Renunciation. Jesus was a proletarian, a beggar without a piece of land, without any earthly attachment. He moved about Galilee, advising people to give up homes and goods, to adopt loneliness and beggary, as ways to attain an abstract blessedness of a heavenly kingdom. He invited others to give up, while he himself was not giving up anything. Buddha, on the contrary, was a prince. Like most Asiatic princes he possessed much power and much wealth. He had experienced love, married and given birth to a son. This prince, this husband, this father, left his palace, his kingdom, his loved wife, and a little son lying in a precious cradle. He put on the clothes of a beggar and went about begging and preaching renunciation of all desires, unlimited love for all beings, contempt for self-torturing asceticism, intense appreciation of redeeming mercy, and confidence in the face of death.

It is undoubtable to me (to the extent these noble issues can be discerned from Paris, in 19th century, and under attack of cold) that Buddha's life is more meritorious. And look at the difference in the teaching of these two masters. Jesus said : I am son of God, and I insist that everyone of you, mortal men, should practise whatever good you can during your short span of lives, in order that I may later reward each of you with an infinitely good and everlasting life in my Father's dwelling beyond the clouds. Buddha simply said : I am a poor mendicant friar, and I want you to be good during your life-time. You will give rise to better persons, and thus every generation will grow in virtue, establishing on earth gradually the universal virtue. The justice of the just according to Jesus only benefits the just man, while the justice of the just according to Buddha benefits every successive generation and is a lasting good on this earth. Jesus creates an aristocracy of saints,

> whom he takes to delight himself in his kingdom. There is no benefit resulting from them for this world, which continues suffering its undiminished share of evil. Buddha with an accumulation of individual virtues leads to an improved humanity, progressively doing away with evil. Buddha himself always remains by the roadside as a mendicant friar. My darling, I am for Buddha. In any case, both these teachers have served mankind and had the largest share of divinity granted to any humans till our days.[3]

Fradique Mendes' understanding of Buddhism may not be correct, but his admiration for Buddhist principles is beyond dispute, and that is a feature of some importance to be taken note of by a student of religious ideas of Eça de Queiroz.

It is very possible that Eça derived his admiration of Buddhism from his friend at Coimbra, Antero de Quental. This leads us to a search of Hindu influence in Antero de Quental's thought. He wrote to Wilhelm Stork in May 1887 :

> My friend Oliveira Martins has presented me as a Buddhist. It is true that my ideas have much in common with Buddhism, but I believe that there is more than Buddhism in them. It appears to me that the modern mind, with its starting points and tendencies, cannot get out of naturalism, which is ever more bankrupt, except through such outlets as psychodynamism and pansychism. This seems to be the nodal point and the centre of attraction of the great nebula of modern thought in its process of condensation. One finds clear signs of this trend everywhere, and more especially in Germany. The West will produce its Buddhism, its mysticism, but with better foundations and of a better quality than that of the East.[4]

Several other references to and appreciations of Buddhism can be found in Antero de Quental's letters. The following excerpts may suffice to get an idea of his religious thought and his conception of Buddism as a moral and philosophical value :

> ". . . . No one may accuse the Being, or calumniate Buddhism. The Being made us for happiness, and Buddhism is

> a source of all satisfaction, all consolation and all happiness.[5]
>
> If Absolute has no reality in itself, a practice of life with reference to such Absolute becomes contemplation of a stationary point according to Buddhism.[6]
>
> I do not know if you have any idea of Buddhism. I wish you did. You can easily distinguish what is there which is space-bound and transitory. What remains is eternal and source of all consolation and moral goodness.[7]
>
> But I am convinced that such reservations are unfounded. There is not only no contradiction, but there is perfect expression in Buddhism of the natural and spontaneous feelings of human heart' and ideals of justice, harmony and beauty. This Buddhist expression frees them from many illusions and imperfections, and raises them to a better awareness of themselves and their goals. It would be surprising if this teaching, which places Good as ultimate truth of human existence had to clash with those natural sentiments which are only less defined and somewhat incomplete manifestations of our fundamental desire for Good.[8]

Antero de Quental did not consider Buddhism only as a doctrine which impressed him from intellectual and ethical angles. It had its psychological impact on the writer, as we can read in his confession :

> My moral life is truly that of a Buddhist. This has had its reflection in my poetry . . . ."[9]
>
> Of a mind that suffers from depressions and Buddhist indifference, which are characteristic of my temperament (. . .) I crave for Nirvana, if not as a great contemplative, at least as a sick person.[10]

We shall conclude our set of excerpts from Antero de Quental's writings with one last excerpt which permits a general critical evaluation of his understanding of Buddhism :

> Buddhism is a nice thing. However, its efficacy, like that of all religions can only manifest itself in collectivity. A community of Buddhists can be heavenly, but an individual Buddhist is a poor man, whose transcendent knowledge can only help him to yawn.[11]

From the above extracts it is obvious that Buddhism assumed great importance in Antero de Quental's way of thinking and in the permanent struggle which took place in his intellectual and moral life.

However, there is another aspect that calls for attention. Though Antero de Quental's poetry is mainly confessional, deeply reflecting his world of ideas, his problems, his doubts, and the anxiety and uneasiness of his soul, he wrote two sonnets in which he repressed his personality and replaced it with two different personalities acting as pseudo-authors of those two sonnets. One is claimed to be composed by a monk of the 13th century, and the other by a lonely disciple of Buddha, 2500 years ago, and whose mind was fixed on a single point according to the precept of his Master, or may be by a German philosopher, who dispaired of the insufficient naturalism in modern philosophy and had recourse to dreams of a primitive religious feeling. The sonnet, as well as the profile of its pseudoauthor were included in a letter that Antero de Quental wrote to Lobo de Moura on 12th April, 1872.

> . . . . its author could be a lonely disciple of Buddha, who 2500 years ago, sitting under the shade of *Baoba* and fixing his mind on one spot (according to his Master's instruction) wished to escape from the anguish of contingency and fragility of life. It is more probable, however, that its real author was some contemporary German philosopher, who could not find ultimate meaning of existence in modern philosophy and sought it in the primitive religious feeling. We are inclined to accept this second author as more probable, because of certain allusions in the text, and because of the national clarity that differs from the profound simplicity and concreteness that characterise the old sages and can be attributed only to the subtlety of the neo-buddhists. Whatever it be, this is the sonnet :

In the jungle of dreams, day after day
My suffering mind finds its way,
In the regions of vague forgetfulness
My phantasy leads me, step by step.

I cross in the darkness the chill fog
Of a strange world that inhabits the wind,
And my querulous and unsure feeling
Trusts solely the visions of night.

What mystical desires are maddening me ?
Depths of Nirvana appear
Before my eyes in the silent immensity !
Along this journey in desert space
I seek you and your hand
Oh Death, sister of Love and Truth.[12]

The poet published this sonnet with the title *Nirvana* in February 1875, but it is included as *Elogio da Morte* in *Sonetos Completos*. There appear in it another sonnet *Nirvana*, which was probably written in 1878.

To conclude our survey of Antero de Quental's religious thought, we can say that Buddhism did not only influence his intellectual and moral world, but also appeared as a recurring theme in his poetry, which marked an innovation in Portuguese poetry.

After discussing the influence of Buddhism upon the work of two of the greatest Portuguese literary figures, we wish to add a reference to a study of the late Prof. Délio Nobre Santos. *O Sentido Histórico da Civilização Hindu* was his graduation thesis and it was published in 1939. It is basically a refutation of Spengler's thesis that Indian culture reflects a non-historical mentality and that the historical consciousness of Western Europe is in contrast with the sharpness of Indian conscience, whose history is like a dream.[13]

The author disproves Spengler's thesis, at least as far as the Hindu civilization is concerned, and questions his methods of analysis. He refutes the allegation that Nirvana is a brahmanic concept. Prof. Nobre Santos was greatly interested in Indian civilization and helped much to develop this interest in Portugal.

NOTES

1. *A Correspondência de Fradique Mendes* (Lisboa, 1946), pp. 155-57.
2. *ibid.*, p. 163.
3. *ibid.*, pp. 257-260.
4. *Castas de Antero de Quental* (Coimbra, 1921), p. 12.
5. *Cartas Inéditas de Antero de Quental a Oliveira Martins*, (Coimbra, 1931), p. 138.
6. *ibid.*, letter 88, p. 155.
7. *Cartas de Antero de Quental* (Coïmbra, 1921), pp. 196-97.
8. *ibid.*, pp. 237-8.
9. *ibid.*, p. 71.
10. *ibid.*, p. 149.
11. *Cartas Inéditas de Antero de Quental a Oliveira Martins* (Coimbra, 1931), p. 257.
12. *Cartas de Antero de Quental* (Coimbra, 1921), pp. 350-52.
13. The author used a Spanish translation of Spengler's work *Der Untergang des Abendlandes.* See *Revista da Faculdade de Letras* (Lisboa, 1939), tome VI, nn. 1-2, p. 256.

18

Asian Trade and World Economy from the 15th to 18th Centuries

NIELS STEENSGAARD

THE theme with which we have been working for three days, have been Indo-Portuguese history, centered upon Goa. In this field I am an intruder, I am neither Indian nor Portuguese, but I have been drawn towards it because I consider the Indo-Portuguese encounter one of the decisive moments in the history of mankind - not less. After the last three days' sessions I find this view confirmed. Again and again the discussions have carried us from specialized topics towards problems of a far more general nature, problems concerning the forces that shaped the modern world.

It is one of these general aspects of our discussions, the relations between Asian trade and World economy in the 15th-18th centuries, I intend to pursue in this lecture. I shall try to review some of the results of the research in the field of Asian trade history done by the historians of the post-war generation and to discuss some of the unsolved problems.

It is about 30 years ago, I began to interest myself in this particular subject. At that time it was quite easy. Three or four good books, a handful or articles and a lot of rubbish was all the information available to the student. Provided one did not get lost in the rubbish, the subject might be mastered in one term.

I want to emphasize—or even exaggerate—this point for

two reasons. One is the fact that for those of you, who are only a few years younger than I, it must be difficult to imagine the colossal dimensions of our ignorance 30 years ago. We now have at our disposal a vast amount of good specialized studies within the general framework of early modern, or as you may prefer to call it, late medieval Asian trade history. But if you look at the date of publication, you will find that they all, with a few notable exceptions, have been written within the last three decades. The other reason, why I want to emphasize this fast accumulation of knowledge is to bring into focus the damage it has done to all preconceived notions. The generation before us had very little information, but most often a firm conviction that they knew what were the essentials. We have a lot of information, but we are not at all sure what the essentials are.

The over-all view which has been discarded beyond dispute by the last generation of historians, was a direct heritage from the evolutionism of the 19th century, but in actual fact we may trace it back right to the beginning of the so-called European expansion. If a Portuguese chronicler stopped to wonder about the causes on a more general level, he would think of God's will, the able leaders and the brave men. The 19th century removed God's will and put evolution instead. The result was, what we may call the Eurocentric paradigm. The higher level of European civilisation, the able leaders and the brave men explained everything.

A reaction against this simplified view had set in already between the wars, the most notable example being the Dutch sociologist, Jacob van Leur, but it was in the years after the second World War that historians in Asia, America and Europe began to ask a new kind of question about the old Asian trade and the so-called European expansion in Asia. The ways of historiography are often difficult to explain, but I find it more than probable that the inspiration for this new Wave was external to the profession of historians. The Eurocentric paradigm, the paradigm of evolution, smart leaders and brave men, did not suit the age of decolonisation. I can add from my own experience, that it did not suit the post-war generation at all.

We had enough of smart leaders and brave men, and we doubted the higher level of European civilization.

One interesting feature about the reaction against the Eurocentric paradigm is, however, that it did not take the shape of a massive ideological battle between losely [founded theories, I mention this is contradistinction to the corresponding revisions in the history of Africa and Latin America, but unfolded itself as patient research in the archives. An academic self-discipline for which we should especially tribute the Indian historians.

So, after the patient work of a generation of historians, we now have a vast amount of information on the old Asian trade. I cannot hope to summarize even a small fraction of this literature. What I shall try to do, is to summarize some of the findings in three points, which to several of you may be obvious and trivial, but which were not obvious 30 years ago, and have become trivial thanks to the labour of numerous historians. After that I shall discuss the long term trends in Asian trade between the discoveries and the age of domination. Finally, I shall try to discuss how far or how close we are to a new paradigm.

The first result of modern research, to which I want to draw your attention, is the dynamics of Asian trade. Not only the trade of the companies, which European historians since the fall of the monopolistic organisations in the 18th century had condemned as unimaginative parasites, but also the trade of the Asian entrepreneurs was shown to be in a constant process of growth and change. The old Asian trade was not, as van Leur had believed, a historical constant. The rhythm of the monsoons might be the same, year after year, but the sailors, the merchants and the commodities were not.

Closely related to this observation of the capabilities of the Asian trade. Again I am talking of something which is obvious, but which was not obvious 30 years ago. The more we know of the old Asian trade, the smaller becomes the distance in capabilities between the Asian merchants and the Europeans. The technique of the sailing ship is one example. The Portuguese ships were the first to establish a direct contact between the trading worlds of Europe and Asia. But the navigational and sailing technique they used, built upon the common heritage of Europe and Asia. The Chinese ships, which visited the ports of Western Asia in the early 15th century, might probably with a few modifications have made the voyage to Europe. The Gujarati ships which roamed from East Africa to Java, might probably have done the same.

The capabilities of the old Asian trade and economy can be illustrated in several other ways. The simplest is perhaps to remind you, that though the Europeans came to Asia to buy spices, they soon turned to high-technology commodities, and that they only had two things to offer in return, bullion, ships and the related services of trade, transport and violence. It was the Asian producers and the Asian merchants, who found ways to produce and deliver the commodities in demand.

The two new insights I have mentioned so far are the dynamics and the capability of the Asian trade. A third, equally important insight concerns the Asian participation in the broad development we usually call the European expansion. I do not have to give many examples to prove the point. It is a feature repeated from the earliest contacts between the Portuguese on one side and Asian navigators, merchants and princes on the other until the astounding development of the nominally European country trade in the 18th century. Asian participation did not only mean, that there was an Asian seller to every European buyer, but without local protection, local know-how and local capital the European buyer, but without local protection, local know-how and local capital the European trade in Asia in the 15th—18th centuries would have been a very small business indeed.

Dynamics, capability and participation. Taken together these features mean, that it was a gross distortion to see the Europeans as dominating the Asian scene before the very late 18th century.

These insights, which I have pointed out, could have been guessed at 30 years ago, but from a scholarly point of view, it was little more than guesswork. They are now proven beyond doubt. This sends the Eurocentric evolutionary paradigm in to the realm of legend. The Europeans did not arrive in Asia as representatives of a higher level of civilization.

The trouble is that this only means the destruction of an old myth, but it does not help us very far, when it comes to understanding what really happened. Because, as you all know, the age of participation eventually gave way to the age of domination. If the initial differences were so small, why was the presence of the Europeans tolerated in Asian waters, and why did this presence eventually lead up to domination ?

We are beginning to have the elements for answering the first of the two questions, though the answer by no means is a simple one. We know that it must be looked for in the relations between government and society in the Asian states. An official preoccupation with core territories which meant that coastal regions and overseas trade were marginal as a source of income and as a political interest for the ruling elites.

The second problem, to which I shall address myself is the following : How or why did presence lead to domination ? This is more controversial. The present tendency among scholars is, I think, to separate the problem from the early period, and see it as a function of European economic growth in the 18th century, ultimately the Industrial Revolution. In fact, this is a reinstatement of the evolutionary Eurocentric paradigm, only shifted to the 18th century. This view can be traced back to van Leur, but has recently been reintroduced in two important books, *World Accumulation, 1492-1789* by Andre Gunder Frank and *The Modern World System*, vol. 2 by Immanuel Wallerstein, the assumption being that the Asian trade was declining or stagnating in the long seventeenth century and that it was an outer arena in relation to the European world economy.

I think both assumptions are wrong. Even if the statistics we can produce are deficient, they are sufficient to prove that at the very least the sales value of Asian commodities imported into Europe doubled during the 17th century and doubled again during the first three decades of the 18th century. Of course the rise was not continuous, but it is impossible to identify a seventeenth century depression in the trade between Europe and Asia.

But of course the trade to Europe was a only a fraction of total Asian trade. Can we identify a seventeenth century depression in Asian trade ? Chaunu thought more than 20 years ago that he had found symptoms of a depression in the 1620's in the course of his studies of far-eastern trade as seen from Manila, but we now know, that what he found was a crisis of the Hapsburg empire, not a global crisis.

From several other studies on the trade history of various Asian regions during the long seventeenth century we get the contrary impression, the seventeenth century was not an age of depression, but an age of growth. The information we have from Bengal, from the Coromandel Coast, from Surat, from Acheh, from Bantam, from Jahore, all point in the same direction. With few exceptions Asian trade was growing along lines that were older than the discoveries and the Europeans presence. And there are several indications that this growth was not only a matter of the quantities handled, but also qualitative in the sense of larger concentrations of capital and new forms of entrepreneurial organisation.

But the regional studies also leave the impression that while Asian trade was growing, the European share in Asian trade grew even faster. While it is highly improbable that the Portuguese owned more than 10,000 tons of shipping in Asian waters apart from the ships of the carreira before 1,600, we know that the governor-general in Batavia had more than 10,000 tons at his command by the 1620's, more 20,000 tons by the middle of the century and more than 25,000 tons by the end of the century. To this should be added the tonnage owned or controlled by the Portuguese, the English, the French and the Danes.

How did the Europeans manage to take over a growing share in the 17th century ? I have on earlier occasions argued, a specific entrepreneurial form, the company, gave the North-west Europeans certain advantages on long distance routes, but here I should like to draw your attention to another feature, the comparative advantage of the Europeans in the age of sailing ships, though not in the trivial sense, that the Europeans knew something the others did not know, but in the sense that shipping and shipbuilding was the technologically most sophisticated and fastest growing industry of the early modern period—apart from war of course.

We have been discussing several aspects of sea power during this seminar, but one aspect is easily overlooked, the simple fact that some parts of the Asia-European continent profited more than others from the development of the high-sea sailing ship. By far the largest part of the sailing ships of the seventeenth century were to be found in the waters of the European far west of the continent. Of course this is no surprise and no tribute to a specific European mearitime genius. It follows logically, one might even say geographically determined, from the state of technological knowledge. The prevailing winds in Europe, the indented coastline and the two inland seas, the Baltic and the Mediterranean, gave the sailing ships much better operational conditions than the monsoon winds and the territorial masses of Asia. On the other hand river and canal transport was in all probability much more developed in Asia—though we know far too little about it—than in Europe.

So even if the initial advantage of the Europeans in the matter of shipping technique was very small, they were able to keep the lead, because they at any given moment had access to the most advanced techniques. The Asian entrepreneurs knew this. We can see that from differential freight rates paid in Asia to European and Asian carriers, and we can find examples of Asian entrepreneurs freighting, chartering, buying or imitating European ships.

The information we have indicate that the volume of Asian trade was growing, that the European share in Asian trade was growing, that the economies of Europe and Asia were steadily becoming more integrated in the 16th—18 centuries. One problem remains to be discussed, however, in order to make this line of reasoning valid. Was the Asian trade of any economic significance beyond the small circle of merchants and consumers of luxury goods ?

I think it was, but it is a difficult thing to prove. One important pointer is the growing diversification of the European import from Asia into commodities with a potentially far larger market than pepper and fine spices : indigo, sugar, silk, porcelain, textiles, coffee and tea. There are also indications that a corresponding diversification took place in the exchange of commodities within Asia. Tobacco was a new commodity on the Asian markets in the 17th century, of course. So was the large scale import of raw cotton and opium from India to China in the 18th century. Only further research can prove or disprove the general impression that there was an increase in long distance trade in commodities like sugar, textiles and metals in Asia in the 17th century.

Of course we are talking of very small figures in absolute terms from the point of view of the consumers. If we assume an equal distribution of the Asian commodities brought to Europe among the European consumers c. 1730 only the supply of pepper appears ample—c. 40 grammes of pepper for each. Each European might get c. 17 grammes of coffee, c. 9 grammes of tea and c. 0.15 m^2 calico—i.e. enough to make a small handkerchief.

From the point of view of the consumers the figures are ridiculous. But if we look at the figures from the point of view of the producers and consider the amount of labour which went into production of these commodities, using the method suggested by Om Prakash, the figures are not ridiculous. The European import of Indian calicoes alone c. 1700 kept 75—100,000 persons fully occupied. We may compare this to a labour force of c. 70,000 slaves in the sugar colonies, producing c. 6000 grammes of sugar a year for each European. It should also be remembered, that it was not until the decades after 1660 that American commodities became of more importance in the London market than the Asian commodities. In Amsterdam the shift of balance in favour of the Atlantic probably occurred even later.

One last illustration is the number of people employed in the Asian-European trade and transport. We have no possibility of estimating total figures, but we know that the Dutch East India Co. by the end of the 17th century employed 22,000 men, nearly half of these on its ships. The Dutch Company was—apart from governments—the largest employer of the age.

As you will remember, in the opening of my lecture, I argued that an old paradigm had broken down, the Eurocentric paradigm of evolution, smart leaders and brave men. And

I raised the question, how close to or how far from a new paradigm are we now.

One possibility, which I have been discussing above, is to revive the paradigm as what we might call "neo-Eurocentrism", that is, to ignore the 16th and 17th centuries and to find the origin of the age of dominance in an exogenous factor, the reversal of the long term trends in European economy in the middle of the 18th century. I hope I have convinced you, that this alternative is not tenable. The long 17th century was a period of vigorous growth in Asian trade and Asian economy, the shift to European dominance was not an externally induced shift from a phase B to a phase A, but a link in a continuous process of growth and change.

So where does this lead us ? I regret to say, it leads us to a lot of unanswered questions and no paradigm. The two comparative advantages of the Europeans, to which I have drawn your attention, the companies and the technique of the sailing ship, cannot have been decisive, because they could be and were imitated or counterweighted by the Asian entrepreneurs.

Then, of course, there is the possibility of chance, perhaps domination after all was only an accident. As we know, the decisive break in continuity occurred in conjunction with two events of a political nature, the opening of the Chinese market and the break-down of political authority in South and West Asia, particularly in India. In a few decisive decades the Europeans held all the trumps. They had a privileged position in the profitable China trade, and in India all traders looked to the European towns for the protection, which the Indian authorities could not provide. And they had the opportunity to appropriate the treasuries of the princes and the taxes of the peasants.

In these decades, as we know from the studies of Holden Furber and Das Gupta, the country trade was given an enormous boost by the capital flowing in, not only from the company employees, who wanted to launder their illicit gains, but also from Asian entrepreneurs, who for a time saw their best chances of survival and prosperity in co-operation with the Europeans and therefore transferred their capital and know-how to the European enclaves. And after these few decades the trend towards dominance was irreversible—at least for a couple of hundred of years.

The hypothesis of the big accident is a tenable hypothesis, but I don't like it, if not for other reasons, because I don't like big accidents history and the sudden change of the political scene in the early 1700's looks like a very big accident indeed.

So I must end my lecture, not by pointing towards a new paradigm, but towards new problems. These problems are related to a concept, which has turned up again and again in our discussions, the concept of coastal society. What were actually the effects upon Asian society of centuries of continuous growth in long distance trade ? On one hand we are talking of negligible quantities, when compared to an Asian population of 300 million or more, that is obvious. But were the effects negligible ? We are after all talking of hundreds of thousands of people becoming dependent upon production for distants markets, and this adaptation took place in the coastal regions, that is, most often in the perifery of the traditional empires. What were the effects on the political and social balance within the empires ?

One other problem, which we have only touched briefly during this seminar. We know that vast amounts of bullion was produced in Asia and imported to Asia in the 16th—18th centuries, but we don't know much about the effects of the bullion in Asian economy and society. We can only assume that disequilibria must have followed from the growing monetisation and accumulation of treasure in certain regions.

There is no new paradigm. Perhaps the most valuable new insight is the growing understanding that we are not talking of two continents, but of one. Ashin Das Gupta some years ago remarked, that the trouble with Asia is that we do not know, if it really exists. We may have the same doubts concerning Europe. It follows logically from the rejection of the Euro centric paradigm that the very concepts of Asia and Europe are artificial. From this insight we should continue our work. I hope the Indo-Portuguese seminars in the future will continue to be one of the most stimulating points of contact between historians from all parts of the continent, as it has been until now.

NOTE

+For references see my survey articles "Asian Trade 15th - 18th Centuries : Continuity and Discontinuities" in *Rapports II, XVe Gongress international des sciences historiques*, Bucarest, 1980 and "Asian Trade and World Market : Orders of Magnitude in the Long Seventeenth Century" in *Ier Colloque—Franco-Polonais, Université de Nice*, 1980, in preparation.

Index

African coasts, 131
African military experience, 151
Aguia (1559), 27
Albuquerque, Afonso de, 59, 185, 186
Albuquerque, Francisco de, 46, 47
Albuquerque, Jorde de, 62
Albuquerque, Motias de, 95
Alcântara 1580, battle of, 74
Aleppo, 87, 88
Algerian Muslim, 125
Ali Apula, 5
Almazen (arsenal), 61
Almeida, Dom Francisco da, 2
Amsterdam Oude-Compagnie, 75
Andrade, Anlónio Banha de, 42
Anglo-Indian Society, 207
Anil seal, 102
Anti-Portuguese feeling, wave of, 74
Arabs, 88 ; merchants, 1 8
Archbishop, 27
Aryans, 217
Asian-European trade, 231, 232
Asian Participation, 228
Aurangzeb (Emperor), 114, 119
Azevedo, D'Almeida, 187

Babylon, 86, 87, 88
Baçaim, geographic origin, 97
Balbi, Italian traveller, 18, 20
Bantam, 23
Bardez, 184, 185, 190
Basra, 86, 137
Batticaloa, 81, 151, 159 ; Burgher community, 155, 157 ; Portuguese-Burghers, use of script, 159-167
Bay of Bengal, 57, 58
Bendaharas, 62, 64, 65
Bengal, embroidery, 136
Bijapur, Bahmani Kingdom of, 184
Black sea, 43
Blockading forees, 80
"Bombay connection", 104, 107
Bombay, Portuguese national domiciled, 107
Bouchon, Genevieve, 16
Brahmin, 186, 187, 188
Brazil, 21
Buddhism, 218
Buddhist Principle, 220

Caba da Rama, 183
Cachil Labuzaza, 64
Calicut, 6, 7, 45 ; fleet, 49
Cambay, 4, 8, 10
Cannanore, 3, 7, 45 ; King of, 2, 6
Canton system, 110
Cape Route, 19, 41, 75
Cargoes, average distribution of, 22
Carreira, return cargoes of, 13-28
Carreira da India, 84 ; Glimpses of, 40-51
Casa da India, 15
Castilian fleet, 15, 44
Castelo Branco, embroidery of, 138; Mariados Remedies, 216
Ceylon, 44, 58, 77, 81, 150, 155
Chekiang, 34, 38
China coast, 32, 35
Chinese conditions, 79 ; embroidery, 134 ; imperial order, 33 ; policy, 37 ; xenophobia, 32
Christ, military order of, 64

Christian empire, 63 ; merchants, 1, 7, 9, 10
Cochin, 1, 6, 14 ; Cherina Marakkar, 4, 5, 6 ; loading of, 51
Colégio Novo, 128, 130
Coromandel Coast, 60, 77, 78, 220
Crown, 25, 92 ; Cargo of, 51

da Costa, A.A. Bruto, 103
da Nova, João, 45
Da Silva, Bernardo Peres, 105
Daman administration, 111
Das Gupta, Ashin, 192
de Castro, João, 4
Deccan politics, 114
de Laval, Pyrard, 14, 26
De Souza, Teotonio R., 102
Dicl oli, Subhedar of, 118
Diogo Ribeiro's Vocabulary, 196-201
Dona Maria da Candia, 149
Dutch East India Company, 23, 73, 110, 150, 232
Dutch aggression, Origin and Rhythm of, 73-81
Dutch-Burgher community, 153

East African Coast, 17
East Africa, in Portuguese Colonies, 148
East Asian economic development, 34
Eastado da India, 73, 78
Edappally, 6, 7 ; Muslim merchant of, 5
Sir Edward West, 108
Ethiopia, Clergy of, 95
Eurocentric Paradigm, 226, 227, 229, 239
Europe, 27
Eurasians, category of, 153
European economic growth, 229
European expansion, 226, 228
Exploitation, 42
Exploratory mission, 45

Faria, Sir Roger de, 108, 109, 110, 111
Fazenda Real (Royal Treasury of) 91, 92, 96
Fernando, C.M., 154
Fleet of 1587, 16
Francisco Pais, 94
French revolution, 208, 212
St. Francis Xavier, 128
Francisco Luis Gomes, 203
Fukien Coasts, 34, 37, 38

Gabrial Holzschuher, 26
Gaspar Correia, 45
George Winius, 84
Goa, 14, 91, 96 ; Archbishop of, 104; customs of, 94 ; freedom struggle, 102-112 ; image of, 181; Jesuits in focus, 125; Jesuits, spoliation and exile of, 123; liberal-constitutional struggle, 103 ; limpert port, 182 ; national movement, 102 ; political development, 105, 107
Goa Dourad image, 187
Godinho, Manuel, 84, 85, 87
Goonatilleka, M.H., 147
Gumão, Francisco de, 128

Haj pilgrimage, 137
Hindu merchants, 9, 59
Hocart, A., 188

Iberian Peninsula, 1
Ifeka, Caroline, 181
Ilhas, 184, 185, 190
Inauspicious Ambience, 32-38
India, 23 ; *aramdas* in, 47 ; cargo loaded in, 50 ; commercial embroidery, 130 ; condition of loading, 49 ; financial improvement, 92 ; financial situation of, 90, 92 ; First War of National Independence, 208 ; global balance, 93 ; west coast of, 10
Indian culture, 216 ; mutiny, 208 ; nationalism, 102 ; ocean, 93 ; Princes, 78
Indo-European culture, 190
Indo-Portuguese embroidery, 134
Indus river, 217

Jacome Abuna, 3
Jaina symbolism, 139
Jajmani system, 186
Sir Jamshetjee Jeejeebhoy, 109
Japanese Politics, 79
Jewish merchants, 7
John Correia-Afonso, 84
Jones, Sir William, 198

Kashatriyas, 186, 187, 188
Kayamkulam, Bragaida Taquatome of, 5, 7
Kellenbenz, H., 43
Khan, Shah Adil, 184
Khoja Shams-ud-din, 3, 5, 7
Kienicisiez, J., 43
Kollam, 51
Konkan, Desais of, 114, 115, 122 ; grammar, 204 ; idiometic expression, 198
Koran, 61
Kudal, Kham Sawant of, 115, 116
Kukali, 117, 118
Kwangtung authorities, 36, 37

Lamartine, Alphonse de, 212
Lampoco, 37
Lane, Frederic, 13
Linschoten, 14, 183, 187
Lisbon, 15, 21, 23, 24, 26, 30, 36, 40, 48, 149 ; *Casa da India*, 97 ; Nosa Senhora da Graça in, 20
Lourenço Moreno, 3
Luso-Indians, 152

Madre de Deus, 25
Magalhães-Godinho, V., 13, 15, 22, 23, 40
Malabar, 1, 4, 7, 44, 46
Malacca, 4, 44, 62, 79, 81, 133 ; custom-house, 63 ; Hindu community, 64 ; Indian merchant community, 56-65 ; Sultanate, 57
Malay Peninsula east coast, 62
Mandovi river, 183
Manuel Botelho, 3, 41
Maratha merchants, 121 ; Power, 114
Martin, Oliveeira, 220
Mascow, 86
Mathew, K.S., 1
Mecca, 5
Medina, 86
Ming dynasty, 32, 33, 36
Miranda, Rocky V., 196
Missing Monsters, mystery of, 25, 27
Mochi embroidery, 139
Mocquet, 15
Moors, 181
Mozambique, 17, 26
Mughal army, 114, 116 ; maratha conflict, 120
Muscat, Imam of, 88
Muslim merchants, 1, 3, 7, 9, 58, 63 ; peasantry, 156

Navigation regulations, 49
Nina Chotu, 59, 61, 64
Noronha, D. Antão de, 92, 94
Nossa Senhora de Jesuits, 21
Nunes Dias, 41

Old Asian trade, 227, 228
Old Goa, churches of, 191
Oliveira, J.P. Bacelar E., 123
Ormuz, 5

Palsgrave, 23
Panhala, 119, 120
Pepper cargo of 1587, 17
Pereira, Bragança, 189
Perera, S.G., 148
Persian embroidery, 135 ; Gulf, 6, 43
Pescadores Archipelago, 79
Philippine administration, 90, 99
Politico-diplomatic, 35
Pombal, machiavellian trait in, 125
Ponda, administration of, 117, 121
Portugal council, 21 ; education system, 205 ; spices import of, 48
Portuguese adventures, 4 ; agreement, 43 ; Burghers, 153-154 ; church, 123; collections, Indian textiles in, 133-140 ; crown, 43, 61; currency,

150 ; education, 158-159 ; estado, 27 ; fleets, 40, 59 ; idle curiosity, 16 ; merchants, 62 ; military problem of, 96, 97 ; rivalry, 119
Prince's agreement, 47
Priuli, Girolamo. 41

Quental, Antero de, 222
Queirez, Eça de, 216
Quintaladas system, 51

Ramusio, G.B., 41
Rau, Virginia, 42
Razzaq Abdur, 187
Red sea area, 5, 84, 88
Ṛgveda, 136
Rogerio de Faria, ghost of, 103
Roman Catholic faith, 203

Salappu Aracci, 148
Sambhaji, 115
Santa Catarina, 76, 77
Santa Cruz, 27
Sanudo diaries, 13, 16
Sanuto, Marino, 41
São Jão Baptista, 27
São Martinho, 21
São Salvador, 17
São Thomé, 24 ; cargoes of, 17
Salcete, 184, 185, 190
Sarparpatyagar, 118, 119
Scholberg, Henry, 203
Second World War, 226
Septa-Sindhu, 217
Seville, Casa da Contratacion in, 15
Shah, Mudhafar, (Sultan of Malacca) region of, 57, 59
Shanteng peninsula, 34
Shivaji, Chhatrapati, 114, 121
Sino-Japanese relations, 33
Smuggling and piracy, 37
Sonda, 117, 118
Spanish authorities, 16
South East Asia, 56

Sri Lanka, emergencies
ironical situation, 1
Portuguese crede in,
Steensgaard, Niels, 13,
Sudra, 186, 187, 188
Sunda, Kingdom of, 12
Sung dynasty, 33

Teixeira da Mota, 42,
Thomaz, Luis Filipe F
Tomé Pires, disastrous mission of, 36
Torre do Tombo, 43
Tristão do Cunha, 50
Tyrannic behaviour, 61
Turks, 86

United East India Con

Vaishnavite influence,
Van Neck, 76
Vasco da Gama, 2, 44, 183
Vasconcelos, Joaquim
Veena Das, 190
Venetian diaries, 16
Venice, 41
Vietnamese coral, 35
Vigo, port of, 21
Vijayanagara empire,
Vithal Pandulik, 116,
V.O.C. Strategic Plan
Von Murr, Christoph

Wake, C.H.H., 14
West Indies, 44
"Westerse Quartieren
White-collar Job, 156
Williams, Lea E., 32
World economy, 225

Zamorin, Sultan of,
Zuari river, 183